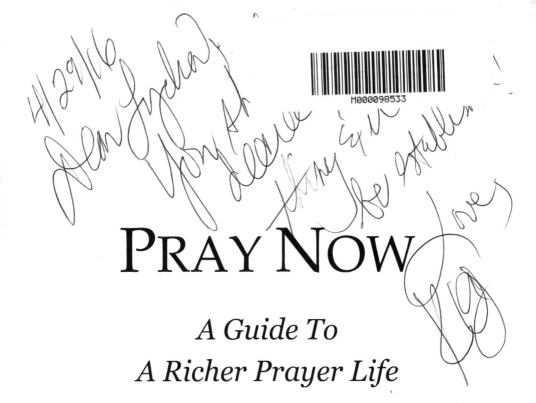

PRAY NOW

A Guide To
A Richer Prayer Life

Karen L. Gardner

BASAR
PUBLISHING

PRAY NOW: A GUIDE TO A RICHER PRAYER LIFE by Karen L. Gardner

DEDICATION

This is the first book I've written and I dedicate it to Abba Father, my family and friends.

To my husband, Anthony L. Gardner, thank you for your support and encouragement during the book writing process. You're a great leader and coach.

To our children: Ashlee, Anthony II, Amber and Austin, and to our grandsons, Jaylen and Tristan, I leave you this book as a part of my legacy. I love you. Prayer is one of the most powerful forces on earth. You can lose everything in life, but if you know how to pray by faith that works by love, you can recover all.

To my precious Mom, Louise Greene, the first intercessor in my life, I love you and I enjoy our prayer times. To Mom Lattie Goodson, my first intercessory prayer teacher, thank you for teaching me how to minister to God and to pray through until I get a note of victory.

To my dear sister-friends, Mini Card, Dr. Debra Lavender-Bratcher, Paula Allen, Jimmie Sue Woelke, Apostle Renée Gray, Kim Bacon, Davina Stallworth and my Alaska Eagle sisters— thank you for your encouragement to maximize my potential.

Lastly, I dedicate this book to all the faithful, loving intercessors that unselfishly and relentlessly stand in the gap praying for souls and to birth the next great awakening and revival, until the kingdoms of this world become the kingdoms of our Lord and of His Christ and He will reign forever and ever.

ACKNOWLEDGEMENTS

With any successful project, there is a team that works together to accomplish a common goal. I'd like to thank my team for giving their time and talent to help publish my first book. I couldn't have done this without you.

I'd like to thank my initial editing team: my husband, Anthony L. Gardner, my sons Anthony L. Gardner, II and Austin Gardner, and my dear friend, Alma Krause. I'd also like to give special thanks to Candace Ford of Love Clones Publishing for substantive editorial and publishing support, and Sandy Holladay for proofreading and formatting.

I give heartfelt thanks and appreciation to Apostle Pamela Hardy, founder of Eagles International Training Institute (EITI), and her husband, Bishop Chris Hardy, for the privilege and opportunity to serve as director/instructor of the Eagles International Intercessory Prayer Institute (EIIPI) and for launching and mentoring me in ministry.

I give special thanks to my pastor, Dr. Ken Friendly and First Lady, Dr. Deb Friendly, of Lighthouse Christian Fellowship. You have both taught me so much, especially about faith, prayer, family and victory in Christ Jesus.

Thank you to the following leaders who have impacted my spiritual development in prayer, prophetic intercession and ministry:

In Alaska: Thank you Rev. Paula Allen, director of the Healing Rooms of Alaska, for giving me the opportunity to coordinate community prayer watches and for hands-on healing ministry training.

Thank you Prophet Jimmie Sue Woelke, founder of A Voice in the Wilderness Ministries, and Lorraine O'Neal, for practical ministry experience and School of the Prophets.

Outside of Alaska: Thank you Apostle Renée Gray, founder of Praise Party School of Dance, for always encouraging me to pursue prayer and worship dance to glorify God and to impact the lives of others for the kingdom's sake.

Thank you Prophet James Hernandez, instructor of Eagles International Training Institute School of the Prophets, for prophetic training and for modeling the humility of God. I appreciate the key prophetic insights you've given me over the years. Alaska for Jesus!

Thank you Apostle Elizabeth Hairston-McBurrows, founder of The Apostolic-Prophetic Connection, Women With A Call International and instructor of Eagles International Training Institute School of Worship, for the teaching, training and mentoring you have given me in prayer, praise and worship, ministry ethics and the School of the Prophets. You are a true Mother of Zion.

Lastly thank you to Pastor Rekesha Pittman, instructor of the Eagles International Authors Institute and an accomplished author, for guiding me on my first book writing journey. I couldn't have done this without you. #STAY WRITE!

TABLE OF CONTENTS

FOREWORD

PRAY NOW is a rich and compelling book by Karen Gardner that will move you into experiencing intimacy in the presence of God like never before. This book will give you keys that will help you to hit your target when you pray. As a prayer leader—as one who hears from God and knows how to discern his voice, Karen has written this book to introduce the body of Christ to a major shift in the area of prayer. As I travel around the nations of the world, I see that there is a call for us to become more strategic in prayer. We must learn how to hit the target. It is imperative that we are biblical in our approach to prayer and that we learn how to integrate it into the fabric of the church.

PRAY NOW. The word now means at the present moment in time, currently, right away, immediately, instantly, promptly, and without delay—as soon as possible; ASAP. There's a fresh sound of God in the area of prayer that must come forth in this day. As we pray, the portals of heaven will be open. God will be able to fill us with his glory and release new passion and power into our lives.

Every day gives us an opportunity to PRAY NOW. We do not need to be at church or in a prayer meeting. We can be bank tellers, teachers or doctors. We can simply be en route as we carry out our daily errands. We can be lawyers in between briefs or firemen reaching for a fire hose. We can be a stay-at-home mom or the president of a nation. Wherever we are and whatever we do, we can pray. We must pray. We have the privilege of partnering with God our Creator. He has given us all kinds of prayer, from intercession to meditation—from persistent prayers to warfare prayers. He has said that we can decree a thing and we will see it happen.

Karen Gardner has given us ample tools and keys to be able to unlock a new level and a new measure of prayer. This book will help you to become the type of effective prayer warrior that you desire to be. Open the pages and take this journey with her.

—Apostle Pamela Hardy
President and Founder of Set Free Evangelistic Ministries
and Eagles International Training Institute

PREFACE

I wrote this book to encourage you to pray and decree with greater passion and accuracy the new desires upon the Father's heart. I encourage you to pray now, in the present moment, because there is urgency in the realm of the spirit to birth the new—new souls, new attitudes, new ideas, new creativity, new businesses, new ministries, new relationships and new life. In these end-times, God is doing a new thing, and He is seeking for those who will partner with Him to fervently and diligently pray His will into the earth.

I pray that this book will give you a foundation in prayer that will stimulate an insatiable hunger to daily commune with God. May the words in this book ignite your heart with passion to intimately know God.

Lastly, I pray the knowledge shared in this book will increase your desire to passionately meditate, memorize, study and read God's Word, so that like Prophet Elijah, you will cause heaven to invade earth on behalf of others as well as yourself.

Prayer is an exciting journey of cultivating an intimate relationship with our heavenly Father. It is not rituals, formulas or techniques. It is all about Him. May this book keep the fire of prayer lit upon the altar of your heart, so that you become a "friend of God"—one He can count on to obey Him like faithful Abraham to "pray now".

INTRODUCTION

There have been many books written on prayer and there will be many more, so what makes this prayer book different? This book is filled with principles, secrets and keys about prayer and intercession gained from my life experiences that will energize and revitalize your prayer life. It also contains reference material and prayers, making it a useful guide for the student of prayer from the beginner to the advanced.

I will share how the pain of my childhood drew me into an intimate relationship with God. The ups and downs of life have taught me that one Word from God trumpeted from the mouth of a faithful intercessor can bring a prodigal child back home, win a worker's compensation case and heal a sick body.

The God-kind of prayer is motivated by the God-kind of love and activated by the God-kind of faith. This type of prayer always gets results. If you want more answers when you pray, cultivate an intimate relationship with God.

What will you get from this book? If you apply the principles, you will pray with greater passion and accuracy. Your prayer life will become supernatural, not routine. You will encounter the glory realm. Like the Psalmist David, you will say, "In His presence is fullness of joy and at His right hand are pleasures evermore" (Psalm 16:11).

This book will teach you how to abide in Him as He abides in you, causing your prayers to go forth as straight arrows that hit the mark. Now, let's get started on our prayer journey together.

"Pray Now"

By Karen L. Gardner

Pray now. Dominate.
Speak God's Word
Turn the enemy at the gate.
Pray now. Activate.
Decree the gospel of salvation
'til God's kingdom replicates
all over the world.
Pray now. Celebrate!
Trumpet thanksgiving and praise
to Him alone, Who is great and
greatly to be praised.
Pray now.

"*I Am God's Intercessor*"

By Karen L. Gardner

I am God's intercessor devoted to Him alone.
I rise up when He calls me
to decree what He has shown.

I check with Him daily and often throughout the day.
The voice of another I will not answer;
Him alone I obey.

I am God's intercessor, clothed with His mighty armor and
zeal. I'm dressed to kill the enemy with the spiritual weapons
I wield.

No weapon formed will prosper, as I boldly decree
the will of the Father and His divine strategies.

I am God's intercessor. I pray His prayers and decree His
will, dancing and singing in the Spirit with anointing and
skill.

Advancing the kingdom of God in prayer is what I do best,
as I rely upon Holy Spirit to help me win every test.

Wisdom, prophecy, discerning of spirits and knowledge
are keys I use, causing the enemy to flee far from me
as he becomes confused.

I am God's intercessor. In His presence I live,
gazing upon His beauty, hearing and obeying His will.
I am God's intercessor.

SECTION I
PRAYER FOUNDATIONS

CHAPTER 1

THE STARTING LINE

It's not where you start; it's where you finish.

When I first started praying, I would bring my wish list to God like he was a candy man. All I knew about prayer back then was to cry, whimper and beg God to take care of my family like I was a second-class citizen. I had no revelation of how much God loved me and desired to bless my family because I was bound by rejection, fear, shame and condemnation. I could only hope God would answer my prayers because I had no understanding of the authority I had in Jesus' name to decree a thing.

Therefore, whenever I approached God in prayer, I hoped that I had performed everything perfectly. I thought you had to earn answers to your prayers from God through perfect performance.

My relationship with God was very shallow. I knew nothing about "koinonia" (coy-nuh-NEE-uh)—a Greek word meaning "communion, fellowship, intimacy, partnership, joint participation, social intercourse or communication"— because I didn't trust God. This "koinonia" would eventually become a new spiritual reality—my secret place with God—as I cautiously let down the walls surrounding my heart.

Back then I saw myself as a victim that had to constantly perform like a hamster running on a wheel, in order to receive

God's love and acceptance. I had a deep sense of inferiority that caused me to feel that I didn't deserve to have the best. I was an emotional wreck; consumed by rejection, fear, insecurity, anxiety, shame and anger, all stemming from having an unhealthy relationship with my earthly father.

Nonetheless, in all my mess, I always loved God and spent time with Him in prayer, mostly interceding for others. I just didn't know how to connect with Him for *myself,* even though I wanted this deep down in my soul.

It was impossible for me to fully receive inner healing and deliverance because I was projecting the strained relationship I had with my Dad onto God. I reasoned that if my Dad didn't love me, surely God didn't either. Boy, was I wrong. I would discover just how wrong later in life as circumstances taught me to trust God.

It took hitting a brick wall in my mid-20's for me to begin to shake loose from the bondages of my childhood. I'll never forget the day. I had just been handed a pink slip shortly after returning to work from maternity leave after having my third child. I was working as a public relations account executive for a top advertising firm in Alaska.

Instantly, my world was shattered. I got into my car stunned, confused and hurt, with tears streaming down my face as I began to drive away from the office. Thoughts bombarded my mind. "What am I going to do now to help my husband take care of our family?" "We have another mouth to feed." "Why can't you ever do anything right?"

I continued sobbing, as I drove nowhere in particular. The rejection, shame, anxiety, fear, anger and hopelessness I felt were unbearable. I couldn't understand why I had been laid off. I did great work, or at least that's what my manager had said. Where had I gone wrong?

I would learn later that while my work was usually excellent, my ability to open up and build good relationships with authority figures hampered my success. I was afraid that if they really got to know me, or if I made a mistake on a project, they would reject me just like my Dad. On top of this, I had so much unforgiveness in my heart towards my Dad that it hindered my ability to open up and trust anyone.

As I continued to drive around town with tears streaming down my face, I told God, "I can't take this anymore!" The shame of losing my job, (which was pride), and the thought of losing our home, (which was fear) caused me to spiral out of control. Then I heard a small voice inside of me say, "Go to church and pray." I made a beeline to the sanctuary.

Once there I lay on the floor at the altar crying out to God to remove the gut-wrenching pain of rejection. I repented for everything under the sun, hoping to ease my pain.

But my great emotional display didn't cause God to fall off His throne or to coddle me. He simply said, "Call your Dad and ask Him to forgive you." "What?!" I erupted. "Call my Dad and ask *him* to forgive *me*?!" I couldn't believe what God was asking me to do because I hadn't rejected my Dad—he had rejected me. Or so I thought.

Still upset, I asked God, "What does my Dad have to do with my job?" I reminded God, (as if He didn't already know everything), that it was my *Dad* who had rejected me as a child. He made promises to me that he didn't keep; like the time he promised to buy my sister and I a pair of lime-green bicycles for Christmas—something I had always wanted.

It was my Aunt Sandy, who stepped in to fill the gap, buying our bikes. However, I would later learn that like me, my Dad suffered from a spirit of rejection from his dad. It was a generational curse that needed to be broken by taking authority over it.

Still not pleased with what God had told me to do, I asked Him repeatedly, "Why do I have to call and ask my Dad for forgiveness when he rejected me first?" Pain and anger pulsated through my heart. I thought I was going to explode. I was angry with God, my Dad and the whole world!

But God had spoken. Now I had to choose whether or not I was going to obey Him. The pain in my heart was so excruciating that I decided to call my Dad to ask for his forgiveness. This was a task easier said than done.

I don't know how many times I picked up the phone, dialed my Dad's number and hung up just before he could answer. But by the grace of God, I finally made the call and waited for my Dad to answer because I was sick and tired of being sick and tired. I wanted freedom.

It seemed like the phone rang forever before my Dad picked up. Then I heard his voice. I braced myself. My heart seemed to skip a beat as I held my breath. I hadn't heard my Dad's voice in years because I had written him off. Speaking as fast as I could, I said, "Hi Randy, this is Karen. I'm calling to ask you to forgive me for being rebellious and disrespectful towards you." At this time, I called my Dad by his first name, Randy.

These were the hardest words up to this point in my life that I ever had to say. They were also the most liberating. It felt like a ton of bricks that I had been carrying since I was a child slid off my shoulders, crashing to the ground. I was FREE!

He said, "Hi daughter. You know, I always loved you. I just got stuck on those drugs and alcohol. I want to ask you to forgive me for not being there for you. I love you daughter."

Oh my gosh! My heart melted with love. And I was speechless because my Dad had just said that he loved me! Tears of joy flowed from my eyes. I felt a huge wave of God's healing love penetrate my heart. The burden of rejection with its associated negative emotions that I had been carrying for so long lifted from my shoulders. Thank God Almighty, I was FREE!

After we hung up, I began to sing like a little girl, "MY DADDY LOVES ME! MY DADDY LOVES ME!" I kept rolling these words over and over in my mind and speaking them aloud. I had received a major breakthrough because I met with God in prayer and obeyed Him.

As I began to spend time with my earthly father, my trust in him increased. As a result, I experienced a breakthrough in my spiritual relationship with God. I began to trust Him because I had released all of the unforgiveness towards my father that had hindered me from drawing closer to God.

The reverse is true, however, that as long as I harbored unforgiveness in my heart towards my earthly father, it blocked my ability to build a more intimate, personal relationship with my loving, caring, sharing heavenly Father. This unforgiveness also prevented me from building healthy relationships with physical authority figures because I was afraid they would hurt me.

A child's relationship with his or her earthly dad significantly impacts how that child sees and relates to God. I didn't trust my Dad, so with my childlike understanding, I concluded that I couldn't trust God. I reasoned as a child that if my Dad didn't love me, God didn't either. Therefore, when I prayed to God, I struggled to receive the grace of His love, favor, acceptance, protection and provision for me. I could pray for others to receive (intercession), but not for myself.

Even now when I recall this memory, I can still feel God's healing love reminding me that He will never leave me, nor forsake me. Exercising the power of forgiveness revolutionized my walk with God and with others. It opened the door for me to enter into a realm of fellowship and communion with God that is indescribable. I call this the glory realm, where all things are possible. And it is available to every child of God that chooses to obey.

You cannot effectively fellowship and commune with God in prayer if you have unforgiveness or sin in your heart because sin hinders your relationship with a holy God. Prayer is about *a genuine relationship* with a holy God. It's not a ritual. It's not performance.

It wasn't until I forgave my Dad (as God commanded) that I experienced a paradigm shift in my thinking that affected the way that I saw and related to God. It was a process that didn't happen overnight, so don't despair. Be patient with yourself. The longest journey begins with *one small step of obedience.*

As a result of forgiving my Dad, prayer is now a joy, not a chore, because I know God loves me, and I *trust* Him with all my heart (Proverbs 3:5-6). "No good thing will He withhold from me" is not just black ink on paper, but it's the living Word of God's love that burns in my heart. Moreover, in prayer I encounter my heavenly Father in all of His glory. He alone is everything you need. He is the object of prayer, not things, positions or people.

Now I eagerly anticipate spending time with God. I enjoy ministering to Him with thanksgiving, praise and worship. I would never have experienced such freedom had I chosen to harbor unforgiveness towards my Dad. Choosing to forgive my Dad was one of the best decisions I have ever made. It transformed my relationship and prayer life with God.

I have learned that our parents, in most cases, do the best they can to raise us. However, they are imperfect human beings that make mistakes. If you have unforgiveness in your heart towards your earthly dad or mom, I invite you to forgive them today, right now, so you too can fully experience God's love for you.

It has been said that unforgiveness is like drinking the poison that you intend for the one that hurt you. It is an enemy that hinders your ability to fully experience God in all of His goodness.

Our heavenly Father cannot be compared to an earthly dad or mom. He loves you unconditionally because He is love. His love (agape love) is not based on your performance. He loves you simply because you are His—fearfully and wonderfully made in His image and likeness. God loves you so much that He promises in His Word that He will never leave you, nor forsake you:

> *Let your conduct be without covetousness; be content with such things as you have. For He Himself has said, "I will never leave you nor forsake you. So we may boldly say: "The Lord is my helper; I will not fear. What can man do to me?" (Hebrews 13:5-6 KJV).*

In Psalm 27:10, the Psalmist David also declares concerning God's love:

> *Although my father and my mother have forsaken me, yet the Lord will take me up [adopt me as His child] (AMP).*

Not only do these passages in Scripture reveal that your heavenly Father will never abandon you, Hebrews 13:6 also says that the Lord will help you resist the fear of man (fear of rejection).

I was so fearful of my Dad as a little girl that whenever I saw him I ran the other way. This spirit of fear carried over into my adulthood until I obtained deliverance.

God makes no mistakes when He chooses our parents. However, our parents sometime make mistakes in their choices because they don't cast their unmet needs and unresolved issues onto God, continuing a destructive cycle. I can say this because I'm a parent that has also made mistakes.

But God's mercy and grace is always available to turn the situation around to work for the good of *all* concerned. No human being is perfect. The only perfect human being that has ever lived was our Lord and Savior Jesus. Parents are human. Therefore, it's inevitable that they will make mistakes, some more costly than others. However God will never fail you. He will heal, deliver and restore you. He is faithful. You can trust Him. He is the same yesterday, today and forever (Deut. 7:9; Joel 2:25-27; Heb. 13:8).

The emotional pain and rejection I experienced as a child actually drew me closer to God. It drew me into His healing, delivering love, power and presence. Again, it was only after I forgave my Dad that I developed a more intimate relationship with our heavenly Father that continues to grow until this day.

Right now I want to invite you to experience the same breakthrough that I did so many years ago when I chose to forgive my Dad. *I encourage you to choose to forgive your dad, mom or anyone that has hurt you.*

If you have any unforgiveness towards anyone, forgive him or her right now. Even if they have passed away, you can still forgive them. Just pray "The Prayer of Forgiveness" at the end of this chapter from your heart. Or pray in your own way. Either way, you'll experience healing and freedom that will positively impact your relationship with God, causing you to connect with Him more intimately. Your relationship with others will improve as well.

Your prayer life will grow leaps and bounds in intimacy, authority and power if you will choose this day to forgive those who have hurt you. Your fellowship with God will no longer be hindered, and God will forgive your sins when you ask Him, according to Mark 11:25-26:

> *And whenever you stand praying, if you have anything against anyone, forgive him and let it drop (leave it, let it go), in order that your Father Who is in heaven may also forgive you your [own] failings and shortcomings and let them drop. But if you do not forgive, neither will your Father in heaven forgive your failings and shortcomings (AMP).*

Jesus tells us in the Bible to bless and not curse our enemies. If Jesus told you to do this, He will give you the grace to do it:

> *But I say to you who hear: Love your enemies, do good to those who hate you, bless those who curse you, and pray for those who spitefully use you (Luke 6:27-28).*

In addition to forgiving others, also forgive yourself for the mistakes you have made. Now by faith, pray the "Prayer of Forgiveness" below and experience the burden of unforgiveness as it lifts from your shoulders. In Jesus' name. Amen.

PRAYER OF FORGIVENESS:

Dear God,

Thank you for life and health this day. Thank you for bringing me this far by faith and for saving my soul in Jesus' name. Thank you for your protection, mercy and grace. I bless your holy name.

Lord, I've been so hurt in the past by my parents, and/or (name/s) that I trusted. I confess that I have unforgiveness in my heart towards them. And right now, in the name of Jesus, I repent for this unforgiveness I have held in my heart towards (name/s). I choose by faith to forgive my dad, mom and/or (name/s) for hurting me.

I hold nothing against them. I release them right now. They don't owe me a single thing. Bless those who have hurt me Father. And Lord, I forgive myself for the mistakes I have made. And bless me to fulfill my purpose and destiny on earth by the power of Holy Spirit living in me. In Jesus' name, I pray. Amen.

Now write in the lines below the date and time you prayed the "Prayer of Forgiveness" to seal it into your memory. You can also write down any directions or prophetic words the Lord may have spoken to you regarding your prayer.

For example, you can write, "On this day, Tuesday, January 22, 2014, I forgave (name/s or yourself). Thank you, Father God, for forgiving me as I have forgiven those that offended me and for washing away my sins by the precious blood of Jesus."

After you have prayed this prayer, if you see anyone that hurt you in the past, resist and ignore any negative emotions that may try to tempt you to question if you forgave your offenders. Forgiveness takes place by faith.

Faith is not based on your *unsanctified emotions*, but on the truth of God's Word. Your holy emotions will follow your faith. Remind yourself that you forgave your offenders by faith on the date you recorded below. The past is in the tomb. Tomorrow is in the womb. Today is your time to bloom. Now move forward and cultivate a rich, intimate prayer life with God. He loves you unconditionally.

_____

_____

_____

_____

_____

_____

_____

_____

_____

_____

_____

_____

_____

_____

_____

_____

_____

_____

_____

_____

_____

_____

_____

CHAPTER 2

WHY PRAY?

It seems God is limited by our prayer life— that he can do nothing for humanity unless someone asks Him.
—John Wesley

Why pray? This is a question that has been asked by people throughout the ages. When I asked Father God why we should pray, He gave me several reasons covered in this chapter.

Prayer is the vehicle God uses to display His splendor, glory and majesty throughout the universe. The focus of prayer is always to glorify God. Jesus said:

Whatever you ask in My name, that will I do, so that the Father may be glorified in the Son. "If you ask Me anything in My name, I will do it" (John 14:13-14 NASB).

The purpose of prayer is to bring your life into harmony with God's will. It's not trying to get God to agree with you, or to bless you with things. Nor is it about trying to manipulate God, which is impossible anyway for He knows all things. Prayer is about extolling the greatness of God, as a loving, caring, sharing, heavenly Father, who deserves all glory, honor, and praise.

Simply put, God is the object of your prayers, not what He can give to you or others. The answers He provides to your prayers are an outgrowth of accepting His love for you and for those you cover in prayer. He wants you to put Him in first place before all others (Matthew 22:37-38). Here are some other reasons to pray that our Father shared with me:

1. *"You pray because it's the way you partner with Me to establish my will on earth. I have given you, my creation, my Sons and Daughters, dominion and authority on earth to release the creative, faith-filled power of my Word out of your mouth, as an avenue for me to pour my power into the earth and bring radical transformation to lives, regions, nations and weather patterns."*

Let's go to the book of beginnings and take a look at Genesis 1:26-28 to understand our delegated authority and dominion.

Then God said, "Let us make man in our image, according to our likeness; let them have dominion over the fish of the sea, over the birds of the air, and over the cattle, over all the earth and over every creeping thing that creeps on the earth." So God created man in His own image; in the image of God He created him; male and female He created them. Then God blessed them, and God said to them, "Be fruitful and multiply; fill the earth and subdue it; have dominion over the fish of the sea, over the birds of the air, and over every living thing that moves on the earth.

In this passage, we can see that God Elohim (the Triune God) gave dominion of the earth to Adam. Adam then committed high treason against God when he disobeyed Him by eating the fruit from the Tree of the Knowledge of Good and Evil. The authority God had delegated to Adam was then transferred to satan, who became the god of this world and the prince of the power of the air (2 Corinthians 4:4).

But thanks be to God for the last man Adam, our Lord and Savior Jesus Christ, for He has redeemed us by his death on the cross, breaking the power of sin, death, hell, and the grave over the life of every believer. Jesus' death also has restored our rightful authority in His name to rule and reign on earth as it was in the beginning before Adam and Eve sinned.

In other words, we are God's ambassadors, delegated with dominion and authority to reign on earth as kings (Romans 5:17). Therefore, when we pray, say, prophesy or decree a thing by faith that works by God's love, the ministering spirits, God's angelic force, go forth to bring it to pass (Psalm 103:20-22; Hebrews 1:14).

When you earnestly pray by faith believing in your heart, our Father will answer just like Jesus is praying. This is praying from the position of righteousness-consciousness where you know that you are a new creation in right standing with God by Jesus' precious blood, not sin-consciousness based on the old, carnal man. You know that Father God loves you and that Jesus has authorized you to decree covenant promises into the earth that will come to pass.

Jesus backs up your prayer from where He sits in heaven at the Father's right hand, ever interceding for us. He confirms to His Father that you are one of His, causing the angels to deliver powerful answers to your prayers. James 5:16b says:

The earnest (heartfelt, continued) prayer of a righteous man makes tremendous power available [dynamic in its working] (AMP).

As a believer, you must understand that it is only by grace through faith in Jesus that you have freely been given the gift of righteousness. Jesus' blood gives you bold, unlimited access to the Father's throne to make your requests known. The righteous man is one who knows that *only* in Christ Jesus lies the victory, for *our* righteousness is as filthy rags.

The righteous man keeps his heart lit with a fervent, red-hot desire to please God through prayer, seeking to know His heart and mind. Red-hot, fervent prayer will always hit the target, releasing God's plans and purposes on earth as it is in heaven.

As you commune with God, His desires will become yours. As you gaze into His beauty and behold Him, you will yearn to please Him. One way to please our Father is to pray for His will to be done on earth as it is in heaven.

2. You pray because Jesus commanded His disciples to pray to strengthen their spirit man to resist temptation. Before his death on the cross, Jesus took his inner circle—Peter, James and John—to pray with Him in the Garden of Gethsemane for strength to bear the weight of mankind's sin—past, present and future—on the cross. However, the disciples fell asleep at a time when Jesus most needed them. In Matthew 26:41, Jesus admonished them saying:

Watch and pray, lest you enter into temptation. The spirit indeed is willing, but the flesh is weak.

On another occasion, Jesus spoke a parable about the importance of persevering in prayer when He said,

Men always ought to pray and not faint (Luke 18:1).

3. You pray because Jesus and the Apostles taught us to ask for what we need or desire. Jesus said in Luke 11:10:

For everyone who asks receives, and he who seeks finds, and to him who knocks it will be opened (Luke 11:10).

Apostle Paul tells us in Philippians 4:6-9:

Be anxious for nothing, but in everything by prayer and supplication, with thanksgiving, let your requests be made known to God; and the peace of God, which surpasses all understanding, will guard your hearts and minds through Christ Jesus.

Apostle John encourages us to confidently approach God's throne to ask for what we need, according to God's will (which is His Word):

This is the confidence we have in approaching God: that if we ask anything according to his will, he hears us. And if we know that he hears us—whatever we ask—we know that we have what we asked of him (1 John 5:14-15).

4. You pray to fellowship and commune with God. God created mankind because He wanted a family. He looks forward to spending time with you, just like a good earthly parent delights in spending time with his or her child. He enjoys your presence so much that He gave His best, Jesus, His only begotten Son, to die on the cross for your sins to reconcile you back to Him.

After His resurrection, Jesus sent Holy Spirit to lead and guide the believer into all truth. When you confess Jesus as Lord of your life, Holy Spirit instantly comes to live within your recreated human spirit or heart. Almighty God loves you so much that He has chosen to live inside of you, desiring to daily commune with you (1 Cor. 3:16; Ezek. 36:26-27). You are a living tabernacle of God's miraculous glory, releasing His will on earth when you pray, say, decree, or prophesy.

5. You pray to thank and praise God for His goodness and all that He's done for you. In everything give thanks for this is the will of God concerning you in Christ Jesus (Psalms 100:4; 86:12; 1 Thess. 5:18).

6. You pray because Jesus, our Lord, and Master, commanded us to pray. He modeled a lifestyle of prayer for us to follow (Matthew 6:9-13). If Jesus prayed, we must be willing and obedient to pray, too. We are not above our Master (Luke 6:40).

When you read the gospels of Matthew, Mark, Luke and John, you will see that prayer was a priority in Jesus' life. It was more important than physical rest (Luke 6:12). It was more important than socializing. Jesus often went off to be alone with Father God to commune with Him (Matthew 14:23; Mark 1:35; Luke 5:16, 6:12). Prayer was more important than food because Jesus regularly fasted and prayed for long periods of time, especially before making major decisions. He also fasted and prayed to maintain spiritual vitality (Luke 4:2; Matt. 6:18). Jesus knew the secret—that abiding or continuing in God (communion and prayer) and allowing God to abide in Him (intercession) endued Him with spiritual strength to speak the Word in authority and to operate in signs, wonders and miracles.

7. You pray for others to release God's hand of mercy instead of judgment. This is inspired by the love of Holy Spirit in your heart. Isaiah 62:6-7 says:

I have set watchmen on your walls, O Jerusalem; They shall never hold their peace day or night. You who make mention of the Lord, do not keep silent, And give Him no rest till He establishes And till He makes Jerusalem a praise in the earth.

Ephesians 6:18 says:

*Praying always with all prayer and supplication in the
Spirit, being watchful to this end with all perseverance
and supplication for all the saints.*

God is compassionate, and He is seeking for intercessors that
will pray to release His hand of love and avert His hand of
judgment. Ezekiel 22:30 says:

*And I sought a man among them who should build up
the wall and stand in the gap before Me for the land,
that I should not destroy it, but I found none.*

God is seeking faithful intercessors that will pray now, not
later. Will you be one who will stand in the gap to pray for others,
whether you will feel like it or not?

WHAT IS PRAYER?

The Greek word most often used for prayer in the New
Testament is "proseuche." This is the word used in Ephesians
6:18, for the words "praying" and "prayer", where Paul says,
"Praying always with all types of prayer...".

This compound Greek word has an interesting meaning. The
word "pros" means face-to-face, and the word "euche" means
desire or vow. It originally depicted someone making a vow to
God in exchange for an urgent answer to prayer. Putting both
words together, you derive: "meeting God face-to-face in an
intimate relationship and surrendering your life to Him in
exchange for His". Real prayer is a love affair with God, where
you totally yield your life to Him.

Webster's Dictionary defines prayer as the act of asking for a
favor with earnestness. Prayer means "speaking, to request, to
talk, to commune, to fellowship, or to offer petition and
supplication for others or on your own behalf".

Prayer goes beyond just communicating with God, although it does begin there. It's a spirit-to-spirit connection. Effective communication is two-way and static-free. It's a dialogue. One speaks, while the other listens, without any *premeditated* thoughts. Prayer is not rattling off your wish list to God and leaving Him hanging once you get what you want. It's putting Father God first place in your heart, surrendering your will to hear and obey Him.

Prayer is communion with God that extends beyond your prayer closet. It is a lifestyle of holiness. Sometimes your times of prayer will be intense and protracted. Other times gentle and steady. Effective prayer is a spirit-to-spirit dialogue that takes place in an intimate setting, where you behold the Father's heart, crying out to bring to pass His desires because you love Him and His people.

True prayer is motivated by love first for God, and secondly, love for His people based on your love for yourself, according to Matthew 22:37-40, which says:

> *Jesus said to him, "'You shall love the Lord your God with all your heart, with all your soul, and with all your mind.' This is the first and great commandment. And the second is like it: 'You shall love your neighbor as yourself.' On these two commandments hangs all the Law and the Prophets."*

Spirit-inspired prayer is the most selfless, loving act that we can do to demonstrate God's love.

WHAT DOES PRAYER LOOK LIKE?

Prayer is ministering to God with thanksgiving, praise and worship based on how God has wired you. You need to be authentic when you pray. While there are principles and laws that must be exercised to get results in prayer, your heart flow must be transparent, pure and willing.

This time of communion with your Father can include many facets, from dancing and singing prayers of adoration, to prophesying and meditating Scriptures, to silent contemplation as you lay before Him spiritually and physically.

When I initially enter my secret place to pray, the picture looks like two hearts beating at a different rate, until I quiet my soul and center my mind on adoring, praising and worshiping the Lord. This gazing into His beauty causes our hearts to beat as one. At this depth of union, it is very difficult to leave God's presence because nothing else matters when I am surrounded by His glory.

Prayer involves speaking from your mouth with faith in your heart about what concerns Father. God's top priority is seeing people enter into a loving relationship with Him by faith in Christ Jesus. Intercessors are so important because we work in concert with God to pray souls into the kingdom. If we pray as Holy Spirit leads us, God will have the opportunity to work on people's hearts to save them, and to change circumstances to align with His will.

Prayer should be a daily discipline in the life of the believer, who desires to partner with God and establish His kingdom on earth. God admonishes us in the Old and New Testament to watch and pray. The Apostle Paul told us to pray without ceasing (1 Thess. 5:17).

How can you pray without ceasing when you have a full schedule—taking care of your spouse, getting kids ready for school, going to work, or running your own business, ministry or department? The better question is how can you not? When you access God's wisdom and grace through prayer, He provides everything you need to successfully complete your daily activities.

You must learn to live in a "spirit of prayer," making it a way of life. For example, when George Muller, a great man of prayer and intercession, was asked how much time he spent in prayer, he said that He lived in the "spirit of prayer". He prayed as He walked, laid down and rose up. Prayer was a way of life.

Some of you already live a life of prayer. Living in the spirit of prayer is abiding, remaining, continuing or dwelling in the Lord's presence and His Word, and allowing Him to abide in you. It is practicing His Presence and remaining consciously aware of Holy Spirit when He nudges you to pray, meditate or serve.

I have found that the most effective way to learn to pray is to meditate, study and pray the prayers found in the Bible. In addition, meditating the Word is more powerful because the anointing contained within God's Word penetrates your mind, renewing it with the mind of Christ. We will talk more about meditation in a later chapter.

LEVELS OF PRAYER: THE LAW OF ASKING, SEEKING AND KNOCKING (LUKE 11:9-10)

The first level of prayer is **asking.** This is making a simple request to God and getting an immediate answer. The condition to receive is simply to ask in faith, believing in your heart. Sometimes you don't get an answer because you don't ask for what you desire, or you ask with impure motives (James 4:2-3).

The next level of prayer is seeking. At this level, it will take longer for your answer to show up, but it will, in due season. Only believe. An example of this type of prayer can be found on the Day of Pentecost when all the disciples gathered in one accord in the Upper Room as Jesus had commanded them. Suddenly a mighty rushing wind blew into the room, and they were all baptized by fire as they were filled with Holy Spirit. They began to speak with other tongues. These disciples became great witnesses for Jesus, turning the world upside down as they spread the good news of the gospel of Jesus Christ and the kingdom of God. And the early church grew mightily (Acts 1:4-8, 2:1-4).

The third level of prayer is knocking until the answer comes. It is persistent prayer or intercession in the face of opposition. Daniel chapter 10 is a good example of persistent prayer. For 21 days, Daniel fasted and prayed (knocked) to know when God would release the Jews from Babylonian captivity. Even though God heard Daniel's prayer from the first time he prayed, one of satan's evil angels (a principality), delayed Gabriel, God's messenger angel, from delivering the answer. Gabriel delivered Daniel's answer because He prayed God's Word (Dan. 10:12).

Another example of persistent prayer can be found in the parable Jesus taught in Luke 11:5-10:

And He said to them, "Which of you shall have a friend, and go to him at midnight and say to him, 'Friend, lend me three loaves; for a friend of mine has come to me on his journey, and I have nothing to set before him'; and he will answer from within and say, 'Do not trouble me; the door is now shut, and my children are with me in bed; I cannot rise and give to you'? I say to you, though he will not rise and give to him because he is his friend, yet because of his persistence he will rise and give him as many as he needs. "So I say to you, ask, and it will be given to you; seek, and you will find; knock, and it will be opened to you. For everyone who asks receives, and he who seeks finds, and to him who knocks it will be opened."

What's important to note in this parable is that this is an example of intercession by a friend persistently asking for bread on behalf of another friend in need.

God is faithful to answer prayers that agree with His covenant promises. Sometimes there is an immediate answer, as for provision, and sometimes, such as with intercession for salvation for a loved one, revival, court cases and societal transformation, it may take longer. However, be comforted in knowing that God looks over His Word to perform it. He is faithful to answer you just like He answered Daniel. He is looking throughout the world for His devoted ones to show Himself strong on their behalf. Only believe!

PRAYER VERSUS INTERCESSION

All prayer is not intercession, but all intercession is prayer. Some think of intercession as synonymous with prayer, but it is not.

Intercession is a type of prayer where you allow God to use your entire being—spirit, soul, and body—to pray on another's behalf, led by Holy Spirit. When you pray for someone or a situation, you stand in the gap and build a hedge of protection for God to release His power to heal or fill the gap. Intercession can save a nation, deliver a loved one, or heal a sick body. The possibilities are limitless, which makes it so exciting! As Sons of God, intercession is how we legislate for God and write history on earth (Job 22:28; Rom. 8:14-15). We'll explore the prayer of intercession in Chapter 3.

Let's continue with prayer. Prayer is a privilege, a responsibility and a gift from God, giving the believer direct access into the Father's heart, from the position of being spiritually seated in heavenly places in Christ Jesus, your joint heir (Eph. 2:6). In prayer, you can ask God for what you need or desire. God beckons you to come *boldly* to His throne of grace and mercy to obtain the grace you need to endure and win every battle (Heb. 4:16). Every battle can be won because you are a royal priesthood created to rule and reign in life. You have been planted on earth to occupy and expand God's kingdom until He returns. Remember, there's no defeat in God—if you don't quit—because Jesus has already stripped satan and his cohorts of all power over the believer (Col. 2:15; 1 Cor. 15:57). When it comes to getting answers to your prayers, remember that delay is not denial and failure is not final.

As oxygen is to a human being, so is prayer to the believer. Prayer, which includes thanksgiving, praise, worship, fasting, decrees, confessions and meditation, is your spirit-to-spirit lifeline to God. Our Father will always answer Spirit-inspired prayers that agree with His Word, that are motivated by His love and that are in your best interest.

CHAPTER 3

OPERATING IN THE GOD-KIND OF FAITH

But without faith it is impossible to please Him, for he who comes to God must believe that He is, and that He is a rewarder of those who diligently seek Him.
—Hebrews 11:6 NKJV

This book would not be complete without emphasizing the importance of operating in the God-kind of faith, which pleases God. The faith of God is perhaps the single-most important facet of the believer's life. It's how God created everything, including you and me. It's the gift God has given every believer to fulfill his or her godly destiny to advance God's kingdom. Not the destiny you want, but the one laid out for you by your heavenly Father before the foundation of the world.

However, you cannot operate in the God-kind of faith without possessing revelation knowledge of God's Word. This is the reason Romans 10:17 says faith comes by hearing God's Word. This hearing is continuous. The level of faith you have is proportional to how much revelation knowledge you possess of God from the Word. Therefore, daily meditation of the Word is imperative to renew your mind to operate like the mind of Christ, casting down thoughts of fear, unbelief, doubt, distraction and deception (Josh. 1:8; Rom. 12:1-2; 2 Cor. 10:3-5).

WHAT IS THE GOD-KIND OF FAITH?

What is the God-kind of faith? A strong conviction or firm belief in something for which there may be no tangible proof. It's the opposite of doubt. The God-kind of faith is rooted in Jesus as Savior and Lord. It's being certain that you have the thing you hoped for now even though you do not see it. God's faith is not mere human faith. It is a supernatural gift that God has given to every believer that confesses Jesus as Lord. Hebrews 11:1-2 says:

Now faith is the substance of things hoped for, the evidence of things not seen. For by it the elders obtained a good testimony.

Faith is the intangible, spiritual stuff you are confident that God will supply in the natural realm. Do you remember when you confessed Jesus as Lord of your life? The moment you did, your spirit man was instantly born again by grace through faith (Eph. 2:8). If you haven't confessed Jesus as Lord of your life, this is a great time to invite Him into your heart. If you'd like, you can pray the Salvation prayer found in chapter 15 on page 269.

The God-kind of faith is a part of the fruit of the Spirit that every believer received in his or her heart the moment they confessed Jesus as Savior and Lord (Gal. 5:22). However, the measure of faith you have can lie dormant if you do not continually activate it by acquiring revelation knowledge of God's Word; or it can be choked to death if you abide in the carnal knowledge of the world. To have great faith, you must abide in the Word, which is Jesus, our hope of glory (John 1:1, 15:1-7).

According to Mark 11:22-25, the God-kind of faith has two keys—believing in your heart and saying that which you believe out of your mouth.

This kind of faith works based on having confidence that what God has promised, He will perform. Without faith in God, it is impossible to please Him for He is a loving, caring, sharing heavenly Father that desires to give His children the best. However, His hands are tied until you trust and believe His Word in your heart enough to say it out of your mouth.

To arrive at this point, you must have a solid trust in God's unconditional love for you, and His integrity towards you. The only way to obtain this is by consistent, focused meditation, study and reading of God's Word. Matt. 6:22 says:

> *The lamp of the body is the eye. If therefore your eye is good, your whole body will be full of light (NKJV).*

In other words, if you are full of the knowledge of God's Word, this is what will come out of your mouth in the good and bad times. Jesus wanted His disciples to live victoriously above the enemy, so He taught them about the God-kind of faith or the law of faith in Mark 11:22-25.

> *So Jesus answered and said to them, "Have faith in God. For assuredly, I say to you, whoever says to this mountain, 'Be removed and be cast into the sea,' and does not doubt in his heart, but believes that those things he says will be done, he will have whatever he says. Therefore I say to you, whatever things you ask when you pray, believe that you receive them, and you will have them. And whenever you stand praying, if you have anything against anyone, forgive him, that your Father in heaven may also forgive you your trespasses. But if you do not forgive, neither will your Father in heaven forgive your trespasses.*

According to Mark 11:23-24, Jesus told His disciples if you do not doubt in your heart, but believe what you say or pray, it will be done for you. You will receive it. You replace doubt with faith in your heart by eating the Word of God and acting upon it.

The God-kind of faith referenced in the phrase, "Have faith in God", is the same faith our heavenly Father used in Genesis 1:3-4 when He created light to dispel darkness. God believed He could create light. Then He said, "Light be" or "Let there be light" and it was so. The God-kind of faith is an intangible, spiritual substance activated when you believe with your heart and say it with your mouth, creating manifestation.

This is the same faith that you exercised when you became born-again. You believed in your heart that Jesus died for your sins and was raised from the dead, and then you confessed this with your mouth, receiving salvation. You heard the Word and faith came alive in your heart, according to Romans 10:9-10, which says:

That if you confess with your mouth the Lord Jesus and believe in your heart that God has raised Him from the dead, you will be saved. For with the heart one believes unto righteousness, and with the mouth confession is made unto salvation.

The same way that you received salvation, if you are a believer, is the same way you receive anything from God—by faith.

HOW DOES FAITH COME?

How does faith come? Romans 10:17 says faith comes by hearing God's Word. This hearing can be the Holy Spirit speaking directly to your heart, speaking God's Word out of your own mouth, or by listening to the teaching of an anointed man or woman, equipping you for the work of the ministry.

Apostle Paul calls the Word of God the Word of faith. Romans 10:8 says:

> *But what saith it? The word is nigh thee, even in thy mouth, and in thy heart: that is, the word of faith, which we preach. (KJV)*

The Word of faith works for every believer that will hear it, believe it, say it and do it. It is composed of faith-filled words that are containers of the supernatural power of God, with the ability to create new kingdom paradigms, realities and solutions. This is the same kind of faith that God utilized when He created the world and everything therein, according to Hebrews 11:3:

> *By faith we understand that the worlds were framed by the word of God, so that the things which are seen were not made of things which are visible.*

God believed what He said about the world and then He spoke it into existence. He said what He created was very good. Make sure before you speak what you believe that it is very good because it will come to pass. The God-kind of faith works when what you believe in your heart agrees with what you say out of your mouth in agreement with God's Word.

No agreement. No manifestation. When you pray with doubt in your heart, you will not get an answer because your belief is not based on eternal things, but upon carnal knowledge. But child of God, I have good news for you. Beginning right now, you can change this by making a quality decision to invest daily time, meditating the Word of God until it renews your mind, compelling you to take action because faith without works is dead (James 1:22).

According to Romans 12:3, Apostle Paul said that you (the believer) have received "the measure of faith". This measure is the master key for releasing God's divine plan, not your own—for your life and within the seven mountains of culture. The seven mountains are the pillars of society that include arts and entertainment, business, education, family, government, media and religion with subcategories. As believers, we are to position ourselves in the right mountain(s) to impact souls for Jesus, transforming society.

Regarding the law of faith, every great man and woman of God has operated it in increasing measure to advance God's kingdom. These forerunners of faith (see the "Faith Hall of Fame" in Hebrews 11:4-40) trusted in God's integrity and had confidence that what He said, He would do. The proof of their great faith can be seen in the great exploits they performed.

Have you ever seen someone operating at a higher level of faith than you in a particular area, such as wealth, health or relationships and wondered "when will I arrive"? Don't get discouraged because their faith didn't increase overnight. It was a process. They invested consistent time in the Word and obeyed God until it became a habit. They had to crawl, sit, stand, walk and run into maturity of faith.

As a thinking, speaking spirit, you were designed to live by faith, pleasing your heavenly Father by operating just like Him— calling things that be not as though they were. The God-kind of faith is now, not in the future. The moment you believe in your heart and say or pray it without doubt, it is yours. You take it! In my walk with God, I have learned that faith is taking God at His Word. No matter how long the answer takes to show up, I know I received it when I prayed. It's just a matter of time.

The more revelation knowledge of God's Word you can store in your heart, and the more you understand how much God loves you, the greater your faith will be to take action. Habakkuk 2:4, Romans 1:17 and Hebrews 10:37 all declare, "the just shall live by faith". God said it three times, so this is obviously very important. To me this means that any assignment God gives me will be so large that it will require me to use the measure of faith He's given me to accomplish it. In this way, God will always get the glory. If you can accomplish the mission on your own, you do not need the God-kind of faith.

HOW TO INCREASE YOUR FAITH

Can you trust, believe or have confidence in someone that you do not know? Absolutely not. If you desire to increase your faith in God, you must know Him intimately just like a child knows a good parent. Here are some steps you can employ, in addition to what Holy Spirit reveals to you:

1. Immerse yourself in God's presence with thanksgiving, praise, worship, communion, prayer and fasting and intercession to get to know Him.

   Your faith will increase as you continually encounter God's loving presence and feed your spirit with His Word. You see, the God-kind of faith works by love (Gal. 5:6). When you truly understand that God's unconditional love sent Jesus to die on the cross to forgive your sins—past, present and future, condemnation and guilt will be eradicated and you will take your rightful place and operate by faith as a Son of God.

   In other words, you will know you have the right to boldly approach God's throne and make your request known with the expectation of getting an answer because your Father loves you.

2. Immerse yourself in God's Word—meditating, studying, confessing, praying and reading the Scriptures—especially those dealing with faith or an area you desire to grow.

3. Focus on your God-given assignment. Dig into the Word and find a foundational verse to stand upon that will feed your spirit man, inspiring you to persevere and finish your assignment strong, in spite of inevitable opposition.

4. Take action. Do the impossible even if you have to do it with trembling knees. Depend upon Holy Spirit's power to provide the grace you need to finish strong.

You are an authorized ambassador of God in Christ Jesus, indwelled and empowered by Holy Spirit to represent the kingdom of heaven on earth and to enforce the enemy's defeat by Christ Jesus (Col. 2:15).

When you operate in the God-kind of faith, what is impossible with mere man will be possible with God. When I asked Father God about His faith—the God-kind of faith—this is what He said:

Your faith in Me is rooted in knowing Me intimately, not haphazardly or inconsistently. The closer you come to me, the more my faith in your heart will increase, so that you will operate in signs, wonders and miracles. This is my norm, Karen. My faith is my love to arm you to victoriously war on my behalf. I have given each of you that are mine in my Son our faith, so that by it you will wage a good war. As you learn to rest in my faith because you know I love you, and not your own human faith, your battles will become easier though they will become fiercer. Remember, my Son said it best, "It is my Father that does the work". The key of faith I've given you opens the door for me to step in and do what you cannot do on your own. This is why it pleases me when you step out by faith to do my will. It shows that you know me and I know you intimately. It demonstrates that you love and trust me as we work together to extend heaven on earth to deliver my children. Now go. Continue to fight the good fight of faith. And I Am with you always until the end.

In order to increase your faith in God, you must have an ear to hear what God is speaking, especially in the times we live. This requires an intimate relationship with God, which takes time to develop. You must value God's presence, friendship and His Word above everything else, just as He values you above everything else. He's waiting on you to spend time in His presence to validate and equip you to fulfill your purpose and destiny.

In His infinite love, the Most High God has blessed you with His faith to decree, declare, proclaim and pray His plans into the earth.

Son of God, ambassador of Christ Jesus, watchman of God, will you invest the time to position yourself at His gates to receive wisdom, understanding and revelation knowledge that will enable you to co-create with God by faith until the kingdoms of this world become the kingdoms of our Lord and of His Christ?

A prayer for you:

Father, I pray that the eyes of your people's understanding will be enlightened to know and understand the purpose for which you have planted them on earth. As they minister to you Father, I thank you for giving them a revelation of the breadth, length, depth and height of your love for them, as evidenced by

Jesus dying on the cross to forgive all of our sins. Bless them to encounter you in a new and living way, so their faith will increase exceedingly to fulfill the purpose and destiny for which you have ordained them, glorifying you alone. In Jesus' name. Amen.

Here are Scriptures to meditate about faith: Hab. 2:4; Mark 11:22-25; Matt. 9:22, 15:28, 21:21-22; Acts 6:5; Rom. 1:17, 10:9-10, 17, 12:3; 1 Cor. 13:2, 16:13; 2 Cor. 4:13-14, 5:6-7; Eph. 2:8-9, 6:16; Heb. 10:37, chapter 11; 1 John 5:4.

CHAPTER 4

ALL KINDS OF PRAYER

Use every kind of prayer and entreaty, and at every opportunity pray in the Spirit. Be on the alert about it; devote yourselves constantly to prayer for all God's people. —James 6:18 GNT

Our Father is so good! He's provided us with all kinds of prayer to supply our needs and desires, according to Ephesians 6:18. The purpose of defining the different types of prayers is not to restrict you with rules when you pray. It is to help you understand what the Bible teaches about each type of prayer, so you can maximize the power of prayer to accomplish God's agenda.

When you know the Scriptures concerning prayer, the Holy Spirit can fully use you because He works in alignment with God's Word. The Spirit of God can pull out of you the wisdom and revelation knowledge of God to accomplish kingdom purposes. This is like your manager selecting you to lead a special project at work because you possess the most knowledge and experience about a subject. Your manager can fully use you because you're thoroughly equipped.

I want to admonish you that just because we're discussing the laws and principles of prayer, don't become legalistic when you pray. Always flow with Holy Spirit. Don't try to be perfect.

Not by might nor by power, but by My Spirit, says the Lord of hosts (Zech. 4:6).

When you are yielded to Holy Spirit when you pray, your prayers will always strike God's mark.

Praying different kinds of prayers works together like the finger and thumb of your hand or the parts of your body. For example, you can pray the prayer of supplication, which is an earnest, heartfelt request or petition for yourself or others. The prayer of thanksgiving and praise can be prayed with all types of prayer because thanksgiving and praise is the protocol for approaching God (Psalm 100:4).

Your prayers or decrees don't have to be long to be effective, but they must be based on God's Word, inspired by Holy Spirit. Jesus decreed short, powerful prayers that got results, such as casting out devils and healing the sick because His prayers were based on God's spoken and written Word. Now let's dive into understanding the kinds of prayer found in the Bible to advance God's kingdom. First Timothy 2:1-4 says:

Therefore I exhort first of all that supplications, prayers, intercessions, and giving of thanks be made for all men, for kings and all who are in authority, that we may lead a quiet and peaceable life in all godliness and reverence. For this is good and acceptable in the sight of God our Savior, who desires all men to be saved and to come to the knowledge of the truth.

In this passage of Scripture, Apostle Paul mentions different types of prayers:

1. **Supplications**—A specific request or entreaty that is earnest and heartfelt, poured out of your heart to God; a petition

2. **Prayers**—A general request; communion with God; absolute dependence upon God for provision and protection for yourself

3. **Intercessions**—Praying on behalf of another; mediating or standing in the gap to hold back God's hand of judgment against a person, a nation or a situation

4. **Giving of thanks**—Thanking God for His goodness

NO FAITH, NO ANSWERS

The one caveat here is that regardless of the kind of prayer you pray, without faith that works by love, your prayers won't get results. This is because unforgiveness, doubt and unbelief hinder your prayers (Mark 11:22-25; Gal. 5:6). And without faith (that works by love, emphasis mine), it's impossible to please God.

Faith is the currency of heaven. When you pray, decree or prophesy, you must mix your words with the God-kind of faith, or you will not get results. Even when someone teaches or prophesies to you, if you don't mix the words you hear with faith (belief in your heart and action), you will not profit. Hebrews 4:2 reinforces this point:

> *For indeed the gospel was preached to us as well as to them; but the word, which they heard did not profit them, not being mixed with faith in those who heard it.*

God cursed the twelve Israelite spies/tribal leaders and all those over 20 years old that did not believe and act on His prophetic directive to go into Canaan and take it. They were cursed because they feared the giants that they saw in the land, instead of revering, trusting and believing what God prophesied through Moses about Canaan being their inheritance. The Israelites not only refused to believe God concerning the promised land of Canaan, but they tested God ten times, from murmuring and complaining to committing disobedience and unbelief—in spite of the miracles of provision, signs and wonders God performed to care for them in the wilderness (Num. 13:1-2, 27-33).

Without faith (confidence in what has been spoken to you that compels you to act), it is impossible to please Him. Figuratively, without faith in God, you tie His hands, preventing His help. Belief in your heart mixed with the spoken Word is like a supernatural conveyor belt that transfers what you need or desire—in agreement with God's plan for your life—from heaven to earth (Heb. 11:1).

RULES OF THE GAME

Just as there are different sports with different rules, there are different types of prayer with different laws. In the same way that you can't win a basketball game using the rules for football, you can't get answers to prayer when you apply the wrong laws.

For example, when praying the prayer of faith for healing cancer, you would never add the phrase "if it be thy will" like this:

"Father, in Jesus' name, I curse the spirit of cancer in my body. I command cancer to get out of my body right now, in Jesus' name. I call my body healed and cancer-free now by Jesus' stripes, **if it be your will.**"

The words, **"if it be your will"** effectively cancel your prayer for healing. You never use the phrase, **"if it be your will"** when praying the prayer of faith. This is because the prayer of faith is based on the revealed will of God (promises of God in your Bible). One of these promises says that by Jesus' stripes, you are healed (Isaiah 53:5; 2 Peter 2:24).

We'll discuss the prayer of faith later in this chapter. The point I'm emphasizing is that you must immerse yourself in God's playbook, the Bible, to learn the laws that govern prayer, so you can pray by faith.

Daily communion with God in prayer, and fasting along with meditation and memorization of Scripture, and regular studying and reading of God's Word are essential disciplines for solid spiritual growth and development. Again, our Father is so loving and kind that He has given us all kinds of prayer; to pray both for others and ourselves, so that we lack no good thing. Let's take a look at some of the different kinds of prayer.

PRAYER OF THANKSGIVING & PRAISE—
(PSALM 34: 1-4, 100:4; PHILIPPIANS 4:6-9; HEBREWS 13:15; 1 THESSALONIANS 5:16-18)

This prayer is the protocol for approaching God's throne. Psalm 100:4 says:

Enter into His gates with thanksgiving, And into His courts with praise. Be thankful to Him, and bless His name.

This prayer focuses on thanking and praising God for what He has done, is doing and will continue to do in your life. It is audible, demonstrative and animated. It releases the joy of the Lord, which is a spiritual force in your spirit man that strengthens you to endure (Neh. 8:10). Praise is the highest form of faith because you literally thank God in advance for the answer to your problem, or the desire of your heart, before you physically see it.

I have learned that when I'm going through a hard time, the best thing I can do is to kick off my shoes and go into my prayer closet. Then I lift my hands and begin to thank and praise God in word, song and dance for His eternal goodness and lovingkindness. I give God all the honor, all the glory and all the adoration for He is worthy to be praised. And as I praise Him, His presence rushes right into my situation, giving me the strength I need and causing the enemy to flee.

As I focus my mind, will and emotions on the goodness of our God, His presence floods into my soul, providing what I need. As I press beyond my flesh into thanksgiving and praise, I enter into the realm of God's glory, and what seemed to be an insurmountable obstacle, becomes a shadow in the light of Him.

In the glory realm, you forget all about your troubles as you encounter Almighty God Himself. Nothing else matters. The prayer of thanksgiving and praise releases breakthrough, causing negative emotions to dissipate, evil spirits to flee and natural enemies to shrink into perspective. Wisdom comes.

There are many powerful stories in the Bible about the power of the prayer of thanksgiving and praise (Joshua 6:1-20; 2 Chronicles 20:1-30; Acts 16:16-33). Let me share a testimony from my life about the power of the prayer of thanksgiving and praise.

Back in September 2010, I was working as a sales executive for a Fortune 100 company. One day on the job, I picked up too much at one time and hurt my shoulder. I ignored the pain and kept on working because I'm a healthy person and never get sick.

However, instead of getting better, the pain in my shoulder grew worse, preventing me from doing my job. In spite of the pain and having the use of only one arm, I kept working. I didn't want to go to the doctor because I had recently gotten a new boss that I needed to show I could deliver results. However, when my husband noticed how much pain I was in, he told me to go to the doctor.

After my exam, the doctor told me I had injured my rotator cuff. I still had no idea of the seriousness of the injury; until he told me I couldn't go back to work until my shoulder got better. He recommended worker's compensation since I had hurt myself on the job. The healing of my shoulder took longer than anticipated. Soon my employer cut off my worker's compensation benefits, and I had to get an attorney to fight for reinstatement of benefits. Finances got tight. The legal battle was turning up. And I was dependent upon God and my husband for provision in a way that was far outside of the comfort zone of this first-born child.

I was accustomed to helping my husband care for our family. So I was experiencing a lot of frustration not being able to work. The enemy attacked my mind with thoughts of fear about running out of money. He harassed me with lies that I would not be able to dance anymore (I operate a local worship dance school).

I also felt imprisoned inside of my own home, until I tuned into Holy Spirit through thanksgiving, praise and worship and meditating the Word, and Daddy God gave me a strategy. He told me to increase my prayer time for others and myself. So I began to ask family and friends if they needed prayer for anything. I prayed with them for medical exams, court hearings, job interviews, trips and college exams. I watched and prayed at home, while those on the front line that I prayed in agreement with took action and got the victory!

I felt like Moses interceding with Aaron and Hur for Joshua and the army of Israel that was fighting on the frontline to defeat the Amalekites (Ex. 17:8-16). And the Israelites won the battle on the front line through the power of intercession!

However, the enemy was relentless at shooting fiery darts (negative thoughts) to discourage me. His lies included intimidating statements, such as " I got you now. You're going to lose your home. I'm going to destroy everything you've worked to achieve. You worked all those years for nothing. Just look at how they're treating you now. I'm going to ruin your credit. You'll never have anything."

I took authority and resisted those thoughts by opening my mouth and rebuking the lies from the enemy. I would decree faith-filled statements, such as "All is well" and "No weapon formed against me and my family will prosper!" I shouted and danced, thanking and praising God for His faithfulness to give me the victory now, releasing the spirit of the Lion of Judah (praise) to war on my behalf.

I increased the amount of time I spent in prayer and intercession even more, continually thanking and praising God for all of His blessings. I increased my time meditating, reading and studying God's Word, and worshipping God. I increased fasting as well. I sat under sound teaching at my local church and under other anointed teachers. All these actions combined strengthened my trust and faith in God and to outlast the devil.

As the battle ensued, I decreed and declared faith-filled statements, such as, "Thank you Father for giving me favor to win this worker's compensation case, in Jesus' name." And it came to pass in the fullness of time that I won my case and my shoulder was healed! God showed Himself strong, not only on my behalf, but on the behalf of those for whom I interceded. As I continued to war in the Spirit with thanksgiving and praise to God, singing songs of praise, shouting for joy, clapping my hands and dancing in advance that God gave me the victory!

If you would like to tap into the power of thanksgiving and praise, start by praying or singing the Psalms to the Lord from your heart. The book of Psalms is an excellent place to find prayers of thanksgiving and praise because most of the Psalms are prayers that were sung. Some of my favorite ones are Psalm 23, 34, 91, 100, 103, 107 and 145-150. You can also dance a prayer of thanksgiving and praise unto the Lord. I have learned that when you approach God with an attitude of gratitude and faith, you capture His attention, causing the angelic hosts to minister on your behalf (Hebrews 1:14).

The Bible says if you have faith as small as a mustard seed, you will speak to the mountain and it will be removed. Right now, some of you are going through hard times, which is a part of life. But I want you to know that if you keep on thanking and praising God for your answer, if you keep on decreeing what you need or desire based on God's Word, if you keep on worshiping Him, you will receive your breakthrough right on time. As my friend, Pastor Marie Hawkins, says, "Don't give up, don't give out and don't give in. Keep your eye on the prize." Put God in remembrance of His Word, and He is faithful to perform it.

An exciting story in the Bible that illustrates the power of thanksgiving and praise is found in Acts 16:25-33. As previously mentioned, this is the account where Paul and Silas were unjustly imprisoned after Paul cast a spirit of divination (spirit of python) out of a damsel. This woman had a prophetic gift that was being prostituted by two evil men for money.

Once the men found they could no longer make a profit using the damsel's prophetic gift, they falsely accused Paul and Silas, who were then unjustly arrested, beaten and thrown into a dank, dark, wet prison with chains on their hands and feet. But in spite of their chains and the pain in their bleeding backs, at their midnight hour, (the darkest moment of your life, when all seems lost), Paul and Silas began to pray and sing praises unto God. When you thank and praise God at your midnight hour, this is called a "yet praise".

You will always capture God's attention with a "yet" praise". As Paul and Silas loudly praised God with no shame in their game, everyone in the prison heard them. God was so pleased with their sacrifice of thanksgiving and praise that He responded by triggering an earthquake that shook the ground so hard that all the prisoners' chains fell off. This is the power of the prayer of thanksgiving and praise. It compels God to move on your behalf as well for others.

The earthquake so amazed the prison guard that he asked Paul what must he do to be saved. That night the prison guard and his whole family confessed Jesus as Lord of their lives. Later that day, Paul and Silas were released from prison, when it was revealed they had been unjustly accused.

Even though in the natural, Paul and Silas had every right to murmur and complain because of their mistreatment and abuse, they chose instead to turn their face unto God and give Him a "yet praise". What is a "yet praise" you may ask? Again, it's the sacrifice of praise that you give unto God in the midst of your deepest, darkest hour. When it seems like everyone has forsaken you, and that all hope is gone, give God a "yet praise." This is the kind of praise that the Psalmist David gave to God in his midnight hour, according to Psalm 43:5:

Why are you cast down, O my soul? And why are you disquieted within me? Hope in God; For I shall yet praise Him, The help of my countenance and my God.

When you persist in giving God thanksgiving and praise in your midnight hour, you will always encounter the Lord of

Breakthrough and He will give you the victory (Micah 2:12-13; 1 Cor. 15:57). The Psalmist David, a worshiper, was a man acquainted with adversity. But he knew how to ignore his troubles by focusing on God and opening up his mouth to give God a "yet praise".

> *Let them be confounded and consumed Who are adversaries of my life; Let them be covered with reproach and dishonor Who seek my hurt. But I will hope continually, And will praise You yet more and more. My mouth shall tell of Your righteousness And Your salvation all the day, For I do not know their limits (Psalm 71:13-15).*

David's praise turned his situation around. So in spite of your situation, in spite of your problems, in spite of the pain in your body, in spite of what's in your bank account, turn your face unto God and give Him a "yet praise!" He will make a way out of no way, for He is Jehovah Jireh. This means He is our God who sees ahead what you need and provides. He has already provided everything that you need by faith. So right now, give God a "yet praise!"

7 HEBREW WORDS FOR PRAISE

I encourage you to incorporate these seven ways of praise into your time of thanking and praising the Lord, and watch God show up.

1. **Halal** is a primary Hebrew root word for praise. It means "to be clear, to shine, to boast, show, to rave, celebrate, to be clamorously foolish" (1 Chr. 16:4; Psalm 149:3; 150:1).

2. **Yadah** means "the extended hand, to throw out the hand, therefore to worship with extended hand" (2 Chr. 20:21; Psalm 92:1, 142:7).

3. **Towdah** literally means, "an extension of the hand in adoration, avowal, or acceptance". It is used for thanking God for "things not yet received" as well as things that have already been received; a choir of worshippers (Psalm 50:14, 69:30, 100:4).

4. **Shabach** means, "to shout, to address in a loud tone, to command, to triumph" (Psalm 47:1, 63:2, 145:4).

5. **Barak** means "to kneel down, to bless God as an act of adoration" (Psalm 95:6, 63:4, 34:1).

6. **Zamar** means, "to pluck the strings of an instrument, to sing, to praise" (1 Chr. 16:9; Psalm 21:13, 57:9).

Tehillah means "the singing of halals, to sing or to laud, a new song, hymns of praise" (Psalm 22:3, 33:1, 34:1).

PRAYER OF WORSHIP—
(LUKE 24:52-53; ACTS 4:23-24, 13:1-4)

This is the prayer that gives God reverence for Who He is—Jehovah, the Great I Am that I Am. The word "worship" in the Hebrew means to obey God; worship is an act that springs from the heart. It incorporates song, movement, music and the Word of God. It is also called "harp and bowl" worship. The harp represents songs and music and the bowl represents the prayers of the saints mixed with incense in heaven. The speakers say prayers, the singers sing prayers, and the musicians play prayers on instruments, all flowing together in spiritual unity to release a fragrant aroma of worship unto the Lord.

The pattern for the prayer of worship goes on eternally in heaven, according to Revelation chapters 4 and 5. God downloaded this heavenly pattern of "harp and bowl" worship to King David. He instituted it in the Tabernacle of David (TOD), where he employed, according to some Bible scholars, over 4,000 worshipers and 3,000 musicians 24 hours a day, 7 days a week to worship the Lord. The only furniture in the TOD was the Ark of the Covenant, which represented God's holy presence (1 Chronicles 15 and 16). Today, the believer carries the Ark of the Covenant in his heart by the power of the Holy Spirit.

This Davidic-style of worship is now being restored to the New Testament Church, as prophesied in Amos 9:11-12 and spoken again by the Apostle James in Acts 15:13-18. Worship is rooted in having an intimate relationship with God. Thanksgiving and praise precede it. You cannot separate thanksgiving, praise, and worship. It is a three-fold cord of prayer that ushers in God's presence.

Worship makes prayer refreshing and enjoyable. It also enables you to pray longer. It releases the glory realm of signs, wonders and miracles. I believe more people would attend prayer meetings if thanksgiving and praise and worship were incorporated and allowed to freely flow, according to God's heavenly model. The Church of the past with its traditions, agendas and programs has no power. People are hungry for a real encounter with God's supernatural power and love to set them free (Acts. 2:1-4; Mark 6:15-20).

As leaders, we must throw away programs and formulas and yield to Holy Spirit's flow in our church services and prayer meetings, so that God's glory manifests to save, heal and deliver souls. Our heavenly Father enjoys when we lavish Him with pure worship from our hearts. It's not about how beautifully you sing, dance, play, teach, preach or prophesy. It's all about loving Him.

PRAYER OF FAITH OR PETITION—
(MARK 11:22-24; MATTHEW 21:22)

First, every prayer we pray requires faith to generate results. Faith is believing that what God has said, either written or spoken, that He will perform it. Faith includes corresponding action. It is released by speaking God's Word out of your mouth, while believing it in your heart, and then acting upon it.

For example, if you pray the prayer of thanksgiving and praise, you must release your faith to believe that God will respond to your thanksgiving and praise. If you pray the prayer of dedication and consecration, you must have faith that even though you are unclear about God's will for your life, you trust Him to order your footsteps.

However the prayer of faith or petition requires a different kind of faith. It is a targeted faith designed to meet a specific need. This is the prayer that changes things. It is based upon knowing God's will beyond a shadow of a doubt, so that when you pray, you know you have received the answer. After praying the prayer of faith about a matter, feed your faith by thanking and praising God for the answer until it manifests.

In the spirit realm where God, the Creator of heaven and earth lives (third heaven), everything is already complete or done. As a powerful spirit being that predates earth, you have authority in Jesus' name on earth to call things that be not as though they were. This is the God-kind of faith or the law of faith. You can expect the thing for which you pray to manifest in the natural realm because the moment you say it, your faith reaches into the spirit realm to transfer it into the natural realm. Faith is now.

However, before you can effectively pray the prayer of faith, go to your Bible and meditate the Scriptures that apply to your situation until you have this Word firmly settled in your heart, without doubt. This will take daily time spent in God's presence and meditating His Word. Investing this time that will earn you a 100% return on your investment. Again, you must meditate the appropriate Scriptures and visualize what you desire until the matter is firmly established in your heart, so that when you say, pray or decree the promise in agreement with God's Word and plan for your life, it is established on earth.

Sometimes we pray the prayer of faith prematurely because we haven't meditated God's Word long enough to build faith to believe for a thing. You must know God's Word for yourself in order to pray the prayer of faith effectively. Otherwise your prayer will not work. You cannot live off the faith of your spouse, parents, pastor or Bible teacher. You have to wield your own sword of the spirit. This means you must abide (remain, dwell, rest, continue) in God's Word (Jesus), so that He abides in you. Then you will ask what you will (His will) and it will be done for you (John 15:7).

As previously mentioned, the prayer of faith never contains the phrase "if it be your will" because it is unscriptural to pray, "if it be your will", when you know God's will (the Word or promises of God). For example, if you are a blood-bought, obedient child of God, you would never pray "Father, if it be your will, bless me to safely arrive on this flight to Dallas." The Word of God already tells you that God will protect you (Psalm 23, 41:10, 91; Isaiah 54:17; 2 Samuel 22:3-4). The word "if" implies doubt, which hinders your prayer. You say, "Father, I thank you for keeping the pilots alert and for a safe, smooth flight without turbulence or mechanical difficulties, in Jesus' name."

Or you can make a decree: "In the name of Jesus, I command this flight to go smoothly and all my luggage to arrive on time. I rebuke turbulence and engine problems. I command the angels to go before this jet clearing the air highway of all turbulence, in Jesus' name. Amen." As you grow in your authority in Christ Jesus, you will decree more and ask less because you will know the promises in the Bible belong to you as a Son of God (male or female).

Faith is having confidence in God's integrity and power to back up His Word, both written and spoken. Your faith will increase as you meditate God's Word and get a revelation of how much He loves you.

Two of the greatest hindrances to your faith are doubt and unforgiveness. Let's see how Jesus addressed doubt. (We will cover unforgiveness under the "Prayer of Forgiveness".) Jesus said in Mark 11:22-25:

> *So Jesus answered and said to them, "Have faith in God. For assuredly, I say to you, whoever says to this mountain, 'Be removed and be cast into the sea,'* **and does not doubt in his heart, but believes that those things he says will be done, he will have whatever he says. Therefore I say to you, whatever things you ask when you pray, believe that you receive them, and you will have them.** *"And whenever you stand praying, if you have anything against anyone, forgive him, that your Father in heaven may also forgive you your trespasses.*

Jesus clearly states above in bold that if you do not have doubt in your heart, but believe what you say will be done, you will have what you say. When you speak words of faith, you take possession in the spirit realm first. Then your answer shows up in the natural realm, if you don't doubt. The word "will" is future tense. It means it is on the way.

Doubt will hinder your prayers because it disconnects your spirit-to-spirit connection with God, who is your Source. Doubt causes you to focus on the natural realm, which is temporary.

However, the spirit realm is the causal realm, where everything begins.

The word "heart" in the verse above is not referring to the blood pump in your chest, but to your spirit man, the inward man or the hidden man of the heart. To believe God with your heart is to believe God with your spirit, not your mind. When you believe with your spirit/heart, you tap into the highest realm of reality, the truth of God. It's just a matter of time before your answer appears in the natural realm. Just make sure that what you pray or say agrees with God's Word—no ridiculous or selfish prayers.

When you pray the prayer of faith, you must believe you've got the answer before it manifests in the natural realm (Mark 11:24). For example, you may be flat on your back, sick with the flu. However, the moment you take authority over the mountain of flu and speak to it saying, "In the name of Jesus, I curse you, spirit of flu. I command you to get out of my body now. By Jesus' stripes, I am healed!" The moment you prayed, you were healed. Whether you immediately feel like it or not is irrelevant because faith is not based on what you see or feel. It's based on the authority of God's Word that supersedes the natural realm. You believe first in your heart or spirit, and then you speak this forth out of your mouth and your healing will manifest. Believe it, speak it and you will receive it.

> *Therefore I say to you, whatever things you ask when you pray, believe that you receive them, and you will have them (Mark 11:24).*

If you really believe that you have been healed, then you will do something you couldn't do before like get up from your bed and begin to praise God for your healing. To believe with the heart is to believe with your spirit, not based upon what your five physical senses perceive. To operate with the God-kind of faith, you believe first in your spirit, and then you speak it out of your mouth and then you will receive the manifestation in the natural realm.

Mark 11:22-25 in the Amplified Bible says:

And Jesus, replying, said to them, Have faith in God [constantly]. Truly I tell you, whoever says to this mountain, Be lifted up and thrown into the sea! ***And does not doubt at all in his heart but believes that what he says will take place, it will be done for him.*** *For this reason I am telling you,* ***whatever you ask for in prayer, believe (trust and be confident) that it is granted to you, and you will [get it].*** *And whenever you stand praying, if you have anything against anyone, forgive him and let it drop (leave it, let it go), in order that your Father Who is in heaven may also forgive you your [own] failings and shortcomings and let them drop.*

When will you get your healing or what you desire? According to the verses in bold above—when you believe and are confident in your heart that it's your right to walk in wholeness. You don't see or feel the answer first, and then believe. You believe first with your spirit that you have it when you pray or say it based on God's Word. The God-kind of faith is foolishness to the mind, because it's not rational or logical. It's supernatural believing and this is what believers do. We take God at His Word.

As previously mentioned, everything is already completed in the spirit realm or heaven. So after you have prayed, be patient. Continue to feed your faith with thanksgiving, praise and worship, meditation, decrees and faith-filled confessions until your answer shows up.

The prayer of faith is built upon trust, belief and confidence in God and His Word. Physical evidence follows. Trust in the Lord with all your heart (or spirit); don't lean unto your own understanding (carnal mind, sense realm evidence). In all your ways acknowledge Him (Holy Spirit, Word of God, spoken Word) and He will direct your steps (wisdom, knowledge, understanding, revelation, manifestations). Be led by the Spirit, for you are a Son of God.

In closing, your faith is not based on what you do or do not see, hear, feel, smell, or taste (sense realm evidence), but on what God's Word says, period. To increase your faith in any area, worship God and meditate the Scriptures that deal with that particular subject. Feed on the Word of God and it will also strengthen your spirit man to believe God, and resist doubt.

Man shall not live by bread alone, but by every Word that proceeds out of God's mouth. Just as you eat healthy food, drink pure water and exercise to strengthen your physical body, you must do the same to have a strong spirit man. You must eat a healthy daily diet of spiritual food (prayer, fasting, meditating, studying and reading the Word of God, listening to sound teaching, prophesying and speaking faith-filled words over your life and others). These spiritual disciplines will strengthen your spirit man, so you have faith and confidence in God's love that you are already blessed to be a blessing.

PRAYER OF FORGIVENESS—
(MARK 11:25-26; MATTHEW 6:12, 18:32-38)

This is the prayer to forgive others, so that your relationship with God is unhindered and He answers your prayers. In Mark 11:25-26, Jesus says that when you're standing to pray or preparing to pray, forgive anyone that has hurt you, so that your heavenly Father will forgive your trespasses:

And whenever you stand praying, if you have anything against anyone, forgive him, that your Father in heaven may also forgive you your trespasses. But if you do not forgive, neither will your Father in heaven forgive your trespasses.

Unforgiveness in your heart stifles intimacy with God, and it opens the door for the enemy to release torments, such as anxiety, bitterness, frustration, stress, sickness and disease, unhealthy anger and more.

In the parable of the unforgiving servant, his master forgave him for a $10,000,000 debt when he begged his master not to sell him and his family into slavery to pay the debt. But when this same servant came across someone who owed him $20, he grabbed him by the throat and told him to pay his debt. When the poor guy asked for more time to pay the debt, instead of extending mercy, the unforgiving servant threw him in prison. When the master, who had forgiven the unforgiving servant for a $10,000,000 debt, heard the story, he summoned the unforgiving servant, and this is what he said to him:

Then his master, after he had called him, said to him, 'You wicked servant! I forgave you all that debt because you begged me. Should you not also have had compassion on your fellow servant, just as I had pity on you?' And his master was angry, and delivered him to the torturers until he should pay all that was due to him. "So My heavenly Father also will do to you if each of you, from his heart, does not forgive his brother his trespasses" (Matthew 18:32-38, AMP).

Unforgiveness releases tormenting spirits into your life to harass you. It hinders your relationship with God because your heart does not entirely belong to Him. The poison of unforgiveness infects your heart, hindering your ability to draw near to God and build healthy relationships. When you give your heart totally to Jesus, you will experience peace and intimacy that will empower you to hear Him clearly, and to love and obey Him dearly.

PRAYER OF CONFESSION & REPENTANCE—
(PSALM 51; 1 JOHN 1:8-10)

We all sin and miss the mark. This is why it's important to know about the gift of repentance, which is available by faith through the precious blood of Jesus Christ, our Lord and Savior. Repentance means to change your way of thinking to align with God's Word. Through Jesus' sacrificial death, when you sin you have the right to pray the prayer of confession and repentance and God will forgive your sins. 1 John 1:8-10 says,

If we say that we have no sin, we deceive ourselves, and the truth is not in us. If we confess our sins, He is faithful and just to forgive us our sins and to cleanse us from all unrighteousness. If we say that we have not sinned, we make Him a liar, and His word is not in us.

The Apostle John is writing this letter to born-again believers to give us hope, not a license to sin. You don't need a license to sin. When you sin, repent quickly so you remain vitally connected to God. He is your Source for everything that pertains to life and godliness.

One of the most popular prayers of repentance in the Bible is found in Psalm 51 (see verses 1-4 below), where King David repented to God after the Prophet Nathan confronted him for committing adultery with Bathsheba, and for having her husband murdered. When King David was confronted, he made no excuses. He quickly repented in brokenness, asking God to forgive and cleanse Him for His sin, transgressions, iniquity and guilt.

Have mercy upon me, O God, According to Your lovingkindness; According to the multitude of Your tender mercies, Blot out my transgressions. Wash me thoroughly from my iniquity, And cleanse me from my sin. For I acknowledge my transgressions, And my sin is always before me. Against You, You only, have I sinned, And done this evil in Your sight—That You may be found just when You speak, And blameless when You judge (Psalm 51:1-4).

David, who God called a man after His own heart, earnestly asked the Father to create a clean heart in him, so that he could experience the joy of salvation again, and teach transgressors God's ways (Psalm 51:5-17). King David knew one of the great secrets of prayer:

If I regard iniquity in my heart, The Lord will not hear (Psalm 66:18).

Iniquity is a bent or propensity to commit premeditated sin and not repent that is found in your bloodline, such as David's committing adultery with Bathsheba. Because he didn't repent, it lead to murder Transgression is intentionally disobeying God by crossing the line, such as running a red light. And sin is missing the mark in thought, word or deed, such as sexually lusting for someone in your heart. All sin separates you from God because it is evil, while obedience draws you to Him. If you truly repent, God removes your sins as far as the east is from the west (Psalm 103:12). God not only removes your sins, He removes all the guilt, so you can move forward in life just like you have never sinned before. Oh what joy and freedom!

PRAYER OF COMMITMENT—
(1 PETER 5:6-7; PHILIPPIANS 4:6-9)

The prayer of commitment eradicates the spirit of worry from your life as you cast your cares upon the Lord, who is built to carry them for you. 1 Peter 5:7 says:

> *Casting the whole of your care [all your anxieties, all your worries, all your concerns, once and for all] on Him, for He cares for you affectionately and cares about you watchfully (AMP).*

The prayer of commitment is a way to put all your worries in a bag concerning an issue, and give it to God to handle once and for all. This prayer helps you to focus your faith on God's Word, instead of worrying. Remember to always come before God with thanksgiving and praise in your heart. You cast your care by telling your heavenly Father the good, the bad and the ugly concerning your problems. You unload on God. You pour out your heart about what you're going through and what you need. You search the Bible to find the promises of God that apply to your situation and meditate them to build up your faith to believe for the answer. Philippians 4:6-8 says:

> *Be anxious for nothing, but in everything by prayer and supplication with thanksgiving, let your requests be made known to God; and the peace of God, which surpasses all understanding, will guard your hearts and your minds through Christ Jesus. Finally, brethren, whatever things are true, whatever things are noble, whatever things are just, whatever things are pure, whatever things are lovely, whatever things are of good report, if there is any virtue and if there is anything praiseworthy—meditate on these things.*

When casting your cares upon God, you must resist worry and anxiety by meditating on how much your heavenly Father loves you. Think about this. Our Father takes care of all the birds around the world. How many species of birds do you think exist? Now if you are His covenant Son or Daughter made in His likeness or image, how much more do you think He will take care of you?

Keep your mind focused on your desired outcome or a good report. Activate your faith by finding the right seed (verses) in the Word of God that addresses your need. Then decree it into the atmosphere, believing in your heart that the answer is already yours. Apostle Paul says to keep your affection on things above or eternal. God's provision for you is eternal. This means His supply never runs out. You access God's supply by faith. You will know that you have cast your cares on Jesus when you have peace that passes all understanding. Remember, faith rests. It doesn't stress, strain or struggle. Faith rests. Selah.

PRAYER OF CONSECRATION—
(MATTHEW 26:36-46; GAL. 2:20)

The purpose of the prayer of consecration, also called the prayer of dedication, is to dedicate your life to and for the service of God. It involves daily dying to your will to glorify God. It's the only prayer where you can use the phrase "if it be thy will" without it being considered unbelief.

The prayer Jesus prayed three times in the Garden of Gethsemane before his death on the cross is an example of the prayer of consecration. For Jesus, it was the ultimate test of dying to His will and yielding to the Father's. This prayer is found in Matthew 26:36-46. It says:

Then Jesus came with them to a place called Gethsemane, and said to the disciples, "Sit here while I go and pray over there." And He took with Him Peter and the two sons of Zebedee, and He began to be sorrowful and deeply distressed. Then He said to them, "My soul is exceedingly sorrowful, even to death. Stay here and watch with Me." He went a little farther and fell on His face, and prayed, saying, "O My Father, if it is possible, let this cup pass from Me; nevertheless, not as I will, but as You will." Then He came to the disciples and found them sleeping, and said to Peter, "What! Could you not watch with Me one hour? Watch and pray, lest you enter into temptation. The spirit indeed is willing, but the flesh is weak." Again, a second time, He went away and prayed, saying, "O My Father, if this cup cannot pass away from Me unless I drink it, Your will be done." And He came and found them asleep again, for their eyes were heavy. So He left them, went away again, and prayed the third time, saying the same words. Then He came to His disciples and said to them, "Are you still sleeping and resting? Behold, the hour is at hand, and the Son of Man is being betrayed into the hands of sinners. Rise, let us be going. See, My betrayer is at hand."

Three times, Jesus' flesh, the human part of Him, battled with His spirit man that always desired to do the Father's will, which was to die on the cross (Matt. 26:39, 42, 44). Strengthened by angels as He travailed in the prayer of consecration to bear the burden of the sin of mankind, Jesus' spirit man prevailed. Had he not, we would be eternally lost to sin, death, hell and the grave. Thank you Jesus!

Our Lord and Savior, Jesus Christ, understood that His life purpose was to please His Father by doing His will. Everything Jesus did was to glorify the Father (John 5:30). Likewise every believer that will fulfill his or her godly purpose will utter the prayer of consecration at different seasons of life to please our Father. In fact, you have the opportunity every day to consecrate or rededicate your life to God when you encounter those who mistreat, hurt or misunderstand you. Will you choose to forgive or overlook an offense, or will you react in the flesh?

It's not easy to die to your flesh, but it is essential to be transformed into the image of Christ Jesus. When you trust and willingly obey God's will for your life, instead of your flesh, you will eat the good of the land and receive a crown of righteousness in eternity.

PRAYER OF SUPPLICATION—
(JAMES 5:16B; PHILIPPIANS 4:6; EPHESIANS 6:18; 1 TIMOTHY 2:1-2)

A supplication is a specific humble, earnest entreaty or request for others or yourself. It is not casual. It is fervent and persistent. It involves bowing low to God and may include weeping. This prayer always delivers results. James 5:16b (AMP) says:

> *Confess to one another therefore your faults (your slips, your false steps, your offenses, your sins) and pray [also] for one another, that you may be healed and restored [to a spiritual tone of mind and heart]. The earnest (heartfelt, continued) prayer of a righteous man makes tremendous power available [dynamic in its working].*

The supplications of a righteous man open up a conduit for God to release His power on earth. A prayer of supplication can be prayed for many reasons:

- For believers or saints (Eph. 6:18)

- For leaders and all men, believers and unbelievers alike (1 Tim. 2:1-2)

- For the spiritual needs of others (Eph. 1:16; Phil. 1:9; Col. 1:9, 4:12)

- For forgiveness of your sins and others (1 Kings, 8:34; Dan. 9:3, 17-18)

- For yourself (Psalm 28:2; Phil. 4:6)

A biblical example of the prayer of supplication (and travail, which will be covered later) is Hannah's prayer found in 1 Samuel 1:10-17. She wept as she earnestly and fervently asked God to bless her with a child, whom she vowed to dedicate to the Lord. The child grew up to become the Prophet Samuel, a great prophet and judge of God in the Old Testament. You can see the supplication of Hannah in verses 10-11 below:

And she was in bitterness of soul, and prayed to the Lord and wept in anguish. Then she made a vow and said, "O Lord of hosts, if You will indeed look on the affliction of Your maidservant and remember me, and not forget Your maidservant, but will give Your maidservant a male child, then I will give him to the Lord all the days of his life, and no razor shall come upon his head."

Hannah's supplication moved God and He blessed her with not just one child, but six. She later prayed a prayer of thanksgiving and praise to God, prophesying about the coming of the Jesus, the Messiah in 1 Samuel 2:10.

He will give strength to his king and exalt the horn of his anointed (NIV).

The prayer of supplication, like the prayer of faith, changes things because the believer relentlessly cries out to God and will not let go until He answers.

PRAYER OF AGREEMENT— (MATT. 18:19-20; 1 JOHN 5:14-15)

The prayer of agreement requires agreement with someone else with like or greater faith regarding something specific that you desire from God. It is a powerful prayer because you combine your faith with another believer, exponentially increasing the amount of faith released to obtain your answer.

The Holy Spirit must be the One that harmonizes the prayer of agreement. He produces the power to answer the prayer. The true power of the prayer of agreement is that we are in agreement with God. This means your prayer must be based upon the promises of God. Matt. 18:19-20 (AMP) says:

Again I tell you, if two of you on earth agree (harmonize together, make a symphony together) about whatever [anything and everything] they may ask, it will come to pass and be done for them by My Father in heaven. For wherever two or three are gathered (drawn together as My followers) in (into) My name, there I Am in the midst of them.

The prayer of agreement must be voiced before it can come to pass. It is always best before praying this prayer to build up your faith by meditating God's Word in the area you desire an answer. An anointed husband and wife praying in agreement is an unstoppable force in the kingdom of God. This is because of the multiplied power of their combined faith that releases the power of God. Deut. 32:30 says:

How could one have chased a thousand, and two put ten thousand to flight, except their Rock had sold them, and the Lord had delivered them up? (AMP).

A three-fold cord isn't easily broken. The passage above describes the power of agreement in prayer. You are in agreement with the other person and the Holy Spirit is present to bring to pass what you desire (Ecclesiastes 4:12).

PRAYER OF UNITY—
(ACTS 4:24; PSALM 133)

The prayer of unity or corporate prayer is generated by a group of believers praying together in one mind by the Spirit. As with all prayer, it should begin with thanksgiving, praise, and worship from the heart. It produces powerful results because it creates an open heaven for God to move freely—affecting people, regions and nations (Acts 16:25-34).

Acts 4:23-31 is a biblical example of the prayer of unity by the first disciples, who asked for boldness and power to preach the gospel. Because of their unity, God responded with signs following:

So when they heard that, they raised their voice to God with one accord and said: "Lord, You are God, who made heaven and earth and the sea, and all that is in them, who by the mouth of Your servant David have said: 'Why did the nations rage, And the people plot vain things? The kings of the earth took their stand, and the rulers were gathered together Against the Lord and against His Christ. And when they had prayed, the place where they were assembled together was shaken; and they were all filled with the Holy Spirit, and they spoke the word of God with boldness.

Notice in the first verse above "they raised their voice to God with one accord and said". They prayed as one united in the Spirit, causing God to command the blessing of His power upon them, shaking the meeting place and filling them with His Spirit.

The prayer of unity can be prayed for many reasons, including the following:

- To seek guidance from God (2 Chron. 20:13-18)

- To solve a crisis situation (Acts 12:1-7)

- To ask forgiveness (Joel 2:15-17)

- For corporate praise and worship (2 Chron. 5:11-14)

United prayer causes God to show up. This is why we must pursue peace and resist strife, discord and division in our homes, churches, businesses and work places. When we die to ourselves and seek to fulfill the vision and mission inspired by Holy Spirit, and communicated by the set man or woman (or leader), we will experience an open heaven that releases the supernatural blessings of God to advance His kingdom.

PRAYER OF TRAVAIL—
(ROMANS 8:26-28; JER. 4:19; LAM. 1:16)

The prayer of travail is a very powerful, intense intercession initiated by Holy Spirit that births something new into existence. It is sometimes called "liquid prayer" because strong weeping and groaning characterize it. Not understood by most, travail is agonizing. It is like a woman laboring to have a baby. It opens up a spiritual birth canal for God to birth His burdens, dreams or longings into the earth. Travail always births something new.

Merriam-Webster Dictionary defines "travail" as "work, especially of a painful or laborious nature; a physical or mental exertion or piece of work; agonizing." Jesus' prayer in the Garden of Gethsemane is an excellent example of travailing prayer.

Travail occurs after you have carried something in your heart for a long period of time and then comes the time to birth it like a woman having her baby. Let's look at how Jesus agonized in prayer for the grace to carry the weight of mankind's sin and to die upon the cross to birth us back into God's family in Luke 22:42-45:

> *Saying, Father, if You are willing, remove this cup from Me; yet not My will, but [always] Yours be done. And there appeared to Him an angel from heaven, strengthening Him in spirit. And being in an agony [of mind], He prayed [all the] more earnestly and intently, and His sweat became like great clots of blood dropping down upon the ground. And when He got up from prayer, He came to the disciples and found them sleeping from grief, (AMP).*

God is looking for those that will not fall asleep on their watch, but that will travail now to birth His kingdom on earth. Jesus travailed in desperation until He sweated blood to do the Father's will, which was to die on the cross to forgive our sins because of His great love for us. Do you love someone enough to travail for them in prayer? When you travail, you feel deeply and intensely what God feels. Again, travailing always births something new into existence from a barren place. Remember Hannah's travailing and supplications to have a child? What was the result of Hannah's travail? She bore the Prophet Samuel, the first prophet and judge of Israel (1 Sam. 1:10-17), whose prophesies never failed because God was with him. (1 Sam. 3:19)

You respond best to travailing when you allow the pray-er to pray without disruption. When it is time to stop travailing, the intercessor will notice that the sadness or burden has lifted and will discern a note of victory.

PRAYING IN TONGUES—
(ROMANS 8:26-28; JUDE 1:20)

This prayer is an exciting gift from God that you can receive after you have accepted Jesus into your heart by faith (the gift of salvation) (Rom. 10:9-10). To receive this wonderful gift, you must ask Holy Spirit by faith to fill you with His presence, so that you can speak in other tongues or your heavenly prayer language (Luke 11:13).

Praying in tongues is one of two ways to pray in the spirit. It takes place when you believe in your heart and receive the baptism of the infilling of the Holy Spirit. You receive the baptism of Holy Spirit the same way you received salvation—by faith. You believe in your heart that you have received your heavenly prayer language and then you open your mouth and begin to pray—fully expecting Holy Spirit to give you utterance or the syllables for your heavenly prayer language. Only God can understand what you're saying (1 Cor. 14:14-15). You can also ask Holy Spirit to bless you with the gift of interpreting tongues (1 Cor. 12:10).

When I don't know how to pray in my native language concerning a problem, person or situation, I ask Holy Spirit to pray through me and then I open my mouth and begin praying in tongues. Holy Spirit's prayers always hit the target for He is the Supreme Prayer Strategist and Master Sharpshooter. Rom. 8:26-28 says:

Likewise the Spirit also helps in our weaknesses. For we do not know what we should pray for as we ought, but the Spirit Himself makes intercession for us with groanings which cannot be uttered. Now He who searches the hearts knows what the mind of the Spirit is, because He makes intercession for the saints according to the will of God. And we know that all things work together for good to those who love God, to those who are the called according to His purpose.

Praying in tongues has many benefits. I could write an entire book about this subject and still not cover it all. This prayer builds up or edifies your spirit man, so you can resist temptation and fight the good fight of faith. It charges up your spiritual battery, so you are always ready to minister to others. Let's face it. If your spirit man is depleted, you're not much good to anybody else (Jude 1:20; 1 Cor. 14:4). Praying in tongues gives you spiritual power to be a witness for Jesus, one that operates in signs, wonders and miracles, saving the lost, healing the sick and setting free the captives (Acts. 1:8, 2:4).

The enemy cannot understand or intercept your heavenly prayer language. So if you have a problem to solve, pray in tongues. To do this, I simply say with thanksgiving in my heart, "Father, in Jesus' name and by the power of Holy Spirit, I'm praying about this situation in tongues." Then I begin to pray until I get a note of victory or Holy Spirit says, "It's done". Glory to God!

While it is true that Holy Spirit inspires all godly prayer whether you're praying in your native language or in tongues, when you pray in tongues, you are praying the mysteries of God into reality, though you may not understand a single word you're saying (1 Cor. 14:2). You can also pray to fulfill your predestinated, godly purpose on earth.

Praying in tongues is a surefire way to strengthen your faith. It is the doorway that leads into the realm of the supernatural, where you can operate in the gifts of the Spirit as Holy Spirit wills (1 Cor. 12: 4-11). Praying in the spirit or in tongues revitalizes your walk with God. It will keep you sharp and energized in the spirit. Moreover, your prayer life will stay continually ablaze with passion to pray to God and on behalf His people (Lev. 6:13).

PRAYER OF INTERCESSION—
(ISAIAH 59:16, 62:6-7; EZEK. 22:30; ROMANS 8:26-28; 1 THESSALONIANS 5:17; EPHESIANS 6:18; 1 TIMOTHY 2:1-3; JAMES 5:16)

Intercession is standing in the gap for people or a situation to hold back God's hand of judgment. An intercessor takes the place or pleads another's case like an attorney, mediator or advocate representing his client before a judge. The intercessor stands between a holy God and sinful man as a priest that brings reconciliation.

We must pray the prayer of intercession because God does nothing in the earth without a godly man's permission and cooperation. This is because God has given man dominion and authority on earth (Gen. 1:26-28). Intercession is the way God births His will on earth and intercessors are the midwives and law enforcement agents He uses to do it.

The Hebrew word for intercession is "paga". It is a term for warfare or violent meetings. According to Strong's Concordance, it means to encounter, meet, reach, entreat; make intercession; light upon, join; to meet (of kindness); fall upon (of hostility); entreat (of request); to strike, touch (of boundary); to cause to light upon; to make entreaty; interpose; to make attack and to reach the mark.

The Greek word for intercession is "enteuxis". Found twice in the New Testament, (1 Timothy 2:1 and 4:5), its literal meaning has the sense of meeting with God, drawing near to him, or falling in with Him to talk. According to Strong's Concordance, it means a falling in with, meeting with; an interview; a coming together; to visit; converse or for any other cause; that for which an interview is held; a conference or conversation, a petition and supplication.

Intercession is not:

- Having intellectual knowledge of prayer

- Praying Scriptures verbatim without faith

- Praying the longest or loudest to get attention

- A ritual or religious duty to check off your list

- Information, manipulation or witchcraft (controlling) prayers

- Begging God in self-pity without faith

Intercession is:

- The highest demonstration of God's love for mankind (Isa. 53:12; John 3:16)

- Partnering with the Lord to pray for mercy on behalf of others (Psalm 2:8; Ezek. 22:30; Isa. 59:16, 62:6-7; 1 Tim. 2:1-3; Eph. 6:18)

- Communion and fellowship with God in your secret place, in the process becoming one with Him to advance His kingdom (John 5:19; 30, Matt. 6:10)

- Developing an intimate, spirit-to-spirit relationship with God fueled by His love, faith and righteousness (John 4:23-24; Gal. 5:6; Heb. 11:6; 2 Cor. 5:21)

Our intercession invokes or calls forth God's hand of mercy, while sin provokes or calls forth God's wrath or judgment. Abraham's prayer for Sodom and Gomorrah is a biblical example of intercession that saved a nation.

Then the men rose from there and looked toward Sodom, and Abraham went with them to send them on the way. And the Lord said, "Shall I hide from Abraham what I am doing, since Abraham shall surely become a great and mighty nation, and all the nations of the earth shall be blessed in him? For I have known him, in order that he may command his children and his household after him, that they keep the way of the Lord, to do righteousness and justice, that the Lord may bring to Abraham what He has spoken to him." And the Lord said, "Because the outcry against Sodom and Gomorrah is great, and because their sin is very grave, I will go down now and see whether they have done altogether according to the outcry against it that has come to Me; and if not, I will know.

Then the men turned away from there and went toward Sodom, but Abraham still stood before the Lord. And Abraham came near and said, "Would You also destroy the righteous with the wicked? Suppose there were fifty righteous within the city; would You also destroy the place and not spare it for the fifty righteous that were in it? Far be it from You to do such a thing as this, to slay the righteous with the wicked, so that the righteous should be as the wicked; far be it from You! Shall not the Judge of all the earth do right?" So the Lord said, "If I find in Sodom fifty righteous within the city, then I will spare all the place for their sakes (Gen. 18:16-26).

ABRAHAM

Abraham pleaded the case for God to spare Sodom and Gomorrah, in order to save his nephew Lot, his wife and family— going so far as to ask God if there were ten righteous found, would He spare Sodom and Gomorrah? Abraham's nephew, Lot, and his family, were the only righteous people that lived in Sodom.

Even though there weren't ten righteous found in Sodom and Gomorrah, Abraham's intercession still saved the lives of Lot and his family from imminent destruction. Let's read:

When the morning dawned, the angels urged Lot to hurry, saying, "Arise, take your wife and your two daughters who are here, lest you be consumed in the punishment of the city." And while he lingered, the men took hold of his hand, his wife's hand, and the hands of his two daughters, the Lord being merciful to him, and they brought him out and set him outside the city. So it came to pass, when they had brought them outside, that he said, "Escape for your life! Do not look behind you nor stay anywhere in the plain. Escape to the mountains, lest you be destroyed (Gen. 19:15-17).

God in His lovingkindness is always seeking intercessors like faithful Abraham to build up the hedge and stand in the gap for sinners and saints, so that He can extend His hand of mercy (2 Chron. 7:14; Ezek. 22:30, 33:11; Micah 7:18). God's highest and best is that sinners repent and confess Jesus as Savior and Lord (John 3:16; 2 Pet. 3:9).

MOSES

Another biblical example of intercession is Moses' compassionate intercession on behalf of the rebellious Israelites, who are God's chosen people. They had murmured and complained so much that God told Moses He was going to wipe them out and start a new race of people through Moses. Without hesitation, Moses' stood in the gap for them, boldly pleading with God to spare their lives (Ex. 32:7-14). Psalm 106:23 says:

*Therefore He said that He would destroy them, had not
Moses His chosen one stood before Him in the breach, to
turn away His wrath, lest He destroy them.*

Moses' bold, compassionate intercession saved a nation, and
so can your intercession, inspired by Holy Spirit.

QUEEN ESTHER

Another bold example of intercession is Queen Esther. Upon
risk of losing her life, she called a 3-day corporate fast for her
people, the Jews, to pray for favor for her to approach her
husband, King Ahasuerus, to make a request to stop a deadly,
genocidal decree planned to wipe the Jews off the face of the
earth. The king had unknowingly signed the decree that had been
deceitfully proposed by Haman, an Amalekite and one of the
king's ruling princes that hated the Jews.

Based on protocol, Queen Esther, who was not in the king's
good graces at the time, knew that if she approached him to
reverse the decree without being called by him, she could be
killed on the spot. However, to save her nation and at the
insistence of her Uncle Mordecai (see Esther 4:14 below) to help
her people, Esther risked her life to stand in the gap for such a
time as this.

*For if you remain completely silent at this time, relief
and deliverance will arise for the Jews from another
place, but you and your father's house will perish. Yet
who knows whether you have come to the kingdom for
such a time as this?*

After the fast had ended and at the strategic time, Queen
Esther boldly approached the king's throne to make her request
known, resulting in the king later issuing another decree to
protect the Jews and to destroy Haman's entire family. The same

noose that Haman had prepared for Uncle Mordecai was the same one used to hang him and all of his sons.

Later, Uncle Mordecai, who had earlier saved the king's life by exposing an assassination attempt against him and who had pleaded with Queen Esther to go before the king to save their people, was promoted into Haman's position.

In intercession, you must be willing to pour out your life as a drink offering to intercede on behalf of others. Also like Queen Esther, you must be willing to risk your very life by taking strategic action. Note that the queen didn't approach the king haphazardly. She (and her people in unity) prepared with fasting and prayer. She also praised and adored the king. You can glean more revelation knowledge about Queen Esther's intercessory prayer strategy by reading the Book of Esther.

Today, as a New Testament believer covered by the blood of Jesus, you can boldly approach your Father's throne and make your requests by faith—expecting an answer when you pray in agreement with Father's Word. However, corporate fasting and prayer is still an effective strategy to produce unity that God will command the blessing upon, annihilating stubborn demonic opposition to save a nation.

Who knows if it is for such a time as this that you been born to intercede and save the nations?

JESUS' MINISTRY OF INTERCESSION

Lastly, our Lord and Savior Jesus' very life embodied intercession. He died on the cross to reconcile sinful man to a holy God, restoring us through His righteousness as sons and daughters of God, as it was in the beginning in the Garden of Eden. Jesus gave up everything in heaven to gain us as His prize (Phil. 2:7-8). That's love. Every drop of His blood ratified the New Covenant of grace that provides us with better promises than the Old Covenant ratified by Moses. Jesus, our Messiah, now sits at the Father's right hand in heaven ever making intercession for us. When you sin and repent, it is Jesus who reminds the Father that you are one of His, and His blood has cleansed you from all sin and unrighteousness (Heb. 7:25). Thank you, Jesus!

Jesus' sacrificial death on the cross—where He paid in full the penalty for our sins by shedding His sinless blood—has bought for every believer the right, authority and freedom to come boldly to God's throne of grace and obtain mercy, as well as the grace we need to overcome every adverse situation (Heb. 4:16). Jesus' ministry of intercession caused the mercy of God to triumph over judgment. First Timothy 2:5 says:

For there is one God and one mediator also between God and man, the man Christ Jesus.

God is looking for intercessors who will build up the hedge and stand in the gap to avert His judgment, save souls and deliver nations. A major responsibility of intercession is to guard (or watch) on behalf of others.

On your walls, O Jerusalem, I have appointed watchmen; All day and all night they will never keep silent. You who remind the LORD, take no rest for yourselves (Isaiah 62:6 NASB).

Every believer is called to participate in Jesus' present day ministry of intercession. God is calling you to partner to make up the hedge and stand in the gap for others. Will you answer the call?

In conclusion, God has blessed the believer with all kinds of prayer for every situation. The best prayer to pray is the one needed at that moment as Holy Spirit prompts you. As a Son of

God made in His image and likeness, you are already equipped in your spirit man with everything you need to renew your mind, so that you are always victorious in Christ Jesus. Rise up and pray now for God's will to be done. Rise up, I say, and watch and pray without ceasing and take action for God's kingdom to come on earth as it is in heaven!

INTERCESSORS IN THE BIBLE

There are many great intercessors in the Bible. In addition to the ones mentioned above, here are several more to read about and study:

Old Testament: Noah, Joseph, Zipporah, Miriam, Deborah, Esther, Abigail, Hannah, Joshua, Samuel, Huldah, Noadia— Isaiah's wife, Major & Minor Prophets, Elijah, Nehemiah, King David, King Solomon, King Jehoshaphat and Job.

New Testament: Zechariah, Elizabeth, Anna, Mary the mother of Jesus, the first 12 Apostles, Stephen, Agabus, Apostle Paul, Silas and Epaphras.

CHAPTER 5

TEACH ME TO PRAY

Lord, teach us to pray. —Luke 11:1

Jesus, who is our Chief Apostle and Chief Intercessor, always got results when He prayed; whether healing the sick or casting out devils. One of his disciples noticed this, and wisely asked Jesus to teach them how to pray.

From my research, I discovered three main reasons why Jesus' prayers were effective, although there are more:

1. He lived to please and glorify His Father God. Therefore, He spent much time fellowshipping and communing with God to understand His will and do it. His heart was united with our heavenly Father. He revered God, both as His loving Abba Father who tenderly supplies provision, and as the infinite, majestic, transcendent God that holds all power in His hands (John 4:34, 5:19, 30, 6:38).

2. Jesus prioritized meditating and studying the Scriptures, so He always prayed in agreement with God's will. He *knew* God's nature, attributes and character, again both as our Father and as Creator of the universe (Matt. 4:4; Josh. 1:8-10; 2 Tim. 2:15).

3. Jesus, the Master Teacher of all times, was disciplined, which meant he stayed focused on doing the will of God, completing His assignments on time, whether He was

praying for others, or submitting His will to die on the cross for the forgiveness of our sins.

In the midst of his Sermon on the Mount, Jesus compares the false religion, or religious spirit of the Pharisees and scribes with God's true standard, as He taught his disciples how to pray. He first covered prayer ethics, which focuses on your motives for praying. For example, in Matthew 6:5-8, he told the disciples two things to avoid when praying. He said:

> ***"And when you pray, you shall not be like the hypocrites. For they love to pray standing in the synagogues and on the corners of the streets, that they may be seen by men. Assuredly, I say to you, they have their reward.*** *But you, when you pray, go into your room, and when you have shut your door, pray to your Father who is in the secret place; and your Father who sees in secret will reward you openly.* ***And when you pray, do not use vain repetitions as the heathen do. For they think that they will be heard for their many words. "Therefore do not be like them.*** *For your Father knows the things you have need of before you ask Him.*

When Jesus told the disciples to pray in secret, He wasn't telling them that public prayer is wrong, because the Apostle Paul says later in 1 Timothy 2:8:

> *Therefore I want men everywhere to pray, lifting up holy hands without anger or disputing (NIV).*

But he was warning the disciples to resist the temptation to meet in public places to pray to impress people with long-winded prayers, like the scribes and Pharisees. In verse 5, Jesus called the scribes and Pharisees hypocrites because they only prayed to impress man. They had no love or relationship with God as Abba Father, or as reverence for His awesome majesty. The attention they craved was from man. Jesus said, that was the only reward they would get.

Ron Mattoon in *Treasure from Proverbs, Volume One* said, "The Pharisees were like actors in a play, speaking from under a mask. Their mask was that of self-righteousness, which men would look at and be deceived, thinking that they were something they were not. They were not praying to honor God, but themselves! They sought the esteem of men, not that of God."[1]

Jesus encouraged the disciples to cultivate an *intimate* relationship with our Father. They were to pray in their prayer closets from a pure heart, glorifying Abba Father and worshipping the Most High God who holds all power in His hands. In return, the disciples would receive an eternal reward.

Jesus continued in Matthew 6:9-13 to teach the disciples the Model Prayer or the Lord's Prayer (also called the Disciples' Prayer). This is our blueprint or pattern for effective prayer. It is a pattern of prayer that you must follow when you pray to get results.

Prayed over the centuries by millions, do not let the Lord's Prayer become rote to you. It is more than black ink on white paper. It's more than a poem to be memorized and recited without meaning. It's more than six points to check off to prove that your prayer life is alive.

It is the living Word of Almighty God—powerful, super-natural and transformational. Jesus, our Chief Apostle and Intercessor, was the best teacher that has ever lived. The Lord's Prayer is authorized by God to superimpose His kingdom on earth as it is in heaven by the power of Holy Spirit.

Jesus opened the door to a richer prayer life for His disciples when He taught them the six principles of His Father's heavenly kingdom agenda. You are not born knowing how to pray. You must be taught just like Jesus taught the first disciples.

On a deeper level, the Lord's Prayer is an invitation to enter into a divine encounter with our caring heavenly Father, who is to be exalted in all the earth. We must humbly and confidently draw near to Him expecting to experience His tender loving care as He provides for us. He is eager to provide for our needs. We must be eager to meet with Him daily, and lavish Him with praise and worship that is due Him. He is Jehovah, the Most High God. Relational and majestic. Powerful and personal.

The Lord's Prayer encompasses thanksgiving, praise and worship, love, relationship, kingdom decrees, intercession, provision, forgiveness, protection and adoration. Getting answers to your prayers is a *natural* outgrowth of your intimate relationship with our heavenly Father.

Let me share an example. If I sent you an invitation to attend an elegant, five-course meal at my home, but we've only met informally one or twice, you may have a seat at my table. However, it probably wouldn't be where I would seat my closest friend. But if you and I had talked every week for the past five years eating together and sharing our ups and downs, my friend, you would sit at my right hand, because I know and trust you. You have looked into me, and I have looked into you. We have an intimate relationship.

I believe Jesus was teaching the disciples that if they did cultivate an authentic relationship with God, He would hear and answer their prayers because His prayers have become their prayers.

The supporting pillars of the Lord's Prayer are praise and worship, adoration and devotion to God as Father and Creator. These pillars help you prioritize God's initiatives above your own. This overarching desire to please your Father through fellowship and communion while dialoguing with Him, I believe, catches His attention. He then expands Himself within your heart; birthing a richer, intimate prayer life.

Here are some benefits you will derive when you pray, according to the pattern of the Lord's Prayer:

1. You will glorify God, which is fulfilling. This prayer is God-centered, not *self*-centered. It focuses on worshiping God, communicating with God, and partnering with God in prayer and action to advance His kingdom on earth as it is in heaven.

2. Your relationship with God will deepen as you move from being an acquaintance to a son or daughter of God. You will know that you have immediate access to your Father's heart.

3. You will strengthen your faith in God and His trust in you. As you pray, you will witness the hand of God moving in people's lives and circumstances to accomplish His will.

4. You will pray with a greater accuracy. Jesus told his disciples to pray these specific points as an apostolic mandate from God. This heavenly pattern is designed to cascade the glory of God's power and love upon the nations.

5. God will take care of your business. The Lord's Prayer is provisional. As you focus first on worshiping God and decreeing His business, He will take care of yours.

6. You will become a catalyst for societal transformation as you decree God's kingdom initiatives, impacting the seven mountains of culture with His glory. The seven mountains are arts and entertainment, business, education, family, government, media, and religion.

Just as God gave Moses a pattern for constructing the Tabernacle of Moses and He gave King David a pattern for David's Tabernacle and Solomon's Temple, Jesus has given us the Lord's Prayer. It is a pattern that will cause you to be one with God, a conduit for Him to extend heaven to earth.

If you've never prayed the Lord's Prayer following this pattern, give yourself time to practice it because it works. This pattern is not designed to restrict spontaneous praying, but to ensure that your spontaneity aligns with God's will.

In His teaching, Jesus was not telling the disciples to pray the Lord's Prayer verbatim. The phrase, "After this manner therefore pray ye" is the Greek word "houtosoun" which means "thus, therefore," or you could translate it, "along these lines, pray". It is not saying to pray these exact words. Jesus is saying that prayer should follow this model or *outline*.

Jesus taught the disciples specific facets of the Lord's Prayer (Matthew 6:9-13). Each focuses on an aspect of our Father's nature. Let's look at them.

- **Our Father which art in heaven** speaks of His paternal love.

- **Hallowed be thy name** speaks of His reverence.

- **Thy kingdom come** speaks of His vision.

- **Thy will be done in earth, as it is in heaven** speaks of His mission.

- **Give us this day our daily bread** speaks of His provision.

- **And forgive us our debts, as we forgive our debtors** speaks of His mercy.

- **And lead us not into temptation, but deliver us from evil** speaks of His protection.

- **For thine is the kingdom, and the power, and the glory, forever. Amen—** speaks of His supremacy.

Now let's examine each facet and apply it to prayer:

1) Praise and worship—Matthew 6:9

2) Decree God's will—Matthew 6:10

3) Pray for your needs—Matthew 6:11

4) Ask for forgiveness—Matthew 6:12

5) Pray for protection—Matthew 6:13a

6) Kingdom worship—Matthew 6:13b

Praise and Worship—"After this manner therefore pray ye: Our Father which art in heaven, Hallowed be thy name" (KJV).

Here Jesus is teaching several things:

First, He says pray to "our Father", not to Him. The use of the word "our" in this passage is significant. Jesus is setting the pattern that our prayer begins with recognizing that God is your Father who personally provides for you. He loves you the same way He loves Jesus—unconditionally.

The use of the word "our" points to the fact that if you have confessed Jesus as Lord of your life, then you have been adopted into the family of God. You are now an heir of God, and a joint heir with Jesus Christ. There should be no selfishness among God's children because He loves each of us unconditionally.

Your adoption into the family of God is not like some natural adoptions. You're not treated second-class like an unwanted stepchild. Adoption into the family of God gives you the same rights and privileges as that of a biological child. With our Father, there is no partiality. Remember, He loves you the same way He loves Jesus, unconditionally.

Your adoption by faith in Christ Jesus gives you bona fide access to come boldly to the Father's throne room to minister to *Him*, talk with Him and to ask for what you need or desire, according to His will, which is His Word.

But this adoption can put a strain on your relationship with God if you have had an unhealthy or abusive relationship with your earthly parents. This is because we often unconsciously project upon our heavenly Father (if we don't get healing and deliverance) the same unhealthy relationship that we have had with an earthly parent.

For example, I had a dad who rejected me at a very young age. His dad rejected him. Because I had rejection, fear, anger and unforgiveness towards my earthly Dad, this caused me to put up walls to protect my heart from my Father God. I was very distant and aloof.

As a result, my relationship with God was distant and aloof. I thought if I couldn't trust my Dad; I couldn't trust God. If I wasn't good enough for my Dad, why would God love me? I saw God like I saw my Dad. He was there, but He didn't care. I was on my own. If you're feeling like that right now, I understand. And I have good news for you. God loves you with an everlasting, unconditional love that far surpasses human, partial love. And He can heal your heart right now, if you let Him.

Your parents or guardian, may not have been there for you, but your heavenly Father will never leave you, nor forsake you. You can receive His healing touch right now by praying the prayer for Inner Healing in chapter 15 on page 270. God is faithful to do it. I'm a living witness. If He did it for me, He'll do it for you. He loves you with an everlasting love. You are special to Him.

Let's continue with the Lord's Prayer. In these next two passages of Scripture, Jesus explains that the right way to pray is to our Father in Jesus' name, according to John 16:23-27:

And in that day you will ask Me nothing. Most assuredly, I say to you, whatever you ask the Father in My name He will give you. Until now you have asked nothing in My name. Ask, and you will receive, that your joy may be full.

And in John 14:16, Jesus says:

I tell you the truth, my Father will give you whatever you ask in my name.

Jesus does not take any glory away from the Father. When He walked on earth, He always modeled how to pray to the Father. Yet many believers don't know this principle and instead, direct their prayers to Jesus. I used to pray like this myself before I received training. My prayer went something like this:

"Jesus, would you please bless my mom with safe travel passage? Would you give my husband favor for a job promotion? Would you heal Larry's body of cancer? Thank you Jesus."

I believe God answered my prayers because they were aligned with His will, in spite of my ignorance, because my heart was in the right place. So don't be hard on yourself if you're just learning this. God will meet you right where you are. I don't mean to criticize anyone. We all do the best we can with the knowledge we have. Many of us have never taken the time to really study prayer in the Bible nor have we taken a prayer course. Nevertheless, the Model Prayer teaches us how to pray to accomplish God's mission.

As you learn more, you're accountable to do more. It behooves all of us to press into learning how to pray in these end times because God's people perish for a lack of knowledge and for rejecting His knowledge. Prayer is the vehicle that God has given us to fellowship, commune and communicate with Him, and to execute His will on earth as it is in heaven.

Second, in Matthew 6:9, Jesus teaches us that we must approach God, our King with thanksgiving and praise. We must come before Him with a reverential, worshipful attitude, giving Him all the honor and glory that is due to His name.

Just as there is a natural protocol for approaching a king or queen—for example, if you live in a monarchy like Great Britain—there is a spiritual one for approaching our heavenly Father. The two Scriptures below describe the protocol for approaching our King in prayer. It says:

> *Enter into His gates with thanksgiving, And into His courts with praise. Be thankful to Him, and bless His name (Psalm 100:4).*

> *By him therefore let us offer the sacrifice of praise to God continually, that is, the fruit of our lips giving thanks to his name (Hebrews 13:15).*

Your approach to God in prayer should always be preceded by heartfelt thanksgiving and praise, in spite of your circumstances.

Many times we skimp or skip over praise and worship because we're too focused on our needs and wants. Our prayers are self-centered, not God-centered. If you want answers to your prayers, start praying God-centered prayers that produce *fruit*.

Third, you must acknowledge and honor our Father's name, for He is holy. The Greek word for "hallowed" is "hagiazo". It means "to make holy, i.e. (ceremonially) purify or consecrate; (mentally) to venerate. When you "hagiazo" God, you exalt, adore, honor and esteem Him. You give Him reverence and regard Him with great respect.

When you pray, take time to worship God. The best way to learn how to worship God is to pray or sing prayers from the Bible. Many of them are found in the book of Psalms. They will hit the bullseye every time because they are Holy Spirit-inspired. You can also pray the names of God. For example, you can invoke God's name for Healer—Jehovah Rapha, to worship Him.

To "invoke" means to make an earnest request, or to petition for help or support, according to Merriam-Webster's Dictionary. An example of prayer with the names of God can be found in chapter 15 on page 260. Here are a few examples of Scriptures you can pray to exalt our Father. Look up the meaning of words you don't know, so that you pray with passion and understanding.

O Lord, our Lord, how excellent is thy name in all the earth! (Psalm 8:9).

Give unto the Lord the glory due unto his name; worship the Lord in the beauty of holiness (Psalm 29:2).

O magnify the Lord with me, and let us exalt his name together (Psalm 34:3).

Again, the book of Psalms is a book of prayers that were actually *sung*. It is filled with prayers of thanksgiving, praise and worship. When you say or pray the names of God, you invoke God's presence, and He responds by releasing His power. His name is worthy to be praised.

Also, please see Appendix A for a list of the names of God with their meanings.

Decree God's Will—"Thy kingdom come, Thy will be done in earth, as it is in heaven" (KJV).

This verse is a decree stating God's vision and mission. His desire is for the earth to be established as an outpost of heaven. It is serving the enemy notice that the kingdom of God is advancing.

A decree is written in the imperative tense, which means it's a command. So in the Greek, this verse says, "Come thy kingdom come! Be done on earth now!"

When you decree a thing, you operate in your kingly anointing. When you pray, you operate in your priestly anointing. You are both a priest and king unto God.

What is a decree? Here are two definitions, according to Merriam-Webster's Dictionary:

Decree (noun)—an official order given by a person with power or by a government

Decree (verb)—to order or decide (something) in an official way

A decree is legislating an official order in the heavenly realm, backed by God's authority to accomplish His divine will on earth. It is the vehicle that transfers answers from heaven to earth.

For example, a king has the power and authority to issue a decree that must be carried out. Failure to obey is punishable by law. You must declare or voice a decree to establish it. To declare means to announce or proclaim.

As God's ambassador on earth, you have the authority in Jesus' name to decree His Word, and He will bring it pass. Your job is to speak the Word. God's job is to bring it to pass. When you decree a thing in agreement with God's Word, you light the fuse that causes the supernatural power of God to explode into someone's life or situation! (Gen. 1:1-3; Mark 11:22-25).

It is important when you decree a thing that you see yourself as God sees you, spiritually seated in heavenly places in Christ Jesus, issuing decrees from heaven to earth, not earth to heaven, causing ministering spirits to bring them to pass. Your decrees are the vehicle God uses to release heaven on earth.

God will permanently establish your decrees if you do first things first: hear and obey God. Ask Holy Spirit what you should decree and declare. To declare means to proclaim or announce what already belongs to you. One way to know what to decree in your life is to identify what is lacking. Then speak the applicable promise of God into the atmosphere to create it.

Thou shalt also decree a thing, and it shall be established unto thee: and the light shall shine upon thy ways (Job 22:28).

In this passage of Scripture, the word "shall" is used. This is a synonym for "will". God is commanding you to open your mouth and speak forth His decrees, so His kingdom can come. Don't stop decreeing until it comes to pass.

When I pray, say, confess or decree something, I visualize myself sitting next to Jesus in the heavenly realm. In the beginning, this was difficult because I struggled with a poor self-image, rooted in an unloving spirit that I had to cast out

I began to regularly meditate the Word of God to uproot this false image including the "I Am" Scriptures. I wrote them on 3 x 5 cards that I carried with me to remind me. I also did the same with the 365 Scriptures that deal with fear, to drive it out of my life. This progressive deliverance was achieved through eating or meditating the Word of God daily and often throughout the day. As my pastor says, "The Word works, if you work it."

The anointing within the Word of God renewed my subconscious mind, which generates the majority of your beliefs and actions. I began to perceive, know and understand how much my heavenly Father loves me. He loves you so much that He created you in His likeness and image, and has given you dominion and authority to partner with Him through prayer and intercession to advance His kingdom. This kingdom partnership begins inside of your heart, and you release it as a sweet aroma, wherever you go, effecting heaven on earth.

I highly recommend meditating and memorizing the "I Am" Scriptures to eradicate "stinking thinking." God's grace is sufficient to transform you into who He created you to be—the head and not the tail, above only and never beneath, if you diligently hear and obey His Word and daily abide in His presence.

Pray for your needs, not your greed—"Give us this day our daily bread" (KJV).

Your heavenly Father is willing to supply your needs and desires, when they align with His will for your life. Remember, God only has your *best* interests at heart! Do you know that as a son or daughter of God that you have already been given everything that pertains to life and godliness, according to God's divine power working inside of you and spoken out of your mouth?

Therefore, resist worry and fear, obtain revelation knowledge and open your mouth boldly to ask God for what you need. Better yet, command it into existence in the name of Jesus (Prov. 18:20-21). If you can find the promise in the Bible or God speaks it into your heart, it is yours by faith. Only believe. All things are possible if you believe. Your faith or confidence rests upon knowing the promises of God.

The kingdom of God operates based on operating the law of faith. This is how God created everything. He believed and spoke it into existence. For example, when God said "light be", it appeared as an energy source, followed later by God's creation of the moon, sun and stars on the fourth day of creation (Gen. 1:3, 14-19).

When God changed Abram's name, which means "high father", to Abraham, "father of multitudes", one year before he and Sarah conceived—Abraham and Sarah believed and birthed their promised son, Isaac, from two barren bodies (Gen. 17:5; Rom. 4:17).

God's laws work for anyone who is fully persuaded that God is able to do what He says. God looks over His Word to perform it. Therefore resist fear, lack, sickness and disease, death and all insufficiencies. God will supply all your needs that agree with His Word—from finding a new job to having a baby—if you believe in your heart and confess your desire with your mouth. It will come to pass (Mark 11:22-26).

Forgive the sins of others, so God can forgive your sins—"And forgive our debts as we forgive our debtors" (KJV).

When Jesus shed his blood on the cross to die for our sins, He paid the penalty demanded by God to forgive mankind's sins—past, present and future. Without the shedding of blood, there is no remission (forgiveness) of sin.

What a powerful demonstration of God's love. He exchanged our sin for Jesus' righteousness. Because God has forgiven our sins, reconciling us to Himself through the death of His dear Son Jesus on the cross, we should be quick to forgive those who offend or persecute us. If we fail to forgive the sins of others, God clearly tells us in the Bible that He will not forgive our sins. This means our prayers will be hindered. Jesus commands us to forgive those who have offended us in Mark 11:26, which says:

But if you do not forgive, neither will your Father in heaven forgive your trespasses.

As previously mentioned, unforgiveness hinders your relationship with God. It opens the door for tormenting spirits to vex your soul, including anxiety, bitterness, stress, frustration and unhealthy anger. Again, holding unforgiveness towards someone is like drinking poison intended for the person that offended you.

Won't you choose right now to forgive anyone who has offended you? If the person has passed away, you can still forgive them. Just confess right now, "Father, I confess I have unforgiveness in my heart. I repent of it. Please forgive me for all the unforgiveness I have towards (name/s). I forgive (name/s) right now by faith. I hold nothing against them. I ask you to bless them, in Jesus' name. Amen. Thank you Father for answering my prayer. "

Also forgive yourself, so that you can experience peace in every area of your life and move forward to serve God and others in a meaningful way.

Pray for Protection—"And lead us not into temptation, but deliver us from evil" (KJV).

The moment you confessed Jesus as Lord of your life, you stepped into an invisible war zone for your soul. The devil will continually try to tempt you to sin against God, just like he tempted Jesus in the wilderness. You can defeat Him every time by renewing your mind with God's Word and decreeing what is written in the Bible, like Jesus did when He defeated the devil in the wilderness (Luke 4:1-13).

To resist temptation, you must walk in the Spirit, and you will not fulfill the lust of the flesh. Jesus Christ, our Lord and Savior, has already legally won the battle against satan, sin, death, hell and the grave through His sacrificial death on the cross, burial, resurrection and ascension (Col. 2:15). Now we must enforce His victory by faith.

During the intense spiritual warfare that took place in the Garden of Gethsemane, Jesus admonished his disciples to watch and pray (Matthew 26:41). To watch and pray many times includes fasting, which strengthens your spirit man and drives out unbelief, so you are alert to resisting temptations.

Apostle Paul admonishes us in 1 Thessalonians 5:17 to pray without ceasing. When you live in the spirit of prayer, you're sensitive to the leading of the Holy Spirit, discerning and demolishing the enemy's strongholds. When God allows you to be tested (to promote you), pray for wisdom to pass the test. Continually pray to the Father to protect you, your family and those in the body of Christ from yielding to temptation. God always provides a way of escape when the enemy tempts us. Invoke His name, El Gibbor, which means Mighty God and Man of War, and He will war on your behalf, always causing you to triumph!

Kingdom Worship—"For thine is the kingdom, and the power, and the glory forever. Amen" (KJV).

We began the Lord's Prayer with praise and worship and we end it with Kingdom worship that focuses on decreeing and declaring the supremacy of our God. He alone is to be revered and extolled because He is God all by Himself. He upholds this entire universe together by the Word of His power.

We joyfully proclaim the greatness of Jehovah, the Great I Am, as the Creator of the universe. He alone is worthy to be worshipped and adored forever more. Until ...

The kingdoms of this world have become the kingdoms of our Lord and of His Christ, and He shall reign forever and ever! (Rev. 11:15).

In closing, if you will pray according to the pattern of the Lord's Prayer, it will transform your prayer life into a passionate time of fellowship, communion, thanksgiving and praise, intercession and kingdom worship. It pleases the Father when you exalt His name. May His hand of mercy, grace and power rest upon you, both now and forevermore.

CHAPTER 6

JESUS CHRIST: OUR CHIEF INTERCESSOR

Wherefore he is able also to save them to the uttermost that come unto God by him, seeing he ever lives to make intercession for them. —Heb. 7:25

Jesus is our Intercessor, High Priest and Mediator. You can come boldly to God's throne of grace and obtain mercy (God's love) and find grace (unmerited favor, supernatural enabling power) to help in your time of need, because of Jesus' substitutionary death on the cross, burial, resurrection and ascension.

Jesus, as your Chief Intercessor, became acquainted with your needs and made them His own on the cross—because of His great love for mankind.

The Hebrew word for intercession is "paga", which means to come (between), cause to entreat, fall (upon), make intercession, intercessor, entreat, lay, light (upon), meet (together), pray, reach, and run; impinge (to make an impression; have an effect or impact upon), by accident or violence, or figuratively by importunity (urgent or persistent in solicitation).

It is a meeting with an outcome.

In addition, from the Old Testament Lexicon, "paga" means to encounter, to meet (of kindness), to strike, touch of a boundary, interpose, to make attack and to reach the mark.

The Greek word for intercession is "enteuxis", which means a falling in with, meeting with, an interview, a coming together; to visit, converse, a conference, a petition or supplication.

When Jesus mediated between sinful man and a holy God by dying on the cross for our sins (paga), He reached the mark set by the Father to redeem us (enteuxis). Jesus demonstrated the highest example of godly love through His embodiment of intercession.

JESUS OUR CHIEF INTERCESSOR

The prophet Isaiah, more than any other prophet in the Old Testament, prophesied that Jesus would make intercession for mankind's sin, 750 years before the Virgin Mary gave birth to Him. In chapter 53, Isaiah prophesied about the rejection, pain, and death that Jesus would suffer, to redeem us from the power of sin by dying on the cross as the perfect Lamb of God. Jesus suffered all this pain and anguish, because of the Father's and His great love for us.

Jesus' very life is the embodiment of intercession. Before the foundation of the earth, He agreed to be slain as the Lamb of God to forgive our sins (Revelation 13:8). Isaiah 53:12 says of Jesus, our Chief Intercessor:

> *Therefore I will divide Him a portion with the great,*
> *And He shall divide the spoil with the strong,*
> *Because He poured out His soul unto death,*
> *And He was numbered with the transgressors,*
> *And He bore the sin of many, and made intercession for*
> *the transgressors.*

Jesus who knew no sin became sin for us that we might become the righteousness of God in Christ Jesus (2 Corinthians 5:21). When He hung on the cross, spilling His blood, He said, "It is finished". He was decreeing that He was the last sacrifice that would ever have to be made to pay the penalty for our sins.

Through the veil of His flesh ripped open on the cross, He opened up an eternal way for the true believer to come boldly to the throne of God to fellowship, commune and make your requests. Everything that Jesus can access in the Father, you also can access as a joint heir with Christ Jesus. Our Chief Intercessor has reconciled us to the Father, restoring us to the family of God. It can be as it was in the beginning before Adam sinned in the Garden of Eden that we walk as one Spirit with God (Genesis chapters 1-3).

JESUS OUR HIGH PRIEST

In the Old Testament, once a year the high priest took the blood of animals and sprinkled it on the mercy seat in the Holy of Holies in Moses' Tabernacle to cover mankind's sin, but this blood could never pay our sin debt in full. In truth, the continual sacrifices were a reminder of how much we *needed* a savior. Jesus is the perfect sacrifice, the Lamb of God that shed His sinless blood once on the cross of Calvary, to satisfy the debt of our sin. Now *that's* love.

After His resurrection, Jesus ascended to heaven to apply His blood on the mercy seat in the heavenly Holy of Holies. This one act sealed our redemption, restoring those that confess Jesus as Lord as sons and daughters of God.

This means that when you confessed salvation in Christ Jesus, He forgave all your sins—past, present and future. He forgave them all (Col. 1:14; Acts 10:43). This is not a license to sin, because if you're really a child of God, you will *desire* to please God by obeying His commandments and walking in love, not the lust of the flesh or sin.

But if you fall into sin, you have an Advocate with the Father—the Lord Jesus Christ, our High Priest, who is faithful and just to forgive your sins and to cleanse you of all unrighteousness when you repent (change your way of thinking) and confess them, according to 1 John 1:9. The word "confess" means to agree with or to speak the same as. When we confess our sins, we agree with God that we have sinned.

Jesus' ministry in heaven is also to serve as your High Priest, who forever sits at the right hand of the Father, interceding for *you*. He is your representative before the Father, acknowledging your prayers. He washes away all of your sins by the eternal, living, cleansing power of His blood.

Having lived 33 years on earth as a man, Jesus is intimately acquainted with your weaknesses, fears, and infirmities. Therefore you can come boldly to His throne, and confidently make your request, because He understands your weaknesses. Hebrews 4:14-16 says:

> *Seeing then that we have a great High Priest who has passed through the heavens, Jesus the Son of God, let us hold fast our confession. For we do not have a High Priest who cannot sympathize with our weaknesses, but was in all points tempted as we are, yet without sin. Let us therefore come boldly to the throne of grace that we may obtain mercy and find grace to help in time of need.*

Jesus' blood has made you righteous before God, just as if you had *never* sinned (2 Cor. 5:21). Therefore, you should have no guilt or condemnation, but conviction only, when you stand before the Father's throne to fellowship and commune with Him.

In the Old Testament, this was not so. The earthly Jewish high priest would take the blood of bulls and goats, and sprinkle it on the mercy seat annually. This act could only cover, but not wipe out the sin of man. It could not remove the bondage, guilt and condemnation of sin.

The animal sacrifices foreshadowed the coming of our Lord and Savior Jesus, who would shed his blood and die on the cross once and for all for our sins, satisfying God's demand for justice. Jesus' blood didn't just cover our sins—He wiped them *out*. Without the shedding of blood, there can be no remission or forgiveness of sin (Isa. 53; Heb. 9:22). As His Body on earth, we are responsible to partner with Jesus, continuing His present day ministry of intercession to stand in the gap to save the lost and to set people free.

JESUS OUR MEDIATOR

Jesus as our Mediator or Advocate has obtained a better covenant for us through His blood, without which there is no remission (forgiveness) of sin (1 Tim. 2:5). An advocate is like an attorney that pleads your case, so that you can have a *fair* trial.

Jesus is the Perfect and only Mediator between a holy God and sinful man because He never sinned. His sinless blood ratified a new and better covenant for the New Testament believer to exercise authority and live the abundant life. Hebrews 8:6 says:

> *But now He has obtained a more excellent ministry, inasmuch as He is also Mediator of a better covenant, which was established on better promises.*

The New Covenant is better in many ways than that of the Old Covenant. It falls under the dispensation of grace, which is God's unmerited favor. Grace is the mercy, love and favor of God that cannot be earned through works. It is the foundation of the ministry of righteousness in Christ Jesus, as opposed to the ministry of condemnation in the Old Testament. Here are a few other ways the New Covenant is more superior than the Old:

- It guaranteed that through faith in Christ Jesus, the whole world would be blessed. This is a physical blessing as well as spiritual (Gen. 22:18; Eph. 1:3).

- Only Jesus' blood could take away the sins of the world once and for all, restoring us as heirs of God and joint heirs with Christ (Matt. 26:28; Luke 22:20; Heb. 1:8, 9:12,15, 10:1-4).

- Jesus was a better Mediator than Moses, who ratified the Old Covenant, because Jesus knew no sin. Therefore He was the Perfect Sacrifice to forgive the sins of the world (1 Pet. 2:21-25).

- The New Covenant promises are written upon the tablets of our hearts by Holy Spirit, symbolizing a personal relationship with God, not on tablets of stone as under the Old Covenant. We can have an intimate relationship with God.

These examples are just a few of the ways that the New Covenant is superior to the Old.

JESUS' PRAYER LIFE

Jesus lived a lifestyle of prayer when he walked the earth. There are numerous scriptural accounts in the gospel of Matthew, Mark, Luke and John that reveal Jesus' prayer life.

For example, He arose a great while before day to pray. He often climbed mountains alone to pray to the Father. Here are some Scriptures that speak of Jesus' prayer life. Let them inspire you to fellowship and commune in prayer with our Father:

And when He had sent the multitudes away, He went up on the mountain by Himself to pray. Now when evening came, He was alone there (Matthew 14:26).

Then Jesus came with them to a place called Gethsemane, and said to the disciples, "Sit here while I go and pray over there" (Matthew 26:36).

Now in the morning, having risen a long while before daylight, He went out and departed to a solitary place; and there He prayed (Mark 1:35).

And when He had sent them away, He departed to the mountain to pray (Mark 6:46).

So He Himself often withdrew into the wilderness and prayed (Luke 5:16).

Now it came to pass in those days that He went out to the mountain to pray, and continued all night in prayer to God (Luke 6:12).

And I will pray the Father, and He will give you another Helper, that He may abide with you forever (John 14:16).

"I do not pray for these alone, but also for those who will believe in Me through their word; that they all may be one, as You, Father, are in Me, and I in You; that they also may be one in Us, that the world may believe that You sent Me. And the glory which You gave Me I have given them, that they may be one just as We are one: I in them, and You in Me; that they may be made perfect in one, and that the world may know that You have sent Me, and have loved them as You have loved Me" (John 17:20-23).

JESUS ALWAYS GOT PRAYER RESULTS

There are many reasons why Jesus always got results with prayer. Here are some reasons that I gleaned from my study of Jesus' prayer life.

1. Jesus had an intimate personal relationship with His Father that caused Him to obey God. He possessed love and compassion for people, like our Father. He knew His Father's voice, and instantly obeyed Him, whether fasting or praying, teaching or preaching, serving or healing. Jesus understood that His purpose was to do the Father's will. This is revealed in the Scriptures below:

    So Jesus added, When you have lifted up the Son of Man [on the cross], you will realize (know, understand) that I am He [for Whom you look] and that I do nothing of Myself (of My own accord or on My own authority), but I say [exactly] what My Father has taught Me (John 8:28 AMP).

    This is because I have never spoken on My own authority or of My own accord or as self-appointed, but the Father Who sent Me has Himself given Me orders [concerning] what to say and what to tell (John 12:49 AMP).

    And I know that His commandment is (means) eternal life. So whatever I speak, I am saying [exactly] what My Father has told Me to say and in accordance with His instructions (John 12:50 AMP).

    Do you not believe that I am in the Father, and that the Father is in Me? What I am telling you I do not say on My own authority and of My own accord; but the

Father Who lives continually in Me does the (His) works (His own miracles, deeds of power) (John 14:10 AMP).

2. Jesus got results when he prayed because He lived a fasted lifestyle, pushing away from the plate and the world to commune in prayer with God. His diligence in practicing the spiritual discipline of fasting and praying strengthened Him to resist the devil's temptations, unlike the first Adam in the Garden of Eden, causing His name to be exalted above all. Matthew 4:1-4 says:

Then Jesus was led up by the Spirit into the wilderness to be tempted by the devil. And when He had fasted forty days and forty nights, afterward He was hungry. Now when the tempter came to Him, he said, "If You are the Son of God, command that these stones become bread." But He answered and said, "It is written, 'Man shall not live by bread alone, but by every word that proceeds from the mouth of God."

Jesus fasted 40 days and nights in the wilderness, and passed the test of obedience that the first Adam failed when He was tempted by the devil and disobeyed God (Matt. 4:11-13). Afterwards, Holy Spirit anointed Him with power and He began his public ministry. Luke 4:14-15 says:

Then Jesus returned in the power of the Spirit to Galilee, and news of Him went out through all the surrounding region. And He taught in their synagogues, being glorified by all.

Regarding fasting, Jesus told His disciples in Matthew 6:16-18:

Moreover, when you fast, do not be like the hypocrites, with a sad countenance. For they disfigure their faces that they may appear to men to be fasting. Assuredly, I say to you, they have their reward.

A mature disciple will live a fasted lifestyle because He yearns to draw closer to God through fellowship and communion in the secret place. Your strength comes from waiting on and ministering to God in the secret place (Isa. 40:31).

3. Jesus got results when he prayed because He meditated and studied the Scriptures to know His Father's will, so that He could do His Father's will. Therefore, He always knew the right thing to say or pray, causing the enemy to flee. Luke 4: 4,8,12–14 says:

   But Jesus answered him, saying, "It is written, 'Man shall not live by bread alone, but by every word of God.'" ... And Jesus answered and said to him, "Get behind Me, Satan! For it is written, 'You shall worship the Lord your God, and Him only you shall serve.'" ... And Jesus answered and said to him, "It has been said, 'You shall not tempt the Lord your God.'" Now when the devil had ended every temptation, he departed from Him until an opportune time. Then Jesus returned in the power of the Spirit to Galilee, and news of Him went out through all the surrounding region.

God commands us to meditate in His word day and night, so we will prosper and have good success (Joshua 1:8–10). He also commands us in 2 Timothy 2:15 to study the Scriptures:

   Be diligent to present yourself approved to God, a worker who does not need to be ashamed, rightly dividing the word of truth.

4. Jesus got results when he prayed, because He sought to please God, not man. He said in John 8:29 and 5:30:

And He who sent Me is with Me. The Father has not left Me alone, for I always do those things that please Him. ... I can of Myself do nothing. As I hear, I judge; and My judgment is righteous, because I do not seek My own will but the will of the Father who sent Me.

Jesus, our Chief Intercessor, humbled and emptied Himself of His omniscience, omnipotence and omnipresence to be born as a man on earth. The Bible says, God anointed Jesus with the Holy Spirit and with power, and He went about doing good and healing all that were oppressed by the devil, to show you how to walk in your authority as a Son of God (Acts 10:38).

Contrary to what some believe, Jesus operated as a man on earth, which is why He needed to be anointed by the Holy Spirit. God doesn't need to be anointed because He is the anointing. Through Jesus' life of intercession, He has paved the way for us to walk in His footsteps and do greater works (John 14:12).

Jesus died for our sins and was raised from the dead, so that we could be raised from spiritual death as new creations in Him who rule and reign in life as kings and priests. If you are a blood-bought child of God, you have been entrusted with authority in Jesus' name to do greater works to expand His kingdom on earth through prayer, intercession and service to mankind. Philippians 2:7-8 says:

But made Himself (Jesus) of no reputation, taking the form of a bondservant, and coming in the likeness of men. And being found in appearance as a man, He humbled Himself and became obedient to the point of death, even the death of the cross.

Love motivated God to send His best gift, Jesus, His only begotten Son, to die in your place and mine. He died like a seed of wheat in the earth to bear many joint heirs. His passion to save us sent Him to die on the cross. John 3:16 says:

For God so loved the world that He gave His only begotten Son, that whoever believes in Him should not perish but have everlasting life.

If you are a true believer, the God-kind of love has been shed abroad in your heart like Jesus to intercede for others (Rom. 5:5). Will you deny yourself and take up His cross and build up the hedge to stand in the gap for the lost, backslidden and the oppressed, until they come into the saving knowledge of the gospel of Jesus Christ and the kingdom of God? Will you be a house of prayer like Jesus for the nations?

All these I will bring to My holy mountain and make them joyful in My house of prayer. Their burnt offerings and their sacrifices will be accepted on My altar; for My house will be called a house of prayer for all peoples (Isaiah 56:7).

Then He taught, saying to them, "Is it not written, 'My house shall be called a house of prayer for all nations'? But you have made it a 'den of thieves'" (Mark 11:17).

CHAPTER 7

FREQUENTLY ASKED QUESTIONS

Prayer is not learned in a classroom, but in the closet.
—E. M. Bounds

WHO DO I PRAY TO?

You should direct your prayers to our heavenly Father, as Jesus instructed us in the Lord's Prayer, which is also called the Disciples Prayer or the Model Prayer.

In this manner, therefore, pray: Our Father in heaven, Hallowed be Your name. Your kingdom come. Your will be done On earth as it is in heaven (Matt. 6:9-10).

You should pray in Jesus' name, and by the power of Holy Spirit living within you. Jesus has given you "power of attorney" to pray to the Father in His name. A power of attorney is a legal document that gives you the right to operate on behalf of the one you're representing.

This means Jesus has given you a legal right to transact business in the spiritual realm through prayer, according to His purposes and in agreement with the Word. You represent the love, integrity and compassion of Jesus when you pray in His name (John 14:13-14, 15:16, 16:23-24, 26-27).

It's the power of Holy Spirit who enables your prayers, who prays for you when you don't know how to pray and who comforts you (Rom. 8:26-28).

HOW LONG SHOULD I PRAY?

When Jesus was in the Garden of Gethsemane before His crucifixion, He asked Peter, James and John to pray with Him for one hour, as He spiritually prepared Himself to fulfill the purpose for which He was born. His death was a cruel death on the cross of Calvary for sins He did not commit, but was required to redeem mankind—because without the shedding of blood, there can be no forgiveness of sin (Mark 14:32-42).

But his disciples fell asleep when He needed them most. Not once, but three times. I can relate to this, because I have fallen asleep while praying. But Jesus didn't condemn His disciples, even though it must have disappointed Him. He admonished them saying, "Simon, are you sleeping? Could you not watch one hour? Watch and pray, lest you enter into temptation. The spirit indeed is willing, but the flesh is weak" (Mark 14:37-38).

Jesus often prayed through the night to make important decisions, such as when He chose His first 12 disciples, whom He designated the first Apostles (Luke 6:12-13). He often went alone to mountains and isolated places to pray for hours (Matt. 6:6, 14:23; Mark 1:35-36; Luke 5:16).

Other times Jesus' prayers were short and powerful like when He healed the woman who had suffered with an infirmity for 12 years. If praying for one hour is difficult, start by praying for 15 minutes and build up gradually. The important thing is to make it a habit to spend time every day in fellowship and communion through prayer to deepen your personal relationship and intimacy with God.

WHAT POSITION DO I PRAY?

The most important position when you pray is the position of your heart.

And whatever you do, do it heartily, as to the Lord and not to men, knowing that from the Lord you will receive the reward of the inheritance; for you serve the Lord Christ (Col. 3:23-24).

When I pray, I move through various positions, from prostration to standing. I sing and dance my prayers unto the Lord like Miriam did in Exodus 15:20. Here are seven positions of prayer:

1. Sitting—1 Chronicles 17:16
2. Kneeling—1 Kings 8:54; Ezra 9:5; Luke 22:41; Acts 9:40
3. Bowing—Exodus 12:27, 34:8; Nehemiah 8:6; Psalm 72:11
4. Standing—Nehemiah 9:5; Mark 11:25; Luke 18:13
5. Walking—2 Kings 4:35
6. Prostration—Joshua 7:6; Ezra 10:1; Job 1:20; Matthew 26:39; Mark 14:35
7. With uplifted hands—2 Chronicles 6:12; Psalm 63:4; 1 Timothy 2:8
8. Dancing, clapping, shouting & singing—Exodus 15:20; 2 Chronicles 20:19; Psalm 47:1; 95:6; 149:3

God is pleased and hears your prayers when you come humbly to worship Him in Spirit and truth and pray by faith.

WHEN DO I PRAY?

Jesus prayed early in the morning and sometimes all night. He was always in the spirit of prayer. This is one reason why He operated in such power.

I like to say, ***"Much prayer, much power. Little prayer, little power. No prayer, no power."*** It is not the length of your prayer, but the faith mixed with your prayer that moves God. A 90-second, faith-filled decree can be just as effective as a longer prayer. Without faith, it's impossible to please God (Heb. 11:6). Faith is built upon revelation of how much God loves *you*. The more revelation knowledge you have of God's love for you, the more your faith increases. The more you believe in God's love for you, the easier it is to go to Him in prayer and receive your answer.

God will let you know when and what He wants you to pray. One thing is for sure—He is always seeking faithful intercessors and prayer warriors with devoted hearts towards Him to stand in the gap. We must pray without ceasing for His love and compassion to be released into people's lives and circumstances to bring salvation and transformation (Ezek. 22:30).

The most important thing to remember is that when God calls you to pray, don't procrastinate. **PRAY NOW.** Your prayer can save someone's life, alter an outcome or change a nation. Prayer advances God's kingdom, glorifying Him.

Paul tells us to pray without ceasing (1 Thessalonians 5:17). This doesn't mean to literally stay in your prayer closet and pray all day if you have other duties and responsibilities, but I believe it does mean to be sensitive to Holy Spirit's promptings to pray, whether in your prayer closet, or out and about.

My husband Tony likes to pray first thing in the morning. I enjoy praying from midnight to 6am in the morning. This is when I most like to commune with God and command the day, making decrees and canceling the curses of witches and warlocks. I decree the blessings of God over my family, leaders, students, ministry partners, the body of Christ and myself. I decree and declare to the nations, governments and regions to be filled with God's glory. I ask God for my instructions for the day. I write in my journal important insights, directions, prophecies, strategies or ideas God gives me. Don't wait to write it later, you may forget.

Jesus tells us in the Bible to watch and pray, and that men ought to always pray and not faint (Matt. 26:41; Luke 18:1). We should possess a spirit of prayer, meaning whether we are in our prayer closet or running an errand, we obey Holy Spirit's voice when He says to pray for someone. We're instant in season and out with prayer.

WHERE DO I PRAY?

I have learned over the years of praying that some places work better than others. Ask the Lord where you should pray and consecrate it as holy ground.

I like to pray in my prayer room or my bedroom closet because I'm shielded from distractions. I have set up my altar complete with anointing oils, candles, prayer shawls, Bibles, devotionals, my journal, pen, pillows and music. My prayer closet is also my war room where I decree and declare the prophetic Word of God to establish godly strongholds in the seven mountains of culture: arts and entertainment, business, education, family, government, media and religion.

What's in my prayer room isn't as important as being 100% available—spirit, soul and body to commune spirit-to-spirit with God. Sometimes I sing new songs and dance new movements unto the Lord. This is pure and unedited praise and worship, straight from my heart, to let my Father know how much I love and appreciate Him for who He is, my loving, caring, sharing heavenly Father and to tear down strongholds.

No one or anything can compare to my Beloved. Selah. I meet with God sitting or lying on the floor. There are no chairs in my prayer room. But you may have a favorite chair or sofa where you like to meet with God. Maybe your favorite place is outside close to nature. Wherever your favorite place, it is a holy place, a secret place where you can privately fellowship and commune directly with Almighty God, the Creator of heaven and earth, who is your loving, caring, sharing heavenly Father and the Most High Judge who rules in your favor. He delights to see your face because He made you. You are His delight and He is well pleased with you. Every day you should meet with Daddy God in your secret place to praise and worship Him and to receive daily instructions. In this way, you'll always be prepared for whatever comes.

In Matthew 6:5-6, Jesus tells us "And when you pray, you shall not be like the hypocrites. For they love to pray standing in the synagogues and on the corners of the streets, that they may be seen by men. Assuredly, I say to you, they have their reward. But you, when you pray, go into your room, and when you have shut your door, pray to your Father who is in the secret place; and your Father who sees in secret will reward you openly."

The Father abides in the secret place of your heart. You connect to Him best when there are no distractions. Therefore, close the door and shut yourself into His presence where there is fullness of joy and at His right hand pleasures evermore (Psalm 16:11).Set a standing appointment every day to commune with God in your secret place. This is where He will serve your portion, which cannot be taken away. It can be the oil of gladness to defeat depression and oppression, meat from His Word for spiritual strength to endure, and godly wisdom and revelation to possess your soul and expand your territory.

Most importantly, this is where you have the privilege and honor to serve or minister unto the Most High God, the Creator of heaven and earth and everything in it After you leave your prayer closet, continue to commune with the Lord by staying alert to Holy Spirit when He needs you to pray.

HOW DO I HEAR GOD'S VOICE?

First, you must be a born-again believer, committed to obeying God and His Word. As you read, meditate and study God's Word, you will learn His character, which will help you recognize His voice. His voice is different from your voice of reasoning, and from the voice of the enemy, which is condemning, accusatory and guilt-ridden. There are many voices in the world. This is why you must spend time in your Word and in your secret place, cultivating an intimate relationship to know Him.

God speaks in many different ways. Some of these ways are through the written or logos Word of God. It could be the spoken or "rhema" Word of God, prayer, prophecy, dreams, visions, dances, songs, art, sermons, nature and creation, circumstances, or through the anointed teaching and preaching of other believers.

Here are 4 keys to hearing the voice of God, or "rhema" (spoken) Word of God, based on Habakkuk 2:1-4 from the teaching of Dr. Mark Virkler, Chancellor of Christian Leadership University and the creator of the "Hearing the Voice of the God" course and curriculum:[2]

> *I will stand on my guard post And station myself on the rampart; And I will keep watch to see what He will speak to me, And how I may reply when I am reproved. Then the Lord answered me and said "Record the vision And inscribe it on tablets, That the one who reads it may run (Hab. 2:1-2).*

Key 1—God's voice in your heart will sound like a flow of spontaneous, random thoughts, visions, feelings or impressions. Prophet Elijah described God's voice as a "still, small voice". He had to be very quiet to hear God (1 Kings 19:12).

Have you ever experienced a random thought that seemed to come out of the blue (heaven) at 3am in the morning, or while driving down the road to pray for someone that you haven't seen for years? This is how God often speaks.

The Hebrew word for intercession is "paga". One of its meanings is a chance encounter; accidental intersecting. God prompts us to pray for people through "paga," or chance encounters.

Key 2—"I will stand on my guard post and station myself on the rampart", which means be still and know He is God. God is God all by Himself! (Psalm 46:10). Quiet your soul and body. You may want to sing a worship song to the Lord to quiet your soul. If random thoughts pop up in your mind while praying, write them down. If thoughts of sin or unworthiness rise up, cast them down by decreeing that you are the righteousness of God in Christ Jesus. Focus on Jesus by opening your heart to receive the spontaneous flow of thoughts from the throne of God.

Key 3—"And I will keep watch to see what He will speak to me, and how I may reply when I am reproved" means to keep the eyes of your heart or spirit man focused on God or Jesus. When Habakkuk was praying, he expected to see a vision from God or to encounter God. God speaks to us through dreams and visions of the spirit realm. The spirit realm is the causal realm where everything is created. It is intangible, eternal and alive, whereas this world that we see and feel is tangible, temporary and its deadness is subject to be changed by faith, if you know who you are in Christ Jesus and how to exercise your God-given authority.

You are a spiritual being that lives in a body and you have a soul, so it should be normal for you to operate in the spirit realm. Again, the spirit realm is the causal realm, where everything you see originated. You are naturally supernatural, if you would just invest the time to see through your eyes of faith.

The Lord Jesus lived in continual, spiritual communion with Father God, which is why He could declare that He only did what He saw the Father doing or saying (John 5:19-20, 30). Jesus has ripped open the veil, giving you complete access to our Father's glorious presence and unfailing love (Luke 23:45-46). Draw near to Him and He'll draw near to you (James 4:8; Heb. 10:19-22).

As you pray, expect to see Jesus through the eyes of your spirit man. You have eyes to see and ears to hear in your spirit man. You have been given the God-kind of faith to receive fresh revelation in your inner man from our Father God.

Key 4—"Then the Lord answered me and said, 'Record the vision and inscribe it on tablets that the one who reads it may run.'" This means write out your questions, prayers, and what you believe that God is saying to you by faith. Just let it flow. This will help you learn how to hear God's voice.

Resist the doubt that what you are writing is not from God. Just write it in your journal for now. Afterwards you can compare it to the Word of God, and/or submit it to a solid, trusted, wise counselor like your spouse (if married), pastor, Bible teacher, other five-fold leaders, spiritual mentor or coach. As you practice journaling, you will be encouraged that you can hear and talk to God. Then you must obey God. As you learn to hear God's voice, you will boldly prophesy and decree God's Word, causing transformation.

WHY DOESN'T GOD ANSWER MY PRAYERS?

There are many reasons for unanswered prayer. I believe it's best to ask Holy Spirit, or a minister seasoned in prayer and the Word of God that can teach and pray with you.

Know and understand that we live in a fast food and instant gratification world. However, this is not the way God operates, for He operates outside of time. He is an eternal God. A day to Him is as 1,000 years and vice versa. And He loves you too much to give you something that will hurt you, which is sometimes why He says "no," or you don't receive a fast answer to your prayers.

Here are some other reasons that I have discovered on my prayer journey why God may not answer prayer.

- Your request doesn't agree with God's will, which is His Word. You must hear and read the Word of God to learn His will, attributes, character and nature, or your prayers can be amiss. Find Scriptures that promise or justify what you're praying to receive. God only promises what He's willing to do. And everything He does is *good*. Therefore you can have confidence when you pray His will that you have received, no matter how long the answer takes to show up in the natural realm (1 John 5:14-15, James 1:6-7).

- You're not praying in Jesus' name, the name at which every knee will bow and every tongue will confess that He is Lord. Jesus' name is your power of attorney to represent Him as you transact kingdom business on earth. When you pray in Jesus' name, you pray according to His agenda, not yours. Your desire is to please God as an ambassador of Christ Jesus (John 14:13-14, 15:16).

- You're not asking in agreement or unity, according to Matthew 18:19, which causes God to command the blessing. For example, a husband and wife operating in agreement is one of the strongest forces on earth to advance God's kingdom, because their combined faith releases God's supernatural power on earth. Beware of strife and division, which can hinder your prayers (Gen. 11:6; Matt. 18:19). We must pursue walking in peace and love with one another, so the devil has no place in us.

- Your motives are wrong due to selfishness or carnality, or you do not ask specifically for what you desire (James 4:2-3).

- You don't have faith in God's Word because you're not abiding in Him; therefore you have doubt and unbelief. Jesus says, "If you remain in me and my words remain in you, ask whatever you wish, and it will be given you" (John 15:7). The word "if" is conditional. It means that you must find the promise of God and consistently meditate until it grows inside of you like a baby growing inside of a pregnant mother. Then you will be able to stop doubt from parking in the driveway of your mind.

- If you pray for something—let's say healing—but you don't have belief or confidence in God's promises to heal you, even though you have prayed, you will begin to doubt that you were healed, if the symptoms persist. In Mark 11:24, Jesus says, *"Therefore I tell you, whatever you ask for in prayer, believe that you have received it, and it will be yours."* This Scripture does not say to believe that you **might** receive. It says to believe that you **have** received. You believe you have the answer before you physically see it. Faith is now!

Then praise God for the answer because if He said it, it will appear in due season. God isn't a man that He should lie, and His Word never returns void or empty. It always accomplishes His purposes (Num. 23:19; Isa. 55:11).

Use your shield of faith to resist every negative thought. Confess out of your mouth what God's Word says concerning your desire or need. The mind is the arena where you fight the good fight of faith. You must keep your mind focused on the promises of God to lock out doubt, because it will cancel your faith (Matt. 21:22; Mark 11:22-24; John 15:4-5, 7, 10; James 1:5-8; Heb. 11:6; 2 Cor. 10:3-6; Eph. 6:10-18).

- You have unforgiveness in your heart even though God through Christ Jesus has forgiven your sins—past, present and future. Quickly forgive others when they offend you, so answers to your prayers are released, *not* hindered (Isa. 43:25; Matt. 6:12; Mark 11:25; Eph. 4:26-27). Also forgive yourself, and God, if you are angry with Him.

- You have an ungrateful attitude concerning what God has already blessed you to possess. The Bible says in everything give thanks for this is God's will in Christ Jesus concerning you (Psalm 100:4; 1 Thess. 5:17-18; Phil. 4:6-7).

- You have unconfessed sin or iniquity hidden in your heart that separates you from God. Confess and repent of your sins and received forgiveness by the cleansing power of Jesus' blood and return to your first love, Jesus (Isa.59:1-2; Psalm 66:18; Jer. 14:10-12; John 9:31).

- You grow weary and stop persisting in prayer. Jesus tells us in Luke 18:1 that men ought always to pray and not give up. If you continue to ask, seek and knock, you will receive. It's only a matter of time. Ask God to give you His grace when you are weak. It is sufficient to help you overcome every test, trial and tribulation (Luke 11:9-10; James 5:16b; Phil. 4:6-9).

- You doubt God's love for you because of a deep-seated root of unworthiness, fear, self-hatred, self-rejection, shame, inferiority or low self-esteem that prevents you from receiving His love through answered prayer. Father God loves you relentlessly, so He will never stop believing in you because He created you to WIN in Christ Jesus! You are accepted in the Beloved. God wouldn't have sacrificed His only Begotten Son on the cross for you, if you weren't special to Him. He loves you infinitely (Isa. 65:24; Jer. 29:11-13, 32:27, 33:3; Matt. 6:33; 2 Cor. 5:21).

- You are not giving your tithes, offerings, alms and first fruits cheerfully, honoring God. The principle of giving beyond the tithe is evident in the New Testament. Remember that God sent an angel to Cornelius, who was not a Jew, and said, "Cornelius, your prayer has been heard and your alms have been remembered before God." Alms is money given to the poor (Prov. 3:9-10, 21:13; Mal. 3:8-12; Matt. 5:17-19, 23:23; Luke 6:38; Acts. 10: 2-4, 31, 20:35; 2 Cor. 9:6-10).

Here are several more reasons for unanswered prayer:

- Rejecting God's Word or disobedience (Prov. 28:9; 66:18)
- Mistreating and dishonoring one another (Micah 3:2-4; 1 Pet. 3:7)
- Self-righteousness (Luke 18:10-14)
- Pride and arrogance (James 4:6; 1 Pet. 5:5-6)
- Idolatry (Josh. 7:10-12; Jer. 11:11-14)
- Violence (Isa. 1:15; 59:2-3)
- Fear of man (Prov. 29:25)

When God doesn't answer our prayers on our timetable, we can become frustrated and angry, blaming Him, or worse, *resenting* Him.

I have learned that Father knows best. Almighty God, the Creator of heaven and earth and everything therein, is the Potter and I am the clay. While my flesh may cry in pain for what I think is good for me, I have learned to crucify my flesh with its affections and lust, because what I want can bring leanness to my soul (Ps. 106:13-15).

It is in the waiting, trusting God for the answer as you continue to obey Him, that you can identify with the turmoil and pain that Christ endured, when He submitted to dying an agonizingly, painful death on the cross for our sins. What we endure in life *pales* in comparison to what Jesus endured on the cross, because of His love for us. He was victorious because He kept His focus on pleasing the Father, not pleasing His flesh.

In the midst of waiting for an answer to your prayer, ask God, "How can I encounter you in this hard place?" "What do you want me to learn?"—instead of asking, "Why haven't you answered my prayer yet" or "When, God, when?" Father God knows best. He will never leave you, nor forsake you. Waiting on God to answer your prayer, if you choose to submit to the process, will purify you like pure gold purified by fire from the inside out. Then you will reflect even more the image of Christ Jesus.

C.S. Lewis writes in "The Problem of Pain", "We are a Divine work of art, something that God is making, and therefore something with which He will not be satisfied until it has a certain character."[3]

It is in the waiting (ministering to God and serving others on His behalf), in the suffering and the brokenness of life, that we become conformed into the image of Christ Jesus.

WHAT ARE SOME OF THE SCRIPTURES IN THE GOSPELS OF MATTHEW, MARK, LUKE AND JOHN THAT SHOW JESUS IN PRAYER?

- At His baptism (Luke 3:21-22)
- Before heading to Galilee (Mark 1:35-36)
- After healing the people (Luke 5:15)
- Before choosing His first twelve disciples (Luke 6:12-13)
- When speaking to Jewish leaders (Matt. 11:25-26)
- Giving thanks to the Father before feeding the 5000 (John 6:11; Matt. 14:19; Mark 6:41; Luke 9:16)
- Before walking on water (Matt. 14:23; Mark 6:46; John 6:15)
- While healing a deaf, mute man (Mark 7:31-35)
- Giving thanks to the Father before feeding 4000 (Mark 8:6-7; Matt. 15:36)
- Before Peter called Jesus "the Christ" (Luke 9:18)
- At the Transfiguration (Luke 9:28-29)
- When the seventy disciples returned (Luke 10:21)
- Before teaching His disciples the Lord's Prayer (Luke 11:1)
- Before raising Lazarus from the dead (John 11:41-44)
- Laying on of hands and praying for children (Matt. 19:13-15; Mark 10:13-16; Luke 18:15-17)
- When He asked the Father to glorify His name (John 12:27-28)
- At the Lord's Supper (Matt. 26:26; Mark 14:22-23; Luke 22:19)
- When He prayed for Peter's faith when Satan desired to sift him (Luke 22:31-32)

- When He prayed for Himself, His disciples and all believers, before going to Gethsemane (John 17:1-26)

- At Gethsemane before being betrayed (Matt. 26:36-46; Luke 22:39-46; Mark 14:32-41)

- After being nailed to the cross (Luke 23:34)

- While dying on the cross (Matt. 27:46; Mark 15:34)

- When He prayed a blessing over the communion bread (Luke 24:30)

- With His last dying breath (Luke 23:46)

- When He blessed the disciples before His ascension (Luke 24:50-53)

Jesus now sits at the Father's right hand in Heaven interceding for the body of Christ (Rom. 8:34; Heb. 7:25; 9:24; 1 John 2:1).

WHAT DO YOU TAKE INSIDE YOUR PRAYER CLOSET?

God wants to spend time with you in your prayer closet. You can bring your Bible, journal and pen or digital tablet (if not a distraction) to capture what He is speaking to your heart.

I also like to anoint myself with oil, symbolizing Holy Spirit. I cover my head with my prayer shawl (tallit) to block out distractions. Although these items are not required, you get to use them to make your time with the Lord a very intimate one.

- Bible

- Prayer shawl (tallit)

- Journal and pen or tablet

- Anointing oil

SECTION II
PRAYER SECRETS

CHAPTER 8

PRAYING IN THE SPIRIT

It is the fusion of Holy Spirit within your human spirit that
helps you accurately pray, if you will yield to Him.
—Karen L. Gardner

A powerful transformation occurred inside of me when I received the baptism of the Holy Spirit. I was a 20-year-old sophomore at the University of Florida, when I rededicated my life to God.

Rhogeana Simmons, a graduate student I had befriended, invited me to a Bible study at the Student Union. I'll never forget when I walked into the room how everyone seemed to glow. I couldn't put my finger on what they had, but I knew I wanted it. They were so peaceful and full of joy.

When Reverend Walter Fleming, also a graduate student, extended the invitation for salvation and rededication, I raised my hand. That night I rededicated my heart to Jesus. When I went outside, the world shined brighter than before. It was like I had taken off my sunglasses. Encountering the person of Holy Spirit when I gave my heart to God, transformed me.

I began to attend Bible study on Wednesday, and church on Sunday, with Rhogeana. A few months later, while standing in a circle with other believers at Bible Study, I received the baptism of Holy Spirit with the evidence of speaking in other tongues. I felt a surge of the power of Holy Spirit move deep inside of me, fusing with my spirit. "To fuse" means to join or blend, so as to become one entity. You can receive the baptism of the Holy Spirit when you confess salvation in Jesus Christ, or subsequent to it.

The evidence that you have received the baptism of Holy Spirit is that you begin to speak in a heavenly language called, "other tongues", which is different than your native language. This heavenly language can only be fully understood by God. It's like your own Wi-Fi connection to God (Acts 2:4; 1 Cor. 14:4; Eph. 5:18).

Speaking in your heavenly language is the doorway into the realm of the supernatural, where you can operate in power like Jesus—teaching the gospel, healing the sick and casting out devils. This infilling of the Spirit gives you power to be a witness of the Lord Jesus Christ, spreading the gospel with signs following. The supernatural should be a natural lifestyle for the true believer.

I was so excited about this gift that I prayed like it was going out of style! When you pray in tongues, which is a powerful, exhilarating way to pray, there are many benefits. One is that you build up your faith, according to Jude 20. I could not get enough of praying in the Spirit as I experienced the healing, liberating power of God. I would sing in tongues to God and worship Him. This is the personal side of praying in tongues or your heavenly prayer language, which recharges or edifies your spirit man and builds your faith.

As I grew in the spirit, I learned to yield more to Holy Spirit, praying and interceding for others. Praying in your heavenly language is the perfect way to accurately pray. You should pray in tongues daily and throughout the day to keep yourself overflowing in the power of God. Apostle Paul told the Ephesians they should be "continually filled with the Spirit, not drunk with wine" (Eph. 5:18).

Over the years, I learned by experience that Holy Spirit is not some mysterious, spooky ghost. He is a loving, powerful, holy Spiritual Being, whose mission is to lead and guide you into all truth. He has feelings, and is grieved when you disobey Him. He is a spiritual being with a mind, will and emotions.

Jesus told the disciples before he ascended to heaven after His resurrection that it was necessary that He go back to heaven, so that He could send another Comforter like Himself. Another name for Holy Spirit is the Comforter. In John 16:7 Jesus said:

> *Nevertheless I tell you the truth; It is expedient for you that I go away: for if I go not away, the Comforter will not come unto you; but if I depart, I will send him unto you (KJV).*

Jesus was saying that the ministry of Holy Spirit was more beneficial to his disciples at this time, than Himself. The Holy Spirit is omnipresent, which means He can be everywhere at the same time, releasing the supernatural power of God to bring salvation, healing, deliverance and transformation. However, Jesus in His physical body was limited to be in one place at a time. Jesus had fulfilled His purpose on earth. Now He was passing the baton to Holy Spirit. God had sent mankind His very best—Jesus, our Lord and Savior—to restore us as His righteous sons and daughters. Now Jesus was sending us *His* best, the precious Holy Spirit— to live inside of every believer—leading and guiding into all truth.

The Greek word for "Comforter" in John 16:7 is "parakletos". It also means "helper" and "counselor". Jesus was saying He was sending another person like Himself—God, the Holy Spirit, to help you.

So who is Holy Spirit, and how does He help you when you pray? Great question. Holy Spirit is the third person of the Godhead, completing the Holy Trinity (Elohim): God the Father, God the Son and God the Holy Spirit. The Godhead operates interdependently like the parts of your body or a well-oiled machine.

Holy Spirit is God Himself, working and living in you to create, speak, pray, heal, deliver and transform. He is a powerful, multi-faceted, holy, intelligent, divine spiritual being. He is your Counselor, Helper, Intercessor, Advocate, Strengthener and Stand-by.

As previously mentioned, Holy Spirit is omnipresent, meaning He can be everywhere at one time (Psalm 139:7-8). He is omniscient, meaning all knowing (1 Corinthians 2:10-11; John 14:26). He is omnipotent, meaning all-powerful (Job 33:4; Psalm 104:30; Matthew 12:28). He is the Power Source of the Godhead, producing and creating what we see in the natural realm from the spiritual realm through your faith-filled Words spoken into the atmosphere.

Many believers do not understand how much Holy Spirit is involved in everything God does. This is because Holy Spirit is God. As previously mentioned, He is the third person of the triune Godhead, which consists of God the Father, God the Son and God the Holy Spirit (Matthew 28:19).

For example, when God (Elohim)—which means God the Father, God the Son and God the Holy Spirit—created heaven and the earth in Genesis 1:1-2 (NASB), it was Holy Spirit who released the power to recreate the earth.

In the beginning God created the heaven and the earth. And the earth was without form, and void; and darkness was upon the face of the deep. And the Spirit of God moved upon the face of the waters.

"Rachaph" is the Hebrew word for "moved". It means to brood, hover, move, shake. To "brood" describes how a hen sits on her eggs to hatch them. Holy Spirit brooded over God's creation waiting for the Word to be released, so He could produce it.

When God the Son said, "Let there be light" (Gen. 1:3), Holy Spirit's power produced the light. Zechariah 4:6 says: "'Not by might nor by power, but by My Spirit,' says the Lord of hosts." Everything we see was created by the power of Holy Spirit. God the Father conceived it. Jesus spoke it. Holy Spirit created it.

Since we are made in the image and likeness of Elohim, we have the same creative power in our tongue. This means when we partner with God and Christ Jesus by praying, saying, decreeing, declaring and prophesying faith-filled Words, Holy Spirit releases His power and the ministering spirits or angels of God go forth to bring what was spoken to pass.

For example, when God the Father was ready for Jesus to be born on earth, He sent Gabriel the messenger angel to deliver the prophecy or Word of God (Luke 1:26-35) to the Virgin Mary. He told her she would birth Jesus, the holy Son of God. When she agreed, saying, "Be it unto me even as you have spoken," Holy Spirit brooded over her and she conceived Jesus. Nine months later, the Word of God was born, as the Son of God, who would later die on the cross to redeem mankind from sin and spiritual death.

Jesus waited until He had been baptized, had passed the wilderness test, and had been anointed by Holy Spirit before He began His ministry. Then He began preaching and teaching that the kingdom of God was at hand. He wholly depended upon Holy

Spirit as He healed the sick, opened blind eyes and deaf ears, and taught on the kingdom of God (Acts 10:38).

I have heard it said that Holy Spirit is "Co-creator of the universe. The Author of divine Scripture. The Generator of Christ's humanity. The Regenerator of the believer. And the Distributor of eternal life for He eternally exists." If our Father and Jesus depended upon Holy Spirit, how much more must we as disciples of Jesus Christ? Our success in life as ambassadors of Christ Jesus requires that we wholly depend upon Holy Spirit to lead us into all truth by faith.

This includes depending upon Holy Spirit for everything, especially when we pray. Prayer is the vehicle God uses to transfer His government and solutions, from heaven to earth. The power of Holy Spirit comes from praying in the realm of the spirit. This spiritual power is like the fuel that ensures the vehicle of faith-filled prayer arrives safely to its destination.

If you want to get answers when you pray, yield to Holy Spirit. Get to know Him in an intimate way. I believe developing a relationship with Holy Spirit is the most important investment you can make in your spiritual growth and development. The reason is not just so that you can learn how to pray accurately, or to live the abundant life that Jesus died to obtain for you, (John 10:10), which is all good, but to get to know Holy Spirit in an intimate way. He's the Spirit of truth, and He knows all things (John 16:13). Otherwise why pray and waste your valuable time? Romans 8:26 says:

Likewise the Spirit also helps in our weaknesses. For we do not know what we should pray for as we ought, but the Spirit Himself makes intercession for us with groanings which cannot be uttered.

So when you are interceding on behalf of someone or for a situation and you don't know what to pray, yield to Holy Spirit, and He will come alongside to help you accurately pray as verse 26 says above. The Holy Spirit is continuously available to help you pray.

Remember, one of the ways He functions is as our Intercessor. His prayers always hit the target because He knows all things. However, the only way that Holy Spirit can perform God's will on earth is through the faith-filled prayers of the believer. This is because God has given legal jurisdiction and authority to His sons and daughters on earth (Psalm 115:16; Matt. 28:18-20; Mark 16:15-18; Luke 10:19). We serve as ambassadors of Christ Jesus on earth to legislate His affairs (2 Cor. 5:20).

THE SPIRIT OF PRAYER

I would like to point out something here. The Holy Spirit inspires all true prayer, whether you 1) are praying in your native language, or 2) are praying in other tongues or your heavenly prayer language. Praying in the Spirit is not praying out of your mind, but out of your spirit. It is depending upon Holy Spirit (1 Cor. 14:15).

Praying in the Spirit in your native language is what the old-timers called "getting lost in the spirit", according to Kenneth Hagin, Sr.4 It's where you become more conscious of God and the spirit realm than your natural surroundings. In this realm, you can pray for hours and never even notice it.

This is also the realm of the prophetic, where Holy Spirit inspires you to decree prophecies of God, beyond your own understanding (Rev. 19:10). The Holy Spirit is the air that an intercessor breathes to know what to decree—the who, what, when, where and how of God's will "on earth as it is in heaven."

Since Holy Spirit is fully and equally God, whatever He prays through man will come to pass.

Praying in the Spirit in other tongues is a valuable gift from God, because it gives you the ability to pray beyond your limited, natural understanding as Holy Spirit gives you utterance with groanings (Rom. 8:26). The enemy also cannot decipher praying in tongues. Whenever you don't know what to pray, switch gears and pray in tongues.

If you desire to go deeper in your prayer life, spend much time praying in other tongues. Begin by praying for 5 minutes, then 15 minutes until you're praying in the spirit for one or more hours a day.

Let me tell you a story about praying in the spirit that hopefully will fire you up to pray in this way. Perry Stone, founder of Manna-Fest TV Program, shared how his dad, Mr. Fred Stone, prayed for hours in the spirit, experiencing the supernatural in an unusual way.[5] Perry said at the end of one church service, his dad was so high in the spirit that after everyone else had stopped praying, he was still praying. So Perry left his dad lying on the floor praying with another man watching over him.

Mr. Stone continued to pray one hour, then two. He kept crying out unto the Lord as he prayed for three hours and then four. Entering into the fifth hour of prayer, Mr. Stone continued praying in the spirit.

Then all of a sudden, the other man became startled when he saw Mr. Stone's spirit start rising out of his body. He was so scared that he shook Mr. Stone right out of the glory zone.

Do you want to experience prayer like this as the norm? Remember the supernatural is natural for the believer. As a child of God filled with His glory, wherever you go and whenever you open your mouth to speak, you release heaven on earth—shifting the spiritual climate. You are a very powerful spirit being that God has sent to be born on earth in a body (earth suit) and with a soul (mind, imagination, intellect, will, emotions) to establish heaven on earth.

When you consistently pray in tongues, you will encounter God's presence, release the mysteries of God and walk in greater spiritual authority.

Would you like to travel in the spirit to different places when you pray? Do you want to release the mysteries of God, so heaven invades earth? Do you want to pray fervent, red-hot prayers that will make it rain like Elijah? Do you want to release the godly destiny of your children, future generations and yourself? Then continually pray in the Spirit, releasing the mysteries of God.

Just think of the power of God that could be released all over the world if we could get believers and churches united to organize prayer watches to pray for His kingdom initiatives: salvation, leaders, marriages, governments, healing and deliverance, revivals, financial increase, and to usher in the next great awakening. Glory to God! As pray-ers and intercessors, let's continually press into God's presence, walking in the Spirit as a lifestyle. In this way, may it be said of you what was said of Prophet Samuel in 1 Sam. 3:19:

So Samuel grew, and the Lord was with him and let none of his words fall to the ground.

As a son or daughter of God, the norm is for you to be led by the Spirit, and this includes praying in your heavenly language. Rom. 8:14 says:

For as many as are led by the Spirit of God, these are sons of God.

If you follow Holy Spirit's leading when you pray, your prayers will always hit the bullseye because they will agree with heaven.

CHAPTER 9

CULTIVATING INTIMACY

I am my beloved's, and my beloved is mine.
—Song of Solomon 6:3

The most profound secret I have learned about prayer is the importance of cultivating an intimate relationship with God through fellowship and communion. For God is the object of prayer.

What is intimacy? Webster's 1828 Dictionary defines intimacy as inmost, near, close in friendship or acquaintance and familiar. It also means something of a personal or private nature or closeness between two people.

Some synonyms for intimacy are affection, communion, confidence, friendship and fellowship. Intimacy is cultivated when two hearts (spirits) beat as one. Jesus emphasized the importance of cultivating an intimate prayer life when He said in Matthew 6:6:

> *But you, when you pray, go into your room, and when you have shut your door, pray to your Father who is in the secret place; and your Father who sees in secret will reward you openly.*

Jesus taught us to seek to cultivate an intimate relationship with God when He told us to go into our room and pray. This requires an investment of quality time. You become one in spirit with God. Pouring out your deepest thoughts, fears, hurts, concerns, desires and expressions of love—and allowing Father God to do the same—is no different than a devoted husband and wife knowing each other in the privacy of their bedroom, or cultivating an intimate relationship with your best friend.

Real intimacy with God is impossible without trust, unconditional surrender and obedience to God. You cannot claim intimacy with Christ if your conduct or lifestyle is marked by disobedience, rather than obedience.

When you see a husband and wife "in love" after 50 years of marriage, you can be assured they were intentional in spending quality time together. Our relationship with our heavenly Father is no different.

The closest word in the Bible to describe "intimacy" is the word "know" or "knew". In John 17:3, Jesus said to our Father:

This is life eternal, that men may know You the only true God, and Jesus Christ Whom You have sent.

The word "know" is the same word used in the Septuagint (Greek) Version of the Old Testament in Genesis 4:1, which says, "Adam knew Eve his wife, and she conceived and gave birth to Cain."

The word "knew" in both cases depicts the deepest intimacy: a physical intimacy between Adam and Eve, and a spiritual intimacy between the true believer and God.

Yes, it is fully possible and necessary for human beings to have an intimate relationship with God to fulfill godly purpose and destiny, for He created us for His pleasure and glory! (Isa. 43:17).

I've heard it said that the chief end of man is to know God and to enjoy Him forever. You can also say that the chief purpose of God is to know man and enjoy him forever. God has always desired to dwell with His children.

I have an intimate relationship with my husband, Tony that has deepened over time. But it didn't start out that way. We invest time to understand what is important to each other to strengthen our marriage. The mutual effort we put into maintaining our relationship has created better communication, unity, deeper understanding, respect and love for each other.

A healthy relationship requires regular attention, and this takes time. The same is true of your spiritual relationship with God. The issues in any relationship, when properly understood and healthily confronted, do *not* detract from intimacy in the relationship. In fact, it should deepen it.

Your heart or spirit is where you connect with God. It's the interface He uses to communicate and commune with you. You can only receive revelation from God as you commune with Him—spirit to spirit. You worship God in spirit and in truth; therefore, you must work consistently to strengthen your relationship with God, repenting quickly to fix any breakdowns in communication. We must practice the disciplines of our faith: prayer, communion, fasting, meditating, reading and studying the Word of God, and fellowshipping with other believers.

The hardest lesson for me to learn in my walk with God was how to be still and know that He is God (Psalm 46:10). I had to learn that I didn't have to figure everything out. Today, in my relationship with God, His grace assures me that all of my deficiencies are covered. God's grace supplies what I cannot. I know I am protected through my intimate relationship with Him.

Intimacy means allowing God's love to swallow up fear and restore joy. It means letting Him lead the dance. Intimacy also means to abide in Him and He will abide in you. Jesus emphasized "abiding" several times in John 15:4-5, which says:

Abide in Me, and I in you. As the branch cannot bear fruit of itself, unless it abides in the vine, neither can you, unless you abide in Me. I am the vine, you are the branches. He who abides in Me, and I in him, bears much fruit; for without Me you can do nothing.

To abide in God means to remain or to stay in continuous union with the Lord. It is a fellowship that never ceases as you continually obey God, especially when you've been wronged. In the process of abiding, you bear fruit that glorifies God.

Abiding is not conveniently forgetting you're saved to give someone who offends you a piece of your mind. Keep your mind to yourself. Be patient and possess your soul (Luke 21:19).

Abiding is not a temporary position where you're saved, born again and filled with the Holy Ghost on Sunday, but on Friday, it's happy hour time. Abiding is remaining vitally connected, spirit-to-spirit with the Lord in prayer and communion. Abiding is a spiritual union of mutual love, respect and integrity.

Therefore, you shouldn't lose your temper, or have a temporary identity crisis when something doesn't go your way. As a son or daughter of the Most High God, you must remember that you carry the eternal, resurrection power of Holy Spirit inside of you. You have been bought with a price (the precious blood of Jesus). Your life is not your own. Abiding is an infinite, spiritual union with God. The fire on the altar of your heart will never go out as long as your heart's desire is to please God.

Enoch is a biblical example of someone who had a very intimate relationship with God. Genesis 5:21-24 says:

When Enoch had lived 65 years, he became the father of Methuselah. After he became the father of Methuselah, Enoch walked faithfully with God 300 years and had other sons and daughters. Altogether, Enoch lived a total of 365 years. Enoch walked faithfully with God; then he was no more, because God took him away (NIV).

Enoch walked faithfully with God. This means he remained or stayed in vital spiritual union with God. He wasn't flaky. Up one day and down the next. This I believe is why Enoch never tasted death. God just took him home.

Abraham, the father of faith, is another who enjoyed a deep level of intimacy with God. Before God destroyed Sodom and Gomorrah for gross sin and idolatry, He came down to earth to talk to His friend Abraham. God needed an intercessor to stand in the gap for Lot and his family. They were the only righteous people living in the area at the time. God said in Genesis 18:17:

And the Lord said, Shall I hide from Abraham [My friend and servant] what I am going to do... (AMP).

It was God's mercy extended through Abraham's intercession that saved Lot and his family from being destroyed in Sodom and Gomorrah (Gen. 16:18-33, 19:15-21). God cannot do anything in the earth unless he finds an obedient man, woman, or child to pray, say, decree, prophesy and proclaim His Word, which is His will. This is because God has given mankind legal jurisdiction and authority to usher heaven into earth.

Moses is yet another intercessor who enjoyed an intimate relationship with God. No one can see God and live; yet God trusted and loved Moses so much that He let Moses see the backside of His glory and live.

And he said, "Please, show me your glory." Then He said, "I will make all My goodness pass before you, and I will proclaim the name of the Lord before you. I will be gracious to whom I will be gracious, and I will have compassion on whom I will have compassion." But He said, "You cannot see My face; for no man shall see Me, and live." And the Lord said, "Here is a place by Me, and you shall stand on the rock. So it shall be, while My glory passes by, that I will put you in the cleft of the rock, and will cover you with My hand while I pass by. Then I will take away My hand, and you shall see My back; but My face shall not be seen" (Gen. 33:18-23).

Do you desire to see God's glory? If He let Moses see His glory, God can do the same for you because He is not a respecter of persons. If you pursue God like Moses, spending quality time, all things are possible, if you believe. Moses had such confidence and trust in God, due to cultivating an intimate relationship, that when God told him that He was going to wipe out the Israelites because of their disobedience, Moses boldly interceded for them. Exodus 32:11-12 says:

Then Moses pleaded with the Lord his God, and said: "Lord, why does Your wrath burn hot against Your people whom You have brought out of the land of Egypt with great power and with a mighty hand? Why should the Egyptians speak, and say, 'He brought them out to harm them, to kill them in the mountains, and to consume them from the face of the earth'? Turn from Your fierce wrath, and relent from this harm to Your people."

Even the apostles in the gospels, imperfect as they were, had transparent, intimate relationships with Jesus that caused Him to impart his authority to them, and they turned the world upside down with the message of the kingdom of God.

A mature spiritual person invests time to engage in an honest, authentic relationship with God. You encounter God in the secret place of your heart. You discover His nature, strength, wisdom, revelation, mercy, love and grace, when you embrace a passionate relationship in the secret place. In this place of intimacy, God reveals strategies, tactics and direction to outwit the enemy. Like Queen Esther, who fasted and prayed to save Israel from genocide, God can also use you to save a nation as you commune with Him in prayer in your secret place.

Do you want your prayer life to grow? Then schedule daily time with the Lord. He looks forward to spending time with you because there is no one else like you in all the earth. You are very special to God. No one can take your place in His heart, for you are fearfully and wonderfully made.

Long after I have left my prayer closet, I am still encountering God's presence, whether running errands or working. This sweet communion happens effortlessly and quietly. It's simply being with Him.

Initially, I had a difficult time cultivating intimacy with God because I suffered rejection as a child. Therefore, I had built up so many walls to protect my heart that not even God could get in. I was full of fear, shame and insecurity.

But through the process of spending time in God's Word— communing with Him in my secret place in thanksgiving, praise and worship, and fellowshipping with other believers—I experienced healing and deliverance. I pursued intimacy with God because I was desperate to heal the aching wounds in my soul. Looking back at what I endured, I know that my experiences, good and bad, have shaped me into the woman of God I am today in Christ Jesus.

What did the process of cultivating an intimate relationship with God look like? For me, the process included and still includes much prayer, thanksgiving, praise and worship, meditation, reading and studying the Scriptures, and sitting under sound teaching. When my home was quiet at night, I would worship God. I would talk to Him about my hurts, fears and dreams, filling up many journals as He responded to me. I would dance and kneel before Him. I sung new songs to Him. I cried myself to sleep some nights. I asked Him questions like "What's on your heart?" "Who do you want me to pray for?" and "Why do you love man so much?"

It was those nights spent on my living room floor in the wee hours of the morning, or kneeling at the side of my bed, or laying at His feet in my closet to thank Him for delivering me, that our hearts were knit together to beat as one. I prayed a lot in tongues and still do. I asked God questions about life. Then I listened to what He had to say. I wrote the healing Words He spoke to my heart in my journal.

I sang to Him, from the book of Psalms. I also serenaded Him with new love songs in my heavenly prayer language, downloaded from heaven straight into my heart. I wept tears of pain that turned into tears of joy. I read my Bible aloud with Him. I sat still in His presence, saying nothing and enveloped by glory. I went to sleep on His lap. Our Father gives His beloved sweet sleep. The more time I spent with Daddy God, the more my trust in Him grew. Outside of my prayer closet, I began to hear His voice more clearly as He ordered my footsteps.

As you cultivate intimacy with God, you will understand that prayer is about being with God and understanding what's on His heart. It's about being transparent. He already knows everything about you anyway. When you have an intimate relationship with someone, you want to hear what's important to the other person because you genuinely care for them. So it is with our heavenly Father. You want to hear what's on His heart, so you can fully cooperate on earth to usher heaven (God's government) on earth through your prayers and faith-filled words.

Do you desire a richer prayer life? Then invest daily quality time in God's presence and His Word. If you don't have this desire, ask God to give it to you. His grace is sufficient.

He made you to abide in Him and in His Word. This is where you draw life and strength to answer your call and fulfill your destiny. Delight in Him and let Him delight in you. Give yourself permission to be God's delight. Everything else can wait. Meditate and study your Bible to renew your subconscious mind. Soak in the fragrant pool of His love. Let Him restore your soul. He's your Bridegroom Lover and you're His bride that He's preparing to be without spot, wrinkle or blemish.

God is faithful to meet you at the place of your brokenness and to anoint every bruised place in your soul with His healing love. Then your spiritual eyes will see beyond the pain of your past or present, into the essence of who you are in Him—whole. Intimacy is crying unto Abba Father, "Into me see! Reveal to me, Father, every place where I need to be broken. Break me and put me back together in the image of Christ Jesus."

Isn't this what salvation is all about?

- ♥ Surrendering to God.
- ♥ Confessing your sins.
- ♥ Dying to self.
- ♥ Being resurrected to new life in Christ Jesus.

- ♥ Saving souls.

- ♥ Serving mankind.

- ♥ Fellowshipping with God and His people.

- ♥ Enjoying the abundant life to be a blessing.

- ♥ Walking in the Spirit.

- ♥ Being transformed into the image of Jesus Christ, the One in whom we live, and move and have our being? Selah.

Because I desire to know and please God, I must live in His presence. One way I do this is by centering my thoughts on Jesus. I imagine us sitting on the beach watching the waves hit the shore and roll back out to sea. No words are spoken. Yet we are speaking volumes about our love for each other. The beach is where I go in my mind to spend quality time with Jesus, and it's also where I go to spend time with God when I travel to my hometown of Ft. Lauderdale, Florida.

INTIMACY IN THE PHYSICAL AND SPIRITUAL TABERNACLE (EX. 39:32-43)

The Tabernacle of Moses (TOM) was a house of prayer. It foreshadowed the New Testament believer becoming a living, spiritual tabernacle filled with prayers of thanksgiving, praise and worship unto the only true, living God. To the extent that we understand the importance of our role as priestly intercessors is the extent that we will grow in intimacy with God.

Let's look at the priests in the TOM. They didn't just make atonement for the sins of the people, nor did they just minister God's words to the people. The bulk of their time was spent ministering to God. This involved intimacy or drawing near to God. This is why David's psalms and prayers are so powerful to me. He ministered to God. He loved on God. He was intimate with God. To be effective intercessors, we must draw nearer to God like David to experience newness of life.

If you have a secret, whom do you tell? Would you tell a casual observer? No, you would tell someone you trust—like Jesus, your spouse or a close friend. Well, God is the same way. He can't tell you His secrets if He doesn't know you. As Alice Smith, author of *Beyond the Veil* puts it, "God doesn't have favorites, but He does have intimates."[6] Enoch, Abraham, Moses, David, Elijah, Deborah, Daniel, Anna, Paul, and most of all, Jesus, enjoyed deep intimacy with God because they spent much time with Him. They trusted God, and He trusted them because they desired what He desired. Trust is the foundation of letting you see into me. It is developed over time.

So how do you develop intimacy with God? You must spend quality time with Him, spirit-to-spirit in fellowship, conversation, thanksgiving, praise and worship. You must immerse yourself in His Word to understand how God's kingdom operates. You value and obey what's important to Him—souls saved and delivered from sin, hell, death and the grave.

I have learned in life that seldom are urgent things important, or important things urgent. For example, worshiping God and meditating Scripture are not urgent, but they are extremely important for your long-term spiritual growth and development. Exercising these disciplines is imperative for the fulfillment of your prophetic destiny. It's more important to spend quiet time with God first thing in the morning, instead of rushing off to work, because He will supply everything you need to have a successful day.

The Tabernacle of Moses foreshadowed the coming of Jesus Christ. It had three compartments that speak of increasing levels of intimacy. As living tabernacles of God, the only way to keep the fire of prayer lit upon the altar of your heart is to pursue His presence in spirit and truth. Let's take a look at the three compartments found in Moses' Tabernacle.

First there was the Outer Court. It was located outside and lit by sunlight, symbolizing natural things. It correlates to our physical body, which is made of flesh, blood and bones that absorb natural sunlight. In the outer court, you present your body as a living sacrifice unto God. The outer court represented death to self. It contained two pieces of furniture—the brazen altar and the brazen laver:

1) **Brazen altar** (Ex. 39:39)—was located outside, and lit by natural sunlight, which was used by the priests for sacrificing animals for the atonement of sin. This is where the confession of sin took place. Today, Jesus is the sinless perfect sacrifice, whose blood has washed away your sins past, present and future. You are no longer a slave to sin, but to righteousness. As a New Testament priestly intercessor, when you confess your sins to God, Jesus' blood cleanses you permanently.

2) **Brazen laver** (Ex. 39:39)—was used by the priests to wash the blood from their hands before entering into the Inner Court, or Holy Place. The water represents the washing of the water of the Word that renews your mind. The bronze laver represents the judgment of man. Today, the New Testament (NT) priest cleanses his soul with the living Word of God.

Second was the Inner Court. It was located inside the tent. The Inner Court represents your soul (mind, imagination, intellect will, emotions) communing with Christ Jesus. It is in the soul where sanctification progressively occurs. What do I mean? You are born again instantly in your spirit, progressively in your soul as you renew your mind, and future in your body, which will be glorified at Jesus' second coming.

You eat the Word of God to renew or reprogram your mind like the mind of Christ. If the enemy can control your mind, will or emotions, then he can control you. Your prayer power will be limited. As intercessors, we should fast and pray to keep our flesh under subjection to our spirit man, and to be sensitive to God's voice. We should meditate, read and study the Scriptures to receive wisdom, understanding, knowledge and revelation from God.

God cannot fully use you in life and ministry, let alone in prayer, if you are not filled with His Word because everything God does, or tells you to do, is built upon the foundation of His Word. He can't pull out of you what has not been planted in you. Man does not live by bread alone, but by every Word that proceeds from the mouth of God. The Word of God is seed that you must plant by faith in the good soil of your heart. You will reap a harvest in due season as you continue to water it with thanksgiving, praise, worship and corresponding action.

There were three pieces of furniture in the Inner Court—the Golden Lampstand, the Table of Shewbread and the Altar of Incense:

1) **Golden Lampstand** (Ex. 39:37)—represents Holy Spirit, who is the Spirit of truth that leads you into all truth. The golden lampstand continually provided light in the Inner Court.

2) **Table of Shewbread** (Ex. 39:36)—represents the Word of God, or Jesus, the Bread of Life, with whom we commune daily to receive wisdom, understanding, knowledge, and refreshing.

3) **Altar of Incense** (Ex. 39:38)—represents the prayers of the saints that are mixed in heaven with praise and worship unto our God. At the right time, God releases answers to our prayers with thundering and lightening. David says in Psalm 141:2, "May my prayer be set before you like the evening sacrifice."

Last was the Holy of Holies, which was the most intimate place in the TOM. It was located behind the veil and was continually lit by the supernatural light of God's Shekinah Glory. Only the high priest could enter once a year to make atonement for his sins and the sins of the people, by sprinkling blood from sacrificed animals upon the mercy seat (Lev. 16; Heb. 9:24-28). There was one piece of furniture in the Holy of Holies—the Ark of the Covenant with the Mercy Seat on top. It contained two golden cherubim, one on either side of the top of the mercy seat with wings outstretched, to guard the "Shekinah" (glory) of God.

1) **The Ark of Covenant** (Ex. 39:35)—represents the presence of Almighty God. It symbolizes your spirit alive in Christ Jesus. It contained the following items:

- **Aaron's Rod that budded**—symbolizing that in an intimate relationship with the Father, He can resurrect the dead areas of your life.

- **Ten Commandments**—the Word of God, engraved on the tablet of your heart, so you will not sin against God.

- **Pot of Manna**—symbolizing God as your eternal Source of supply. He's everything you need.

- **The Mercy Seat on top of the Ark**—where the high priest would sprinkle the blood of bulls and goats to atone for the sins of the people. (This is the place in the heavenly Tabernacle where Jesus applied His sinless blood to forgive mankind's sins once and for all.)

The Holy of Holies correlates to our spirit filled by Holy Spirit. Your spirit consists of three parts: communion, conscience and intuition. In the Holy of Holies, it is no longer you who live, but your spirit is alive in Christ Jesus, the hope of glory. You have new life in Him, who has all power in heaven and earth. When you commune with God, Holy Spirit downloads revelation straight into your spirit.

As a New Testament priest, you can boldly enter into the throne room of God to worship Him and make your request. You can do this because Jesus shed His blood on Calvary's cross for the forgiveness of your sins and mine—past, present and future.

Therefore, brethren, having boldness to enter the Holiest by the blood of Jesus, by a new and living way which He consecrated for us, through the veil, that is, His flesh, and having a High Priest over the house of God, let us draw near with a true heart in full assurance of faith, having our hearts sprinkled from an evil conscience and our bodies washed with pure water. Let us hold fast the confession of our hope without wavering, for He who promised is faithful (Heb. 10:19-23 KJV).

In closing, intimacy transcends the rational, logical mind. It's a spirit-to-spirit relationship eternally connecting you with the Most High God. You are a spiritual tabernacle, a carrier of God's glory. You position yourself to release His glory as you rest, abide and remain vitally connected to our Father. This unity in the Spirit gives the believer legal authority and jurisdiction to decree God's kingdom on earth, as it is in heaven, and it will come to pass. Amen.

CHAPTER 10

EXERCISING YOUR AUTHORITY

*Behold, I give you the authority to trample on serpents and
scorpions, and over all the power of the enemy, and nothing
shall by any means hurt you. —Luke 10:19*

Are you walking in the fullness of your God-given authority
in every area of your life? Authority is exercised when there is a
right to exercise it.

A true believer has a right to exercise authority in Jesus'
name. Yet many walk around in abject hopelessness and fear. It's
as if they don't yet realize that when Jesus died on the cross for
our sins, not only did He pay the penalty for us, but He also
restored our authority in His name to have dominion on earth.
He even imputed or credited His righteousness to us, so that we
can reign in life as kings and priests as it was in the beginning in
the Garden of Eden (1 Peter 2:5, 9; Revelation 1:6). Let's define
authority:

Merriam-Webster's Dictionary defines "authority" as the
power to give orders or make decisions; the power or right to
direct or control someone or something; power to influence or
command thought, opinion, or behavior.

God ordains all true authority. In the beginning when God
made heaven and earth, He delegated dominion to mankind,
according to Genesis 1:26-28. Authority is inherent to dominion.

In other words, you can't have dominion over something if you haven't been given authority or a legal right to oversee it.

In addition, concerning the spiritual, you must have a "knowing" (faith) down in your inner man that God has called you to rule over a particular territory, or you risk losing it. Let's look at the first mention of dominion in the Bible to reinforce the principle of our delegated authority.

Then God said, "Let Us make man in Our image, according to Our likeness; let them have dominion over the fish of the sea, over the birds of the air, and over the cattle, over all the earth and over every creeping thing that creeps on the earth." So God created man in His own image; in the image of God He created him; male and female He created them. Then God blessed them, and God said to them, "Be fruitful and multiply; fill the earth and subdue it; have dominion over the fish of the sea, over the birds of the air, and over every living thing that moves on the earth" (Genesis 1:26-28).

The Hebrew word for "dominion" is *"radah"*. It means to tread down, subjugate; to crumble off; make to have dominion; prevail against; reign, bear, rule over and take.

The Hebrew word for authority is *"rabah"*. It means to increase in whatever respect; bring in abundance; be in authority; bring up; continue, enlarge, excel, exceedingly, be full of; make great; grow up, heap, increase, be long, many a time; more in number; much greater; more, make to multiply; nourish, plenteous, store, thoroughly and very.

God has given the true believer, led by His Spirit, the ability to rule over a particular domain and cause it to increase, expand and multiply.

Before Jesus ascended to heaven, where He now sits at the right hand of our Father continually interceding for us, He restored to us the delegated authority Adam transferred to the devil when He disobeyed God by eating from the Tree of the Knowledge of Good and Evil. Jesus came to earth to take back the authority the devil stole from Adam and Eve and restore it to us. Jesus said:

> *All authority has been given to Me in heaven and on earth. Go therefore and make disciples of all the nations, baptizing them in the name of the Father and of the Son and of the Holy Spirit, teaching them to observe all things that I have commanded you; and lo, I am with you always, even to the end of the age (Matt. 28:18-20).*

> *Then He called His twelve disciples together and gave them power and authority over all demons, and to cure diseases (Matt. 9:1).*

> *Behold, I give you the authority to trample on serpents and scorpions, and over all the power of the enemy, and nothing shall by any means hurt you (Luke 10:19).*

The word "authority" in the three Scriptures above is the Greek word "exousia". It means authority, conferred power; delegated empowerment or operating in a designated jurisdiction. "Exousia" also means privilege, right, force, power, capacity, competency, freedom, mastery, magistrate, superhuman, potentate, token of control, delegated influence, jurisdiction, liberty and strength.

God has given the believer delegated authority in Christ Jesus, authorizing the true believer to legislate His will on earth when we pray, decree and act in accordance with His Word. This means we have been authorized to uphold and execute God's law as written in the Bible, in Jesus' name.

For example, the Bible tells us in Mark 16:17 to cast out devils, which is the first level of spiritual warfare. Therefore, you do not pray for God to cast out the devil because He's already authorized you to do this in His name (Mark 16:15-20). If He's authorized you to do it, you're already equipped by His power residing inside of your spirit. So obey God and step out by faith in Jesus' name and watch as God releases His power to back you up.

Remember, there is no place in the Bible where God tells us to ask Him or Jesus to cast out demons, to heal the sick, or to save souls. This is *our responsibility* as stewards of the earth that God has entrusted us to manage for Him. He's also given us the nations as an inheritance to evangelize, teach and make disciples of our Lord Jesus Christ (Psalm 115:16, 2:8).

When you confessed Jesus as Lord, your spirit man was instantly born again as the resurrection power of God that raised Jesus from the dead came to abide inside of you. This is the power of Almighty God Himself, the Great I Am that I Am, Creator of heaven and earth. It is He that is living and working inside of you both to will and to do of His good pleasure.

Holy Spirit translated you from the kingdom of darkness into the kingdom of His dear Son Jesus. You have been raised to sit in heavenly places in Christ Jesus far above all principality, power, might and dominion, and above every name named not only in this world, but in the world to come. Jesus took back all authority from the enemy and delegated it to you, the believer.

God has placed the enemy beneath Jesus' feet, according to Ephesians 1:21-23. If you're in Christ Jesus, this means the enemy is beneath your feet, too. The authority of Jesus trumps the power of the devil.

JESUS' AUTHORITY

Jesus exercised authority like nobody else in history! This is one thing that made it clear that He was the Son of God. He cast out demons with confident authority:

And they were all amazed, insomuch that they questioned among themselves, saying, What thing is this? What new doctrine is this? For with authority commandeth he even the unclean spirits, and they do obey him (Mark 1:27 KJV).

He cast out demons with His spoken Word:

When the even was come, they brought unto him many that were possessed with devils: and he cast out the spirits with his word (Matt. 8:16 KJV).

He healed the sick with His spoken Word:

Wherefore neither thought I myself worthy to come unto thee: but say in a word, and my servant shall be healed (Luke 7:7 KJV).

And amazement came upon them all, and they began talking with one another saying, "What is this message? For with authority and power He commands the unclean spirits and they come out" (Luke 4:36).

In Jesus' name, you have been given the same authority if you're a believer as a son or daughter of God. Therefore, give yourself permission to exercise your authority when you pray. Expect God's power (dunamis) and His angelic force to back up your Words with signs following (Heb. 1:14).

Dunamis power, authority or ability comes after you have received exousia, or your delegated authority which is a part of your salvation package in Christ Jesus. Exousia ranks higher than dunamis because it is your foundation as a son or daughter of God that all creation is waiting for to bring divine order into a person's life or into a region.

Dunamis is the tangible, explosive, miracle-working power of God. It's transferrable from one person to another. It's demonstrative. It does something. It leaps or jumps on people like electricity. Even though it's spiritual, you can feel it. It can be transferred into inanimate objects and work wonders.

Remember how the handkerchiefs that touched Paul's body healed people? Remember how Peter's shadow healed people? You must be bold to flow in dunamis. You cannot care what people think about you when God tells you to command blind eyes to open or to cast out a devil. You just step out and say it. God's power does the work.

Here are two Scriptures that show exousia, dunamis, or both in action.

Luke 4:36 says, *"Then they were all amazed and spoke among themselves, saying, "What a word this is! For with authority (exousia) and power (dunamis) He commands the unclean spirits, and they come out."*

Luke 9:1 says, *"Then he called his twelve disciples together, and gave them power (dunamis) and authority (exousia) over all devils and to cure diseases."*

JESUS DELEGATED AUTHORITY TO HIS DISCIPLES

Then Jesus called together His twelve disciples, and gave them power and authority over all devils, and to cure diseases (Matt. 10:28).

The Scripture above says that Jesus gave us power and authority over all devils and to cure diseases. This means like a traffic cop who puts up his hand to stop a semi-truck that is much bigger than the traffic cop, when we open our mouths and decree a thing in Jesus' name, Almighty God Himself releases His power, causing the enemy to flee.

The believer who understands that God Himself backs his authority in Jesus' name will be fearless in facing opposition, whether casting out evil spirits, laying hands on the sick or conducting a business deal. He will know and understand that God's power is behind Him. How does authority work?

1) Authority doesn't beg. It doesn't ask. Authority commands! In Mark 16:16-17, again, we are not told to *ask* God to cast out demons, we are told to cast them out! We are not told to *beg* demons to come out, we are told to cast them out!

   This means we must use our God-given authority, which must be spoken from our mouths with faith in our heart. "Life and death are in the power of the tongue", according to Proverbs 18:21, "and they that love it shall eat the fruit thereof."

2) Authority (exousia) is undergirded by your faith. It requires that you believe in your heart and decree or confess with your mouth what the Word of God says or what Holy Spirit speaks directly to your heart about a situation. What you say must always agree with God's Word to qualify for an answer (1 John 5:14-15). In Matthew 8:8-10:13, Jesus applauded the Roman centurion, (who was not a Jew and therefore had no covenant right to healing), but who understood how faith worked in relationship to authority:

The centurion answered and said, "Lord, I am not worthy that You should come under my roof. But only speak a word, and my servant will be healed. For I also am a man under authority, having soldiers under me. And I say to this one, 'Go,' and he goes; and to another, 'Come,' and he comes; and to my servant, 'Do this,' and he does it." When Jesus heard it, He marveled, and said to those who followed, "Assuredly, I say to you, I have not found such great faith, not even in Israel! Then Jesus said to the centurion, "Go your way; and as you have believed, so let it be done for you." And his servant was healed that same hour.

Authority (exousia) can only work if you have faith in the person that has authorized you, in this case in Jesus' name.

3) Authority works in Jesus' name, not yours or mine. Jesus has given you power of attorney to execute his will on earth as it is in heaven. A power of attorney is a legal document that gives you the right to operate on behalf of the one you're representing. For example, imagine Warren Buffet, a multi billionaire, has given you power of attorney to withdraw a billion dollars from his bank account to conduct business on his behalf. You would confidently walk up to the bank teller and make the withdrawal just like you're Warren Buffet, with no hesitation, because Warren Buffet's power of attorney is backing you.

In the same way, Jesus has given you authority in His Name as a joint heir to transact Kingdom business on earth. It is an honor, privilege and responsibility to be given authority by the King of kings and the Lord of lords because every knee will bow and every tongue will confess that Jesus is Lord (Phil. 2:10). When you pray, say or decree a thing, it's just like Jesus is saying it. It must come to pass because God's Word cannot return to Him void or empty. Here are a few Scriptures you can meditate to increase your faith in the authority delegated to you in Jesus' name:

And the seventy returned again with joy, saying, Lord, even the devils are subject unto us through thy name (Luke 10:17 KJV).

And these signs shall follow them that believe; In my name shall they cast out devils... (Mark 16:17 KJV).

Peter said, Silver and gold have I none; but such as I have give I thee: In the name of Jesus Christ of Nazareth rise up and walk" (Acts 3:6 KJV).

If Jesus has delegated authority to the believer on earth through a covenant relationship ratified by His blood, and He's given us over 7,000 promises in the Bible, according to some Bible scholars, what is stopping many believers from walking in their kingdom authority?

There are many reasons, from doubt and unbelief, to unforgiveness and condemnation. I believe many of these hindrances are rooted in having a sin-consciousness, rather than a righteousness-consciousness. We don't fully understand who we are in Christ Jesus. We are joint heirs with Christ and heirs of Almighty God! We have been assigned to earth to expand our Father's kingdom. We suffer from perverse thinking, which must be cast down and renewed by the washing of the water of the Word of God.

Some believers continue to focus on sins and guilt, some of which they committed 25 years ago, instead of accepting the mercy and forgiveness of God. Instead of giving themselves permission to receive God's grace, mercy and forgiveness, they allow the enemy to torment their minds with condemnation. This is not God's best—for Jesus shed his precious blood on the cross to wash away our sins and guilt. Believers that suffer from a sin-consciousness fail to realize that when they confessed Jesus as Lord, He who knew no sin became sin for them, placing His robe of righteousness upon them and taking away their robe of sin and guilt.

This robe of righteousness obtained through the precious blood of Jesus has forgiven the believer for his or her sins, past, present and future. Sin no longer has dominion over you, my friend, if you walk by the Spirit, and not by the flesh. And if you sin, you have an Advocate with the Father, the Lord Jesus Christ, who is faithful to forgive your sins and cleanse you from all unrighteousness (1 John 1:9). As soon as you repent, your fellowship with God remains intact.

Part of the cure for sin-consciousness is to meditate the living Word of God day and night until your mind is renewed concerning God's unconditional love for you and who you are in Christ Jesus. One power Scripture of meditation is found in Joshua 1:8:

This Book of the Law shall not depart from your mouth, but you shall meditate in it day and night, that you may observe to do according to all that is written in it. For then you will make your way prosperous, and then you will have good success.

We'll look at meditation in the next chapter. Greater is He (God) that is in you than he (the devil, principalities, powers, rulers of darkness, spiritual wickedness) that is in the world (1 John 4:4). So be strong in the Lord and in the power of His might, not your own strength (Eph. 6:10). God's power (authority) is greater than the enemy's power, which Jesus stripped from him, guaranteeing you the victory in the knowledge of Christ Jesus.

CHAPTER 11

MEDITATING SCRIPTURE

As a man thinks, so is he. —Proverbs 23:7

Meditation is a powerful way to tap into the spiritual realm and renew your mind to think and your mouth to speak God's Word. It increases your trust and faith in God by deleting old programs of fear, doubt and unbelief from your sub-conscious mind. According to Strong's Concordance, the word "meditation" means to murmur; to converse with oneself, and hence aloud; speak; talk; babbling; communication; mutter; roar; a murmuring sound; a musical notation; to study; to ponder; revolve in the mind; pray; prayer; reflection and devotion. To meditate means to think about something over and over again like a cow chewing the cud, until your thinking is changed.

As you meditate the Word of God, or as you ponder, think about or saturate your mind with God's Word, the anointing contained within the Word penetrates your heart (mind), displacing thoughts of sin, condemnation and lack with thoughts of holiness, righteousness and favor.

One of the secrets to meditation is memorization. Meditation uses both hemispheres of the brain—right and left. The left hemisphere is responsible for man's reasoning and logic, which can birth impure wisdom, or dependency upon man and not God, unless it is in line with God's logic (John 18:10-11, James 3:15). The right hemisphere is where God speaks to you. It is responsible for storing and managing intuition, imagination, art and music.

I asked God what happens when I meditate His Word. This is what He told me: "When you meditate my Word, which is all that I Am, you release my creative power to fill and flow into your heart (spirit and mind). This supernaturally transforms your way of thinking, changing your world."

Meditation is how Holy Spirit programs "kingdom code" into your heart. He downloads heavenly wisdom, understanding and revelation (Isa. 11:2, James 3:17). Meditation displaces the old, rational, carnal way of thinking, creating new neural pathways in the subconscious mind so you will never be the same.

You can experience a "quantum leap" in your thinking when you meditate the Word of God because it is "spirit and life" (John 6:63). Webster's defines "quantum leap" as a sudden and significant change or increase; something sudden, spectacular and vitally important; a sudden, highly significant advance; breakthrough.

Consistent, daily meditation of Scriptures to address troublesome areas, such as finances, healing or relationships, when done over time will tear down limiting belief systems. It will replace them with the truth of God that you are the head and not the tail, blessed coming in and going out. Meditating is not the same as reading, listening or studying the Word of God. Although these are good, they are more intellectual, relying on the mind, rather than the spirit.

Studying the Scriptures teaches sound doctrine. But without an obedient heart, studying Scripture to acquire knowledge can produce pride and religiosity. Remember, the scribes and Pharisees in Jesus' day studied all the time, but they rejected Jesus. Their hearts were disconnected from God. They had no relationship, love or intimacy with God. Apostle Paul tells us that the "letter kills". But meditating Scripture, according to Joshua 1:8 and Psalm 1:1-3, has many benefits. We'll explore these passages later in the chapter.

Reading or hearing God's Word as a part of your daily devotion is a good discipline, but beware that without a relationship with God, these activities alone may not produce obedience in the heart. Remember James admonishes those who are hearers only, but not doers of God's Word (James 1:22).

This means you can read through the Bible in a year or listen to teachings until you're blue in the face, but still practice sin because you have not allowed the truth of God's Word to saturate your heart and change you.

Meditating fully engages the heart. Memorizing Scripture changes your inner man in a way unlike studying, reading, or hearing the Word of God. When you memorize Scripture, which is the secret to meditation, it feeds your inner man, compelling you to obey God. Holy Spirit can instantly bring Scriptures that you have meditated to the forefront of your mind, helping you to resist temptation and walk by the Spirit.

Meditation is like creating a "hologram" or vision in your mind like the crew on "Star Trek—The Next Generation". For example, when Captain Jean-Luc Picard wanted to take a vacation on a beautiful sunny beach, he punched buttons on a big TV screen and engaged his mind visualizing his desire. Instantly, he was transported to his sunny destination. (Remember the mind cannot tell the difference between something real or imagined, so keep your mind on things eternal and stayed on Him.)

When you meditate God's Word using your sanctified imagination, your faith pulls what you desire from the spiritual realm into the natural realm, causing heaven to invade earth. Again, meditation reprograms your subconscious mind, which stores all of your memories, good and bad. Meditation used consistently and effectively will delete old self-defeating programs from your past, replacing them with new, kingdom principles that will propel you into your destiny.

Expect to encounter resistance from the enemy when you decide to meditate God's Word. Even though he will resist you every step of the way, he is a defeated foe that is beneath your feet (Col. 2:15; 1 John 3:8). Exercise your authority in Jesus' name by binding the enemy and loosing yourself from his lies and tactics. Submit to God, resist the devil and he will flee (James 4:7). Continually decree and declare out of your mouth the promises of God over your life, your family and your connections. Here are two foundational power Scriptures that reveal the benefits of meditation. Joshua 1:8-9 says:

> *This Book of the Law shall not depart from your mouth, but you shall meditate in it day and night, that you may observe to do according to all that is written in it. For then you will make your way prosperous, and then you will have good success. Have I not commanded you? Be strong and of good courage; do not be afraid, nor be dismayed, for the Lord your God is with you wherever you go.*

This verse clearly states that the way to prosper and have good success in life is to meditate God's Word day and night and to obey God. To attain good success, you must think God's thoughts and decree God's Word. Where the mind goes, the man goes. You must put God's Word first place in your life. Everything you need is contained inside the seed of the Word of God. The longer you procrastinate, the longer you delay the fulfillment of your prophetic destiny and the opportunity to glorify God by advancing His kingdom.

Another powerful verse of Scripture about the power of meditation is Psalm 1:1-3:

> *Blessed is the man Who walks not in the counsel of the ungodly, Nor stands in the path of sinners, Nor sits in the seat of the scornful; But his delight is in the law of the Lord, And in His law he meditates day and night. He shall be like a tree planted by the rivers of water that brings forth its fruit in its season, Whose leaf also shall not wither; and whatever he does shall prosper.*

The blessed man first and foremost resists sin and sinful associations. He daily crucifies His flesh. He meditates God's laws, bringing forth fruit in due season and whatever he does prospers.

Living a holy life is a prerequisite to effectively meditating and fellowshipping with God (Psalm 1:1). Meditating God's laws reinforces obedience. The man or woman that obeys God will prosper in every area of life—spiritually, physically, mentally, emotionally, relationally and socially. Prosperity apart from God is limited because it brings sorrow.

Meditating God's laws will also enhance your memory, as it engrafts the Word of God into your mind. It will give you the power to resist sin and overcome adversity. The Word of God, called the "sword of the Spirit," is not only wielded by thinking. It is wielded by speaking forth faith-filled Words into the atmosphere, causing heaven's Angelic Air Force to bring it to pass.

The "sword of the Spirit" is the only offensive weapon that is part of the armor of God. It casts down or captures negative thoughts, replacing them with God's thoughts (Eph. 6:10-18). The "sword of the Spirit" is the "rhema," or spoken Word of God. It is "quick, powerful and sharper than any two-edged sword, piercing to the dividing of your soul from your spirit and your joints from your marrow. The "sword of the Spirit" reveals the intentions of your heart—the good, the bad and the ugly.

Here is a meditation exercise I used to free myself from the spirit of fear. I was so bound by fear that I slept at night with the lights on. If my husband was traveling, I could forget about sleep because I stayed up all night to protect my children and myself.

I became so frustrated with living like this that I finally did something about it. I wrote every one of the 365 Scriptures about fear on 3 x 5 index cards and carried them with me to meditate. I had them in my car, planner, desk, briefcase, pockets and purse. As I continued to meditate the Scriptures about fear day and night, my mind was gradually delivered from fear of the dark.

However, my deliverance would not have occurred if I had been inconsistent and undisciplined in meditating the Word of God. I meditated day, afternoon and night. As my Pastor says, "The Word works, if you work it". The Word of God is full of creative power.

Through meditation of God's Word, I replaced fear with trust and faith in God's love to protect me. If you want to overcome fear, anxiety or any negative emotion or situation, find Scriptures in the Bible that address your problem. Write them down and begin to meditate them day and night until you experience divine transformation. God is faithful to perform His Word.

Are you ready to change? Are you tired of going around the same old mountain? Do you want to break through the glass ceiling of limiting beliefs? Are you ready to take a quantum leap into your prophetic destiny? Obey God and immerse yourself in meditating the living Word of God. And like Joshua, you will possess the land. Like Caleb, you will take your mountain.

Here are a few Scriptures about meditation to meditate: Psalm 1:1-3, 19:14, 49:3, 63:6, 104:34, 119:11, 15, 23, 48, 78, 97-99, 143:5, 148 and Joshua 1:8-10.

CHAPTER 12

PERSISTENT PRAYER

And He (Jesus) spoke a parable unto them to this end that men ought always to pray and not to faint.
—Luke 18:1 KJV

The quality of persistence cannot be emphasized enough when it comes to prayer, especially the prayer of intercession, because it is by persistent, fervent intercession that lives have been spared and nations delivered.

Persistence in prayer causes you to examine your motives. Why are you praying so determinedly? Is it God's will you desire? Do you want what you're praying for more than God, and which if He granted, would only cause you to turn your back on Him? Persistence draws you to the object of prayer, which is God, not things.

The Merriam Webster Dictionary defines "persistence" as the quality that allows someone to continue doing something, or trying to do something, even though it is difficult or opposed by other people; the state of occurring or existing beyond the usual, expected, or normal time. Some synonyms for "persistence" are determination, endurance, grit, perseverance, resolution, steadfastness and tenacity.

Persistence in prayer is so important to Jesus that He shared a parable with His disciples, emphasizing the point.

Then He spoke a parable to them, that men always ought to pray and not lose heart, saying: "There was in a certain city a judge who did not fear God nor regard man. Now there was a widow in that city; and she came to him, saying, 'Get justice for me from my adversary.' And he would not for a while; but afterward he said within himself, 'Though I do not fear God nor regard man, yet because this widow troubles me I will avenge her, lest by her continual coming she weary me.'" Then the Lord said, "Hear what the unjust judge said. And shall God not avenge His own elect who cry out day and night to Him, though He bears long with them? I tell you that He will avenge them speedily. Nevertheless, when the Son of Man comes, will He really find faith on the earth?" (Luke 18:1-8).

There are a couple of things to note in this parable. First, Jesus is contrasting the unloving, unjust, reluctant judge to our loving, caring, sharing heavenly Father, who delights in answering your prayers like any good Father, as long as it's good for you. He's telling us that anytime you pray, you should be confident that Father God hears and will answer. Pray from the position of knowing that God loves you, not from the position of having to *earn* or measure up to get Him to answer you. It's not about how long you pray, although there will be long seasons of prayer in your life. You are a child of God and He loves you, so never resort to begging Him for anything that He's already said in His Word belongs to you. Give yourself permission to receive God's love through answered prayer.

What can stop our God from answering prayer? When you lose faith in His love for you, especially during the waiting stage and cease to pray. The failure of prayer is to stop.

The persistent prayer can be a prayer of thanksgiving and praise, which I call a "yet praise" that you continue to offer unto God long after you have prayed by faith (Mark 11:22-26).

It could be one of intercession, in which you persevere in praying as Holy Spirit leads you until you get a note of victory. You continue to pray and believe until the answer manifests in this realm. It will show up, if the prayer agrees with God's will (Word) because God's promises are yes and amen.

There are many examples of persistence resulting in answered prayer in the Bible. Some deal with intercession, others with personal prayers. In every case, it was the quality of persistence that drew the person praying closer to God, exposing their motives. Were they persisting in prayer to please God or to get what they wanted?

For example, in Genesis 18:23-33, Abraham boldly and persistently interceded for God to spare sinful Sodom and Gomorrah from destruction to save the lives of His nephew, Lot and his family. He boldly asked God repeatedly if a certain number of righteous people were found in Sodom, starting with 50 persons, would He spare Sodom for Lot's sake?

Then the men turned away from there and went toward Sodom, but Abraham still stood before the LORD. And Abraham came near and said, "Would You also destroy the righteous with the wicked? Suppose there were fifty righteous within the city; would You also destroy the place and not spare it for the fifty righteous that were in it? Far be it from You to do such a thing as this, to slay the righteous with the wicked, so that the righteous should be as the wicked; far be it from You! Shall not the Judge of all the earth do right?" (Gen. 18:22-25).

Abraham continued to persistently plead with Almighty God Himself, to save their lives. This is what intercessors do. We stand in the gap, no matter the cost. Eventually, Abraham asked God if He would spare Sodom if there were even ten righteous people there, which there was not. However, Abraham's persistent intercession did open the door for God to extend mercy by sending angels to deliver Lot and his family before Sodom and Gomorrah were destroyed.

When the morning dawned, the angels urged Lot to hurry, saying, "Arise, take your wife and your two daughters who are here, lest you be consumed in the punishment of the city." And while he lingered, the men took hold of his hand, his wife's hand, and the hands of his two daughters, the Lord being merciful to him, and they brought him out and set him outside the city. So it came to pass, when they had brought them outside, that he said, "Escape for your life! Do not look behind you nor stay anywhere in the plain. Escape to the mountains, lest you be destroyed" (Gen. 19:15-17).

Then Lot said to them, "Please, no, my lords! Indeed now, your servant has found favor in your sight, and you have increased your mercy which you have shown me by saving my life; but I cannot escape to the mountains, lest some evil overtake me and I die. See now, this city is near enough to flee to, and it is a little one; please let me escape there (is it not a little one?) and my soul shall live." And he said to him, "See, I have favored you concerning this thing also, in that I will not overthrow this city for which you have spoken. Hurry, escape there. For I cannot do anything until you arrive there" (Gen. 19:18-22).

It was because of Abraham's intercession that God dispatched the ministering angels to deliver Lot and his family from imminent destruction. What an amazing display of God's love and partnership with intercessors that He has given legal jurisdiction on earth to intercede on behalf of others.

God answers persistent prayers spoken by faith. You receive faith by continually hearing the Word of God (Rom. 10:17). As you abide in God's Word and He abides in you, ask for what you want and God will do it (John 15:7). The effective, fervent prayer of the righteous man avails much power, dynamic in its working (James 5:16).

In the Garden of Gethsemane, Jesus persisted in travailing, even sweating blood. He asked the Father for strength to endure the painful, humiliating death of the cross to pay the penalty for the forgiveness of mankind's sins (Matt. 26:36-45).

While all persistent prayer doesn't guarantee that you will get what you want, Father God will give you what's best for you. Here are other examples of persistent prayer that generated results:

- Jacob persisted in wrestling with the Angel of the Lord, until God blessed him (Gen. 32:24-32).
- Moses persisted in interceding for Israel, causing God to repent of wiping an entire nation off the planet due to their constant murmuring and disobedience (Ex. 32:31-32; Deut. 9:25-29).
- Hannah travailed in prayer with supplications for a son, who would later become the Prophet Samuel, creating a landing strip for God to send Jesus to be born into the earth as our Lord and Savior (1 Sam. 1:10-11).
- Elijah persisted in prayer, ending a 3 1/2-year drought in Israel (James 5:17-18; 1 Kings 18:36-44).

- The Psalmist persisted in crying out to God (Psalm 88:1-18, 119:147-149, 130:1-6).

- Daniel persisted in fasting and prayer for the fulfillment of God's prophecies about Israel and received great revelations, also about the end times (Daniel chapters 10-12).

When the answer to your prayer doesn't show up immediately, keep praying. We have an enemy that will try to intercept our prayers so they can't pierce the heavenly realm, thereby hindering answers on earth. Therefore, you must be as determined as a bulldog biting a bone to pray until the answer comes. It's only a matter of time, as long as you have prayed in agreement with God's Word (1 John 5:14-15).

Why do you have to persist in prayer? When interceding for others, many times you will have to persist because God must deal with the will of all those concerned. You also must persist in prayer due to demonic interference in the second heaven that will try to stop the answer from manifesting on earth (Read Daniel Chapter 10).

However, when praying for yourself, your answer can show up sooner because only your faith is involved. Continue to water your prayer with thanksgiving, praise and worship and it will surely come to pass. After I have prayed for something—for example, a new job—I say, "Lord, thank you for blessing me with my job." Then I go and look for it with expectation because faith without corresponding action is dead. Your inaction can cancel the answer to your prayer. So *take action*.

If your faith weakens, repent if you must and pray again. To strengthen your faith, fellowship and commune with God. Meditate, confess, study and read the Scriptures,—specifically in the area where you need an answer—until the Word becomes real inside of you. You must become pregnant with the seed of the Word through meditation until the image you see in your mind (of what you want) agrees with the seed of God's Word you have planted in your heart. Then your baby will show up.

The Word of God is like bags filled with a variety of seed. When you mediate, confess, pray or decree the Word of God, you're planting it in the good soil of your heart, where it will grow as long as you water it with thanksgiving, praise and worship. There is seed to cover every need: salvation, family, marriage, children, business, finances, healing and deliverance, relationships, promotion, business, ministry and everything that pertains to life and godliness (2 Pet. 1:3).

Persistence fuels prayer and intercession. Adding persistence to your faith and patience, whether you are praying for yourself or for others, will always release answers to prayer aligned with God's purposes. Luke 11:9-10 says:

So I say to you, ask, and it will be given to you; seek, and you will find; knock, and it will be opened to you. For everyone who asks receives, and he who seeks finds, and to him who knocks it will be opened.

Believe, say, pray, decree and intercede until you receive your answer. The Bible makes it plain that if you don't quit, in due season you will reap the reward.

And let us not grow weary while doing good, for in due season we shall reap if we do not lose heart (Gal. 6:9).

Therefore do not throw away your confidence, which has a great reward. For you have need of endurance, so that when you have done the will of God you may receive what is promised (Heb. 10:35-36).

Once you have prayed the will of God by faith, stand there for it. Make the force of endurance—another word for persistence—work for you. Dig in your heels of faith and don't be moved by circumstances, for you walk by faith and not by sight, Faith is being fully persuaded that what God has said, He is able to perform (Rom. 4:21).

God hears the prayers of the righteous. His arm is not too short that He cannot reach into your situation or those for whom you intercede. Nor is his ear deaf that He cannot hear when you pray. God persisted in pursuing a relationship with mankind after Adam and Eve sinned in the Garden of Eden when they ate from the forbidden Tree of the Knowledge of Good and Evil.

He initiated a persistent strategy of redemption to restore us as sons and daughters of God as it was in the beginning in the Garden of Eden, by willingly sacrificing Jesus, his only Begotten Son, on the cross to pay the penalty for our sins. God didn't give up on you, so don't give up on Him. No matter how bad it feels or how bad it looks, keep looking unto Jesus, the author and finisher of your faith. Pray until something happens. *PUSH!*

Here are some Scriptures to meditate about persistent prayer: 1 Chron. 16:11; Psalm 40:1, 88:1, 116:2; Luke 11:5-10, 18:1-8; Acts 1:14, 2:42; Rom. 12:12; Eph. 6:18; 1 Thess. 5:17.

SECTION III
PRAYER KEYS

CHAPTER 13

EFFECTIVE SPIRITUAL WARFARE

For we wrestle not against flesh and blood, but against principalities, against powers, against the rulers of the darkness of this world, against spiritual wickedness in high places. —Ephesians 6:12

A well-stocked arsenal is useless if you do not know how to use the weaponry. Our Father through Christ Jesus has provided a spiritual arsenal that guarantees the believer victory in the cosmic war against satan and his cohorts. While what I am about to share is not an exhaustive study on spiritual warfare, I hope to quicken your awareness that spiritual warfare is not optional for the believer. It is a way of life. It is a conflict that rages between the kingdom of God and the kingdom of satan until Jesus Christ returns for the second time. The good news is that the fight is fixed because we have already WON in Christ Jesus.

This is not a battle with equal opponents. God created the devil and the fallen angels, and Jesus has already disarmed the enemy through his death on the cross and His resurrection. When you understand this truth, you will confidently walk in your God-given authority in Christ Jesus. The Greek word for this type of authority is called "exousia". It is the intangible, delegated, positional, legal authority that Jesus has given to the believer, in His name, to subdue the enemy. "You are in it to win it" in Christ Jesus.

202 | PRAY NOW

The devil may have a lease on earth and world systems, but not over God's people. His lease will expire soon when Jesus returns for the second time to gather His elect. In the meantime, we must enforce our God-given authority over satan and demolish demonic strongholds. We must pray and give to save souls and occupy our spheres of influence to advance the kingdom of God.

C. Peter Wagner wrote in *Confronting the Powers*, "His (satan's) kingdom consists in the control he possesses over people who inhabit the earth, and he maintains that control by securing their allegiance through various means known as 'the wiles of the devil'" (Ephesians 6:11). Likewise, the Kingdom of God that Jesus brought is not a land that has territorial boundaries, but rather the reign of Jesus Christ over human beings. Wherever people declare their allegiance to Jesus Christ, the Kingdom of God is in their midst."[7]

So how did this spiritual conflict originate? Satan, who was originally called Lucifer in heaven, was a mighty archangel primarily responsible for praise and worship (Ezekiel 28:12-14). However, iniquity was found in his heart when he became filled with pride and rebellion, rising up with one-third of the angels in an attempt to overthrow Almighty God Himself (Isaiah 14:12-15). As a result, God cast out satan and his cohorts from heaven into a pre-Adamic earth. Then God created mankind to praise and worship Him—further infuriating satan (Isa. 43:7, 21; Rev. 4:11).

In retaliation, satan hatched a plot to get Adam and Eve to disobey God by eating fruit from the forbidden Tree of the Knowledge of Good and Evil. The consequence of Adam's sin caused mankind to fall from righteousness into sin, spiritually separating us from a holy God.

But God's great love for mankind compelled Him to put a redemptive plan into action, which was to send Jesus, His only Begotten Son, to shed His sinless blood on the cross to pay the penalty for our sins. Jesus' horrific punishment and death on the cross was the only payment that God could accept to restore mankind back into the family of God (Heb. 9:22).

Thanks be unto God for Jesus, who is also called the last Adam. As our Lord and Savior Jesus Christ, He willingly died on the cross, shedding His precious blood to forgive our sins forever. Not only did Jesus' redemptive death on the cross cause God to forgive our sins and take away our guilt, but Jesus' burial, resurrection and ascension also broke the power of sin in the life of every believer. You have power in Christ Jesus to resist temptation.

However, you still have an adversary on earth called satan that is furious with God for eternally banishing him. The devil is jealous because God created mankind in his likeness and image to give Him praise and worship, replacing Him. This was once the devil's privilege and responsibility. He was known as Lucifer, the archangel that stood before the throne of God to lavish Him with praise and worship (Ezek. 28:14-15). This was the case until iniquity and pride was found in Lucifer's heart, causing Him to try to overthrow Almighty God, His Creator and the Creator of heaven and earth and everything therein. For this reason, God will never forgive the devil. He has already been eternally sentenced to hell. He has a limited time on earth to wreak havoc. This is why the believer will encounter attacks from the enemy, but be of good cheer, Jesus has already placed him beneath your feet (Eph. 1:22; Col. 2:15).

Every believer must understand that he or she is a king with the authority to keep the enemy beneath his or her feet, and a priest with the privilege and honor of praising and worshiping God (Rom. 16:20; 1 Pet. 2:5, 9; Rev. 5:10, 20:6), releasing His power on earth. While we should not blame the devil for every conflict, we should not be ignorant of his devices. Instead, we should focus on the victory Jesus has already obtained for us, in His name. Whether it is subduing your flesh (old man, carnality), the world or the devil, you have the victory in Christ Jesus (1 Cor. 15:57; 2 Cor. 2:14).

Unlike the devil, Jesus Christ's precious blood has purchased for us the gift of repentance! If you confess and repent for your sins, Jesus is faithful to forgive your sins and to cleanse you from all unrighteousness (1 John 1:9). If you want to get it right with God right now, pray this simple prayer of repentance. Or if you are already right with God, continue reading.

PRAYER OF REPENTANCE

Father, thank you for the gift of repentance. I confess that I have sinned against you. Please forgive me. I'm coming back home. I rededicate my life to you right now. Help me to be who you created me to be. Help me to obey you, Father. Thank you for washing away my sins by the precious blood of Jesus. Thank you for the forgiveness of my sins. In Jesus' name, amen.

PRAYER OF SALVATION

If you have never confessed Jesus as Lord and Master of your life, you can right now by praying this simple prayer of salvation. It will change your life forever! Or, if you are already a born-again believer, continue reading.

Let's pray:

Father, I believe in my heart that Jesus died for my sins and that you raised Him from the dead. Jesus, I ask you to come into my heart right now. Save me. I confess that you are my Lord and Savior. Thank you for saving my soul.

If you just confessed Jesus as Lord of your life, welcome into the family of God! If you prayed the prayer of repentance to rededicate your life to Him, welcome back home. Worship and pray to God daily. Read your Bible daily. Find a good Bible-believing church where you can fellowship with other believers. And meditate and study the Word of God daily to renew your mind and walk in victory.

Now let's continue on the topic of spiritual warfare. In the fullness of time, God will sentence satan and one-third of the fallen angels, representing principalities, powers, rulers of the darkness of this world and spiritual wickedness in high places (Eph. 6:10-18) to eternal hell.

In the meantime as previously mentioned, satan will attack the believer, using the tactics of deception (lies), accusations and temptations to get you to sin against God. He wants to take as many souls to hell with Him as he can. God never created hell for mankind, but for the devil and the fallen angels.

As believers, we must continually pray to save the lost, to restore the backslidden and to protect and strengthen leaders and the saints of God to advance God's kingdom. There is a heaven to gain and a hell to shun. We are in a cosmic spiritual war to enforce Jesus' defeat over satan and demonic power. This warfare will not cease until Jesus Christ's second coming. But be of good cheer, we have already won!

Regarding warfare, Sun Tzu, a famous Chinese general and military strategist said, "All warfare is based on deception". This is also true of spiritual warfare, where one of the enemy's main tactics is deception. Satan tempts the believer to doubt the Word of God by planting lies into his or her mind to trigger doubt, unbelief, worry, anxiety, confusion, unhealthy anger, perversion and ultimately rebellion that leads to disobedience.

The battle against the devil takes place in your unrenewed mind. This is why it is critical that you commune with God with prayer and fasting, and thanksgiving, praise and worship. You must meditate, study, memorize and meditate Scriptures to cast down the lies of the enemy and to reprogram your "stinking thinking". You should also fellowship with other believers, share your testimony and sit under sound prophetic teaching. These spiritual disciplines will nourish your spirit man, so that you are strong in the Lord and in the power of His might.

Ephesians 6:12-18 and 2 Corinthians 10:3-6 are two foundational Scriptures you should understand about enforcing your authority in spiritual warfare. I say, "enforcing your authority," because Jesus has already disarmed or stripped the enemy's power when He died on the cross over 2,000 years ago. Colossians 2:15 says:

Having disarmed principalities and powers, He made a public spectacle of them, triumphing over them in it.

The devil is a spiritual outlaw that you must arrest (or serve notice) commanding him to cease and desist in his maneuvers against God's people and your life. According to the Merriam-Webster Dictionary, "disarm" means to take weapons from (someone or something); to give up weapons and to make harmless. Jesus through his death, burial, resurrection, and ascension has rendered the devil harmless against the believer, who understands the delegated, intangible, positional spiritual authority you have in Jesus' name over his ability.

God has also anointed you—if you have received the baptism of the Holy Spirit—with "dunamis" power. This is the tangible, miracle-working, explosive power or ability of God to be a witness of Jesus who casts out devils, saves souls, heals the sick, frees the oppressed and performs creative miracles (Mark 16:15-18).

Jesus Christ, our Lord and Savior, eternally sits at the right hand of the Father—a position of authority. Father God has given Him all authority in heaven and earth. He ever lives, making intercession for us. As His Body on earth, we must use our delegated authority to rule and reign as kingly priests. Kings take territory; they occupy and advance. Priests minister to God and to his people. Both release God's glory on earth, bringing change.

So if Jesus has already disarmed the devil, why must we continue to engage in spiritual warfare on earth? Good question. Even though God has given the believer authority over the devil to expand His kingdom on earth by saving souls, we have an enemy, satan, that is called the prince of this world and He will do his best to stop the body of Christ from saving lost souls until His lease runs out.

When Adam committed high treason against God in the Garden of Eden by eating from the Tree of the Knowledge of Good and Evil (Genesis 2:15-18, 3:11, 17-19), he transferred ownership of the world to the devil. He rules as the prince of this world and as the prince of the power of the air (2 Cor. 4:4). However, the enemy does not have authority or power over the believer (Luke 10:19).

When the devil's lease on earth runs out, God will eternally imprison him and his cohorts to hell. In the meantime, Jesus has authorized you to subdue the enemy, keeping him beneath your feet. The devil only has power over world systems, not over the believer walking in his or her dominion authority. The kingdom of God is a spiritual realm that flows out of your heart. It impacts the physical territory or atmosphere around you, bringing change that saves souls and sets the captives free. Your job as a kingdom citizen is to serve as God's military police or law enforcement agent on earth, enforcing Jesus' victory over satan and demonic power. You do this as you humble yourself unto God (obey His Word) and resist the enemy, causing him to flee.

LEVELS OF SPIRITUAL WARFARE

Many experts on spiritual warfare agree that there are three levels:

- Ground Level
- Occult Level
- Strategic Level

GROUND LEVEL

Ground level is the first level of spiritual warfare. It deals with interceding to cast out devils from people, saved and unsaved. Yes, believers can be influenced, demonized, harassed and tormented by demonic spirits, especially if they harbor negative emotions like unforgiveness. But a believer can never be possessed by a devil. Ground level spiritual warfare also deals with self-deliverance or casting demons out of yourself.

As a believer you should know how to cast out devils because Jesus has given you the authority to do so like Him (Matt. 10:1; Luke 10:17-20; Mark 16:17). If you desire to walk in greater spiritual authority and glorify God by setting people free from demonization, read, meditate, pray and study the gospels to see how Jesus and the early disciples dominated the enemy in this arena. Here are several verses that show Jesus casting out demons:

When evening had come, they brought to Him many who were demon-possessed. And He cast out the spirits with a word, and healed all who were sick (Matt. 8:16).

Then Jesus answered and said, "O faithless and perverse generation, how long shall I be with you? How long shall I bear with you? Bring him here to Me. And Jesus rebuked the demon, and it came out of him; and the child was cured from that very hour (Matt. 17:17-18).

And when the demon was cast out, the mute spoke. And the multitudes marveled, saying, "It was never seen like this in Israel!" (Matt. 9:33).

And He was preaching in their synagogues throughout all Galilee, and casting out demons (Mark 1:39).

When Jesus saw that the people came running together, He rebuked the unclean spirit, saying to it: "Deaf and dumb spirit, I command you, come out of him and enter him no more!" (Mark 9:25).

But Jesus rebuked him, saying, "Be quiet, and come out of him!" And when the demon had thrown him in their midst, it came out of him and did not hurt him (Luke 4:35).

And He was casting out a demon, and it was mute. So it was, when the demon had gone out, that the mute spoke; and the multitudes marveled (Luke 11:14).

Like Jesus, his disciples also exercised spiritual authority by casting out devils. You are qualified to do the same, because you are a joint heir with Christ and an heir of El Elyon, the Most High God of the universe, who has placed all powers beneath Jesus' feet and therefore yours, for you are hidden in Christ Jesus. Let's take a look at how Apostle Paul operated in authority and power to cast out devils and to heal the sick in Acts 19:11-12:

And God wrought special miracles by the hands of Paul: so that from his body were brought unto the sick handkerchiefs or aprons, and diseases departed from them, and evil spirits went out of them.

Apostle Paul was a soldier in the Army of the Lord as are all true believers. Like Jesus and Paul, every believer has been anointed by God to cast out evil spirits. You are not a mere human being. You are a supernatural, eternal spiritual being made in the image and likeness of God with a soul that lives in a body sent to earth to subdue the enemy.

Casting out demons should be the norm for every believer that understands that he or she is a king/queen on earth with the authority and power to veto the enemy's tactics (Luke 10:19). Jesus made this truth plain in Mark 16:17:

And these signs will follow those who believe: In my name they will cast out demons...

Many times the root of lingering sickness and disease can be traced to evil spirits attached to negative emotions, such as unforgiveness, fear, anxiety, sexual immorality, depression, jealousy, self-rejection, self-hatred, unworthiness, insecurity, unhealthy anger, and stubbornness. For you to receive healing, these evil spirits must be exposed and cast out, replaced by the infilling of Holy Spirit in all vacated places.

For example, if you harbor unforgiveness, tormenting or evil spirits have a legal right to oppress you. This is why you must be quick to forgive and resist offense because unforgiveness hurts you.

Read the parable in Matthew 18:23-35 about the "unforgiving servant". Note in verse 35 that Jesus used the word "tormenters". Another word for "tormenters" is demons. Again if you don't forgive others, demons have a legal right to vex you. You can prevent this by being quick to repent. It is impossible for offenses not to come into your life, so learn to possess your soul—resist the offense by walking in love and give the devil no place.

PERSONAL DELIVERANCE

When doing self- deliverance, fast and pray for discernment to determine whether it's your flesh that needs discipline or evil spirits that need to be cast out or both. Always begin with praise and worship, inviting Holy Spirit to show you how to pray. Ask Him to reveal areas of sin in your life or iniquity in your bloodline. Confess, repent and renounce any agreement with any evil spirits Holy Spirit reveals to you. Command all evil spirits to get out of your bloodline, in Jesus' name. If married, your spouse should also do this to cleanse his or her bloodline. Conclude by asking Holy Spirit to fill your bloodline and you with His spirit that is the opposite of what you cast out. For example, if you cast out fear, ask Holy Spirit to fill you with His love because love (God) casts out fear. Continue to praise and worship God for your breakthrough. You should examine your heart daily to make sure you are walking in purity, obedience and holiness before God.

DELIVERANCE MINISTRY FOR OTHERS

When delivering others, it is best to work with another mature believer or a team experienced in deliverance ministry. Fasting and prayer are required to sharpen spiritual discernment. Also, praying in tongues or your heavenly prayer language will increase your faith and strengthen your spirit man to operate in the supernatural. Remember, discerning of spirits is also a spiritual gift that some possess to a greater degree than others (1 Cor. 12:7-11). However, all believers have been given authority in Jesus' name to cast out devils. After a demon has been cast out, ask Holy Spirit to fill every vacated place inside the person's heart with a fresh anointing that is the opposite of what was cast out.

I exhort you to rise up, mighty warrior of God, and walk in your authority as a deliverer. Use your spiritual authority in Jesus' name to set the captives free by the power of Holy Spirit. Fast and pray for increased spiritual discernment. Pray in tongues often to keep your spirit man strong. Meditate and study Scriptures that deal with casting out devils (deliverance) and operating in the supernatural, which is normal for believers. Sit under anointed deliverance teachers. Keep on the whole armor of God, so you stay ready to set the captives free!

OCCULT LEVEL

The occult is the second level of spiritual warfare. People involved in the occult seek power from demons. It is more than a few demons tormenting one person as with deliverance. The believer must confront an organized system of darkness that works through people. The system includes occult channels, such as witchcraft, Shamanism, New Age channeling, satanism, freemasonry, eastern religions, astrology, secular humanism, and perverted programming on TV, radio, and the Internet.

People who operate in the occult desire to be godlike, or to operate outside of the government of the Church as established by God, or to manipulate people, things or situations—which is witchcraft. Those involved in the occult have willingly signed up in the devil's army or the enemy has deceived them. Either way, the enemy's strategy is to draw them deeper into his control by satisfying their lust for power that will eventually destroy them. Apostle Paul, by the power of Holy Spirit confronted with the Word and prevailed against occult spirits, convicting and compelling those who practiced such darkness to repent and renounce their belief in the occult. God says you shall have no other gods before Him. Let's look at what Apostle Paul said in Acts 19:18-20:

> *And many that believed came, and confessed, and showed their deeds. Many of them also which used curious arts brought their books together, and burned them before all men: and counted the price of them, and found it fifty thousand pieces of silver. And mightily grew the word of God and prevailed.*

Demons that inhabit people must be cast out, and ruling spirits in a region must be subdued. Beware of the spirit of deception in these end-times. Flee from anything or anyone that leads you away from worshiping Almighty God and obeying His Word. There is one God—Jehovah the Great I Am that I Am (Ex. 20:3). The Holy Spirit leads and guides the believer into all truth—not spirit guides or mediums (John 16:13). Jesus is the way, the truth and the life (John 3:16, 14:6). He is the only Mediator between God and man. Only Jesus' blood can wash away your sins, not blood sacrifices or false gods; not burning incense or chanting empty mantras (1 Tim. 2:5-6). You can only come to the Father through faith in Jesus.

Many young people are drawn to the occult because they lust for spiritual power and significance. I believe another reason is that God created mankind in His likeness and image to have dominion. We are spirit beings with a natural desire to operate in dominion authority because it's in our spiritual DNA from our

Father God. Our heavenly Father created and gave us a kingdom mandate to have dominion.

For example, let's take the younger generation. Why do young people crave video and digital games? Are they seeking to fill the void inside them for spiritual power that only God can fulfill through a personal relationship with Jesus? Are they hungry to see legitimate spiritual power that the body of Christ (individual believers and local assemblies) should demonstrate in signs and wonders to set people free? Do they understand in the spirit realm that there is something more than settling for mediocrity, complacency and passivity in life?

Let me tell you what drew me into dabbling in the occult. As a little girl, I was drawn to the supernatural, even though I did not have the words to describe my longing. Nor did I know the Bible. This curiosity led me to dabble into the occult during my teen years. I explored everything from Ouija boards to astrology. I did not understand the danger of the profane. Nor did I understand the consequences of what I was doing as I opened myself up to demonic spirits. As a result, fear, confusion, unhealthy control and insecurity were constant companions well into my 20's.

When I came to the saving knowledge of Jesus Christ, I plunged into the Word that dealt with God's love, glory, healing, deliverance, gifts of the Spirit and the angelic realm. I spent hours with Holy Spirit as He led me through personal deliverance. I confessed and repented for sinning against God by putting other gods before Him. I renounced my involvement with the occult. I cast evil spirits out of myself as Holy Spirit revealed them. This didn't happen all at once. I asked Holy Spirit to fill me with His purity and love in all vacated places. And He did. God has delivered me from so much. He can deliver you, too.

Are you ready to be free from the occult? If yes, say the prayer below from your heart. Always ask Holy Spirit to lead you in prayer. He will tell you what to confess and repent of, what to renounce, what to bind and loose and what blessings to release. Deliverance is progressive. It's like peeling layers of an onion. You may have to continue your deliverance prayers for a period of time that will be well worth it. You also may need a seasoned deliverance minister to pray with you. Let's pray:

Father, in the name of Jesus, I come to you right now confessing that I have sinned against you by getting involved in the occult. I repent for my sins, and I stand in the gap for my forefathers and confess their sins too. I ask you to forgive us for sinning against you by putting other gods before you. Wash away our sins with your precious blood, Jesus. I renounce my involvement with the occult and the involvement of my foreparents and children. I break every generational curse and stronghold associated with the occult. I bind up and command every evil spirit to get out of my bloodline and to get out of me. Never return, in Jesus' name. We are loosed from your demonic control. I speak the peace of God, Shalom, nothing missing or broken, into my heart and into the hearts of my family members. Fill us with a fresh anointing of your love in every vacated area. Thank you Father for cleansing my bloodline by Jesus' stripes. I praise and thank you for setting us free, in Jesus' name and by the power of Holy Spirit. Amen.

STRATEGIC LEVEL

Strategic level intercession is the highest level of spiritual warfare. It involves intercession against high-ranking territorial spirits assigned by satan to coordinate activities of darkness in large regions to keep people's minds blinded to the glory of the gospel of Jesus Christ and the kingdom of God (2 Cor. 4:3-4).

In Acts 19:24-41, you will find an example of strategic-level spiritual warfare. There was a commotion in Ephesus because Apostle Paul, through anointed teaching, had confronted the goddess Diana. As a result, the disciples of the goddess Diana diminished, causing the remaining disciples to become infuriated with Apostle Paul.

Daniel chapter 10 is another example of strategic-level spiritual warfare. A certain principality was assigned over Babylon. Principalities are territorial spirits assigned to rule large regions. They are aware of what is happening in their assigned territories, and are stationed to fight against the expansion of God's kingdom.

Strategic-level intercession, including corporate prayer and human intervention, will dislodge satanic forces and evil human agents working with them. Winning at this level involves anointed apostolic, prophetic teams equipped with divine, strategic spiritual mapping technology. Effective prayer involves praying in the Spirit, and taking action in the natural, such as voting for godly leaders and judges, petitioning legislators and running for political office. Apostolic-prophetic prayer teams play key roles in launching effective strategic intercession for a region.

Strategic-level warfare is necessary to spread world evangelism. The lack of consistent, relentless, strategic-level intercession gives a clue as to how world religions like Islam, Hinduism or Buddhism have had such a tremendous impact on its followers. Strategic intercession includes historical research of an area through spiritual mapping, identificational repentance, breaking of unholy covenants and curses, and being ready to die to advance God's kingdom.

Principalities at this level influence and determine the customs, traditions and cultural behaviors of a people. They control marriages, births and deaths. They use mental strongholds to entrench beliefs into people's hearts that are passed into laws. In these parts of the world, missionaries and evangelists risk their lives to pull down these strongholds and need much prayer to succeed. Apostolic-prophetic prayer teams though can influence the mindsets of leaders to pass legislation that favorably impacts God's people.

KNOWING WHO YOU ARE IN CHRIST JESUS

Knowing who you are in Jesus Christ and your delegated authority as a commander of God is critical to successfully routing the enemy from your territory. Although the world is under the sway and power of satan—the believer, who is a new creation in Christ Jesus—is not. First John 5:19 says:

We know that we are of God, and that the whole world lies in the power of the evil one (NASB).

In addition, Apostle Paul in Ephesians 2:1-2 says:

And you He made alive, who were dead in trespasses and sins, in which you once walked according to the course of this world, according to the prince of the power of the air, the spirit who now works in the sons of disobedience.

The enemy has nothing on the believer hidden in Christ Jesus. We have been given spiritual weapons to keep him underfoot. Second Corinthians 10:3-6 is a key Scripture to meditate on how to win spiritual warfare in your mind. It says:

For though we walk in the flesh, we do not war according to the flesh. For the weapons of our warfare are not carnal but mighty in God for pulling down strongholds, casting down arguments and every high thing that exalts itself against the knowledge of God, bringing every thought into captivity to the obedience of Christ, and being ready to punish all disobedience when your obedience is fulfilled.

When you employ these spiritual weapons, you pull down or overthrow the strongholds, or negative thoughts, or fiery darts the enemy shoots at your mind. Your battle is never only against a person or people, but evil spirits operating *through* them.

Strongholds are places in your mind where you have allowed the enemy to lodge his lies and fearful thoughts, affecting your mind, will and emotions. By speaking the Word of God out of your mouth, you resist the fiery darts (lies, thoughts) of the enemy, replacing them with God's thoughts that are for your good.

You must lead every negative thought away captive. You cannot sit passively by and let the enemy's lies dominate your mind. You cannot make negative statements, such as "Oh, I'm so scared!", "I'm going to lose my job," "The economy is crashing!", "I'll never have anything!", "My children are always sick," or "I take one step forward and two steps back."

You must understand that you are in the world, but not of it. Continually speak forth God's promises out of your mouth, tearing down strongholds. Continually spend time in His presence, allowing Holy Spirit to transform your way of thinking, speaking, being and acting.

Possess your soul (mind, will and emotions) by setting a watch over your mouth and keeping the doors of your lips closed, if you don't have any godly thing to say. Remember, you're the prophet of your life. You can have, and do have, what you say— good or bad. Your voice is the most powerful voice in your life, so speak the Word only!

If you want to improve your life, stop meditating on fear and meditate on faith-filled Word night and day to renew your mind. Meditate until you convince yourself that what God has said in His Word about you is true. The more you meditate the Word of God, the more you will prosper and have good success, impacting your life and those around you for the kingdom's sake.

The second foundational Scripture dealing with spiritual warfare is Ephesians 6:12-18, which says:

For we do not wrestle against flesh and blood, but against principalities, against powers, against the rulers of the darkness of this age, against spiritual hosts of wickedness in the heavenly places. Therefore take up the whole armor of God, that you may be able to withstand in the evil day, and having done all, to stand. Stand therefore, having girded your waist with truth, having put on the breastplate of righteousness, and having shod your feet with the preparation of the gospel of peace; above all, taking the shield of faith with which you will be able to quench all the fiery darts of the wicked one. And take the helmet of salvation, and the sword of the Spirit, which is the word of God; praying always with all prayer and supplication in the Spirit, being watchful to this end with all perseverance and supplication for all the saints.

As previously mentioned, in spiritual warfare, you do not use physical weapons. You do not focus on the people coming against you as much as the spirits operating behind them. You will not succeed in spiritual warfare by depending on your talent, abilities, intelligence, money, social standing, associations or good looks. Your natural strength is no match against the enemy who is a fallen archangel. Hosea 10:13 says:

But you have planted wickedness, you have reaped evil, you have eaten the fruit of deception. Because you have depended on your own strength and on your many warriors (KJV).

The good news is that Jesus has given you spiritual weapons, such as the full armor of God, to enforce the victory that Jesus has already won over the devil (Col. 2:15; 1 John 3:8). Therefore, it is the responsibility of every believer that confesses Jesus as Lord—every five-fold gift of apostle, prophet, evangelist, pastor and teacher, and every parent or leader—to understand, teach and model how to effectively wield the armor of God to win spiritual warfare. We will take a look at the armor of God in the next chapter.

You receive training in spiritual warfare by fellowshipping and communing in prayer with God, by meditating and studying God's Word in the areas that the enemy is opposing you and by taking wise action. There are no substitutes for spending daily, quiet time with God and His Word to grow as a believer. There is a direct correlation between the time you spend in God's Word and the amount of spiritual authority you wield. Jesus said in Mark 4:24:

And He said to them, "Be careful what you are hearing. The measure [of thought and study] you give [to the truth you hear] will be the measure [of virtue and knowledge] that comes back to you—and more [besides] will be given to you who hear" (AMP).

It is in the secret place that you connect with Jehovah Gibbor, the Lord mighty in battle, to obtain wisdom, revelation, knowledge, strategies and strength to keep the enemy beneath your feet.

As you speak and decree God's Word, the ministering spirits hear and perform it. I call God our Commander in Chief; the ministering spirits are the Air Force; and intercessors led by Holy Spirit are God's Army. When we work together in Christ Jesus, we are an unstoppable, apostolic-prophetic Prayer Force that always triumphs by the knowledge of God.

Now thanks be to God, who always leads us in triumph in Christ, and through us diffuses the fragrance of His knowledge in every place (2 Cor. 2:14).

CHAPTER 14

WEAPONS OF WARFARE

For the weapons of our warfare are not carnal but mighty in God for pulling down strongholds.
—2 Cor. 10:4

The following is a list of spiritual weapons of mass destruction, that when used by faith, will always give you victory over the enemy and demonic power. Delegated authority means you understand that Jesus has authorized you in His name to subdue the devil in your spheres of influence to save and deliver souls through signs, miracles and wonders. Make sure Jesus is truly your Lord and Savior and that you operate within the boundaries of your spiritual authority. Then the power of God will protect you from demonic attacks as you do ministry.

Remember the seven sons of Sceva. They had no personal relationship with Jesus. Therefore when they tried to cast out an evil spirit from a man, the man jumped on them, beating them severely (Acts 19:11-16). You must have a sincere personal relationship with Jesus by faith to operate in His authority and power, continuing His present day ministry.

In and of ourselves, we have no power, but in Christ Jesus we can do all things (He's called us to do). Jesus only did what His heavenly Father revealed to Him (John 5:19, 30). You release the Word through prayer or decree, and Holy Spirit will release His supernatural power for you to do the work. Now let's take a look at the weapons of our warfare available to wage a good warfare.

FAITH IN GOD

You must have faith in God by taking Him at His Word. When you do, you please Him because it shows that you trust your heavenly Father to take care of you. In fact, without faith, it's impossible to please God (Heb. 11:6). Base your faith upon the law of God's Word, which works every time, if you believe. Faith is the currency of heaven that makes things happen on earth like money is the currency on earth to buy things. God will answer your prayers and move on your behalf when He hears faith mixed with your words, whether prayers, decrees or confessions.

Faith comes by continually hearing the Word of God, over and over and over again until you believe it inside you heart (Romans 10:17). If you want greater faith in a specific area, increase the time that you spend meditating, confessing, memorizing, studying and reading the Bible in that specific area. Add fasting with prayer at least once a week. It will dispel unbelief, doubt and fear, increasing your faith and giving you the victory. First John 5:4 says:

For whatsoever is born of God overcometh the world: and this is the victory that overcometh the world, even our faith (KJV).

The God-kind of faith is built upon the integrity of the nature of God. He alone is everything that you need—for all things consist in Him, by Him and for Him. He is your Source—El Shaddai, the many breasted One that nourishes and supplies. His promises are always yes and amen because He is not a man that lies or changes His mind. If He has said it, you can count on it! (Num. 23:19).

The shield of faith, which is one of the pieces of the armor of God, will enable you to extinguish or cast down from your mind every fiery dart or negative thought or image. In order to cast down negative thoughts or images, you must open up your mouth and decree what God says about you in the Bible, believing in your heart. You are the prophet of your life.

To grow in faith, meditate God's Word in the area where you desire breakthrough. Invest the time to meditate until the image of what you desire becomes so real that you can reach out and touch it. Then speak forth your desire and it will manifest in the natural realm in due season. In the meantime, continue to feed your faith by thanking and praising God for the answer and resisting doubt. If you are faithful to command the promise and you passionately believe it in your heart, it MUST come to pass because you are a Son of God with creative power in your mouth.

WORD OF GOD

You must learn to wield God's Word the same way Jesus did when He overcame the temptations of the enemy in the wilderness. Satan tempted Jesus with the lust of the flesh, lust of the eyes and the pride of life. Unlike the first Adam in the Garden of Eden, Jesus resisted him.

Jesus defeated the enemy by decreeing, "It is written", as He was inspired by Holy Spirit to speak forth specific, strategic Scriptures based on the Torah (Old Testament) (Matthew 4:1-11, Luke 4:1-15). Jesus spoke forth the "rhema" Word of God inspired by Holy Spirit. "Rhema" means "an utterance." It is where Holy Spirit provides guidance for current situations and daily choices. A "rhema" Word is built upon the foundation of knowing the written Word of God or logos. This is why we must study and meditate God's Word. The Holy Spirit can only pull out the Word of God that you have stored inside of you through meditation and study.

Jesus was the embodiment of the Word of God on earth. It was customary for Him, being a Jew, to meditate and study the Scriptures. He was disciplined in the pursuit of God's presence and His Word, which is an integral part of Jewish culture.

If Jesus had to spend quality time, fellowshipping with our Father and meditating His Word to resist satan's temptations, how much more must we, who are called His disciples.

Jesus tells us in John 14:15, 21, 23, that if we love Him, we will obey His commandments. He commands us to meditate the Scriptures day and night, so that we will be doers of the Word. As a result of divine meditation, the Bible says you will make your way prosperous and have good success (Joshua 1:8).

In 2 Timothy 2:15, Apostle Paul directs you to study to show yourself approved unto God, a workman that needs not to be ashamed, rightly dividing the word of truth. There are more than 7,000 promises found in the Bible. There is a seed for every need. However, the power of the Word of God will only work if you invest the time to work it by faith.

I hear some of you saying, "But I don't know how to study the Word. It's so hard to understand. I'll start tomorrow, I promise." But tomorrow comes and nothing changes. Do you really love God? If so, the Bible says you will obey Him (John 14:15–31, 15:10). Ask God for the grace to dig into His Word, so you can fulfill your godly destiny.

I completely understand because I said some of those same words. I do understand the battle that takes place between the spirit (new man) that wants to draw close to God, and flesh (old, carnal man) that does not. However, my life was so messed up and my soul so shattered that I was compelled to get into my

Bible and begin praying, meditating, memorizing and studying the Word, instead of getting drunk to numb my emotional pain.

In addition to my Bible, I bought good teachings on cassette, video, CDs, MP3s and DVDs. These were focused on the areas where I wanted to change. I sat under good teaching at church, workshops, seminars, and conferences. I watched Christian TV and listened to Christian radio to deposit the Word of God inside of me to renew my mind because I wanted to change. I became addicted to the living, life-transforming Word of God.

Hopefully, this will help somebody. As a believer when it comes to obeying God, don't be moved by how you feel, by your circumstances, or by what people say. Only be moved by your love for God and His Word. Daily crucify your flesh. Ignore your unsanctified feelings that pull you away from God. I asked God to give me the grace to meditate and study my Bible. And He did. He'll do the same for you. His grace is sufficient. Today I enjoy God's presence and the Bible more than anything else I do. In His presence is fullness of joy and at His right hand are pleasures evermore. Obey God!

If you really desire to immerse yourself in God's Word, a good passage of Scripture to meditate and build up your faith is Psalm 119. It is the longest chapter in the Bible, packed with mouth-watering passages that will increase your spiritual appetite for more of God's Word and His presence. Choose one or two verses for starters. Meditate them every morning and night before going to bed until your change comes.

In Ephesians 6:17, Apostle Paul mentions a very important piece of the armor of God called the sword of the Spirit. It is a "rhema" or spoken Word of God from Holy Spirit that gives guidance or wisdom for a specific situation. It is the only offensive weapon in the armor of God. The foundation of the sword of the Spirit is the logos or written Scriptures in the Bible. The logos is the law of God that reveals His character. It reveals His nature and heavenly government that He wants every believer to establish on earth.

But how can you establish God's kingdom on earth if you do not know His Word (laws, precepts, commandments)? You must discipline yourself to meditate, study and read your Bible so you operate with the mind of Christ. The devil cannot stop the son or daughter of God who knows how to wield the sword of the Spirit, because God's Word is eternal. Jesus said in Matthew 24:35:

Heaven and earth will pass away, but My words will by no means pass away.

Hebrews 4:12 says:

For the word of God is quick, and powerful, and sharper than any two-edged sword, piercing even to the dividing asunder of soul and spirit, and of the joints and marrow, and is a discerner of the thoughts and intents of the heart (KJV).

Every time you wield the sword of the Spirit by speaking it out of your mouth, the power contained in the spoken Word of God invades your circumstances and forces the enemy to flee. Believing in your heart and speaking out of your mouth the *It is written* Word of God vetoes demonic power. Does this mean you have to speak every Scripture verbatim? No, but it does mean you must have *faith* in your heart when you speak it, to hit the target.

Again, as a believer, you cannot neglect spending time with God or in His Word, if you desire to have dominion and live the abundant life that Jesus died on the cross to obtain for you. If you neglect or despise God's Word, you will lose your battle with satan. The opposite is also true, that if you respect and obey God's Word, you will win your battle against the enemy. He is an ancient demonic spirit that has extensively studied mankind. He knows our weak points. He even knows the Word of God. But the Word of God (Jesus) has already defeated him. Therefore, in a battle with satan, your dependence must be totally based on having faith in the inerrant, infallible, immutable, eternal Word of God.

In *Spiritual Warfare in a Believer's Life*, C. H. Spurgeon said, "Satan cannot endure the infallible truth, for it is death to the falsehood of which he is the father."[8] I cannot emphasize enough the importance of spending time worshiping God and meditating God's Word. What many believers fail to realize is that you cannot draw someone else's sword of the Spirit (*rhema*) from their scabbard. No, my brother. No, my sister. You must draw your *own* sword of the Spirit to fight the good fight of faith.

If you don't wear the sword of the Spirit (meditating and studying it) and practice using it (praying, decreeing, prophesying and confessing it)—when the time comes to fight, you will become a casualty of war. This is not God's best for you. You are the son or daughter of a King, And when you decree a thing, it is established. You must discipline your flesh to abide in God and let His Word abide in you.

John Piper in *Desiring God* says, "If the Word of God does not abide in us (John. 15:7), we will reach for it in vain when the enemy strikes. But if we do wear it, if it lives within us, what mighty warriors we can be!"[9] Rise up mighty warrior, and rule your world with the sword of the Spirit!

PRAYER

Prayer is an invitation to access the presence and power of God, spirit-to-spirit, and transport what you need or desire from heaven to earth. As you commune and communicate with God, becoming one with Him, your prayers hit the target. Prayer is the portal into supernatural intimacy with God. It is the key to effective spiritual warfare to legislate and adjudicate God's plans and purposes on earth and to veto the devil's. You shall decree a thing and it shall be established (Job 22:28).

When it comes to spiritual warfare, prayer delivers the following benefits:

- When you become weak in the battle, pray in the Spirit or your heavenly prayer language (tongues) and you will receive spiritual strength like a dead battery being recharged. You also build up your faith in God to outlast the devil (Jude 20). Further, when you pray with stammering lips (tongues), you enter into the rest of God, pleasing God because it shows that you trust Him to care for you (Isa. 28:11-12, 40:31; Acts. 10:46).

- When you don't know what to pray, let Holy Spirit come alongside to help you pray. By yielding your vocal chords to Him and praying in your heavenly prayer language, Holy Spirit prays perfect prayers through you that God will answer. The ministering spirits or angelic realm will respond by bringing the right answer (Zech. 12:10; Romans 8:26-28).

- God will download mysteries, revelations, strategies, tactics, wisdom, ideas, knowledge and solutions that will help you fulfill your assignments and overcome the enemy (1 Cor. 2:7, 14:6; Ephesians 1:17; James 1:5-8).

- God is all-knowing, all-powerful and ever-present. He is love, and He is your Source. He is everything you need. Therefore, when you pray, you will always receive His grace and divine intervention, whether interceding for others or praying for yourself (Jeremiah 33:3; Phil. 4:6-9).

Prayer is about relationship with the Father in the secret place of your heart. Our loving, caring, sharing heavenly Father desires to reveal His secrets to you (Daniel 2:22). He desires for you to draw near to Him so He can draw near to you and show you great and mighty things that you have not seen before.

Spending time with God in your secret place is the best investment you could ever make because everything you need is found in Him. He is light, life and love. He will strengthen and comfort you. He satisfies. He heals. He revives. He restores your joy. God makes your feet to stand like hind's feet in precarious places. He is your Rock (Psalm 91; Isaiah 40:31; Song of Songs 6:3).

FASTING

Fasting combined with prayer increases your spiritual strength, discernment and faith in God. Fasting strengthens your spirit man's ability to hear the voice of God. It is how you humble your soul and body, making it submit to the leading of Holy Spirit living in your spirit man. According to Isaiah 58:6-9, the God-kind of fasting looses the bands of wickedness, heavy burdens, oppression, yokes, poverty and sickness and disease.

Fasting and prayer drive out unbelief, increasing your faith to cast out stubborn devils like Jesus did when He had to cast out the epileptic spirit from the little boy because His disciples were unable due to their unbelief (Matthew 17:17-21; Mark 9:28-29). Let's take a look at this passage of Scripture in Matthew 17:17-21:

Then Jesus answered and said, "O faithless and perverse generation, how long shall I be with you? How long shall I bear with you? Bring him here to Me." And Jesus rebuked the demon, and it came out of him; and the child was cured from that very hour. Then the disciples came to Jesus privately and said, "Why could we not cast it out?" So Jesus said to them, "Because of your unbelief; for assuredly, I say to you, if you have faith as a mustard seed, you will say to this mountain, 'Move from here to there,' and it will move; and nothing will be impossible for you. However, this kind does not go out except by prayer and fasting."

Fasting is necessary to displace unbelief with faith, and to mature in spiritual discernment. Do you want greater belief in God? Do you want to cast out devils to set people free as Jesus commanded in Mark 16:17? Then embrace prayer and fasting as a part of your lifestyle.

BINDING AND LOOSING

Jesus said, "I will give you the keys of the kingdom of heaven; whatever you bind on earth will be bound in heaven, and whatever you loose on earth will be loosed in heaven" (Matthew 16:19, 12:29, 18:18).

Binding and loosing is a key that signifies authority to grant or deny entry. Jesus has given us authority on earth to prohibit or declare unlawful what has already been prohibited in heaven. He has given us authority to loose or declare lawful on earth what is already loosed in heaven. When you bind and loose, you are advancing God's kingdom.

Eddie Smith in *Making Sense of Spiritual Warfare* says, "Some have mistakenly seen binding and loosing as simply a matter of power. Know this—you will never have the power to bind and loose unless and until you have the authority to do so. If you have the authority, the kingdom of darkness will know it."[10]

The reverse is true as well.

Cindy Trimm in *Rules of Engagement* says, "The question I'm most frequently asked is, What do I bind, and what do I loose? Simply put, you bind the activities of satan and his cohorts; you loose any effect that their presence has had and then you release the kingdom (God's divine rule) counterpart. The devil has no choice in the matter, but to relinquish his position."[11]

Binding means to "tie up". You can bind a demonic spirit, much like tying something up with rope or chains. But you cannot bind a person.

BINDING

To "bind on earth" means Jesus has given you authority to tie up the enemy. When you bind something on earth, it must first be bound in heaven. What does it mean to be bound in heaven? The word "heaven" in the Greek also means "air". Spirits dwell in the second heaven or "air" above the blue sky.

The Bible says that God has raised us up together and made us sit together in heavenly places in Christ Jesus (Eph. 2:6). This is not only a location, but a position of spiritual authority that puts the demonic realm beneath your feet because you are in Christ Jesus (Eph. 1:22-23).

As a believer, you have dual citizenship. You are both a spirit seated in heavenly places in Christ Jesus, and a spirit with a soul that lives in a body on earth with legal authority over the enemy in Jesus' name. Your dual citizenship gives you legal authority on earth to bind demons and to loose people from their grip.

In addition, binding and loosing is a powerful witnessing tool. What stops a person from accepting Jesus into their heart? The god of this world, satan, has blinded their minds from the light of the gospel (2 Corinthians 4:4).

In Mark 3:27, Jesus told us to bind the strong man, and then you can plunder his house. If you are praying for someone's salvation, bind the evil spirits preventing him or her from receiving salvation. Command the scales to be removed or loosened from their eyes, so they can confess Jesus as Lord and Master.

You cannot bind a person's will or force them to accept the gospel, but you can bind demons from tormenting and controlling them. Then you can speak directly to the person without demonic interference. Whenever you bind, you must loose.

LOOSING

Loosing occurs on earth based on what is already loosed in heaven, just like binding. Loosing refers to freeing a person from the effects of bondage. You bind demons, and you loose people from the effects of bondage. Then you release the spirit and blessings of God into their lives.

Binding and loosing work together. You can't have one without the other, according to Matthew 18:18. The Holy Spirit will help you to discern what to bind and loose. Knowing God's Word will aid you. Although there are no cookie-cutter patterns of prayer for binding and loosing, here is a prayer using this key—setting someone free from the spirit of fear.

PRAYER OF BINDING AND LOOSING

In the name of Jesus and by the power of Holy Spirit, I take authority over the spirit of fear and I bind it from operating in (name of person)'s life. (Name of person) is now loosed from fear and its effects. I command the spirit of fear to get out of (name of person) now, in Jesus' name. I release peace and the love of God into (name of person)'s life. I seal this prayer in the name of

Jesus and by the blood of the Lamb. Thank you, Father
for setting (name of person) free, in Jesus' name. Amen.

BLOOD OF JESUS

There is power in the blood of Jesus to save, protect, heal
and deliver. You can see a picture of the protection of the blood
of Jesus in Exodus chapter 12. God commanded the Israelites to
apply the blood of an unblemished lamb on their doorposts. This
blood protected the firstborn children of Israel from being killed
by the angel of death that God sent to destroy Egypt's firstborn.
This evil spirit was sent as judgment because Pharaoh refused to
let God's people go.

When you take communion and drink the wine or grape
juice, which represents the precious blood of Jesus, by faith you
can expect to experience the same saving, protecting, delivering
power of Jesus' blood in your life. There is supernatural power in
the blood of Jesus.

When Jesus shed His sinless blood on Calvary's cross, He
conquered sin, death, hell and the grave to give you overcoming
power to resist sin and to live victoriously (1 Cor. 15:57).

Acknowledging Jesus' substitionary death on the cross to
shed His blood for the forgiveness of mankind's sin is critical to
understand, because only His sinless blood, not the blood of
bulls and goats, gives every believer the right to access the
Father's throne and make your request known (Heb. 4:15-16,
10:19-20). Jesus' choice to shed His blood for us because of His
great love has obtained the following blessings:

- It has completely removed our sin and guilt (John 1:29;
  Isaiah 53:6; Hebrews 9:26).

- It removed God's wrath that we justly deserved, replacing
  it with His favor (Romans 3:25-26; Hebrews 2:17;
  1 John 4:10).

- It has removed our alienation and reconciled us back to God. This alienation was due to sin that once separated us from God (Romans 5:10-11; Col. 1:21-22).

- It has defeated the power of satan to torment us with the threat of unforgiven sin (Col. 2:13-14; 2 Cor. 5:21).

- It redeemed us from captivity of the curse of the Law (Deut. 28; Gal. 3:13-14), the guilt of sin (Psalm 103:12; Rom. 3:24; Heb. 10:22), and the power of sin (1 Pet. 1:18-19). This means that you are no longer a slave to sin. You are free to live a holy life (1 Cor. 6:20; 1 Pet. 1:15-16).

Jesus died in your place and mine. We deserved to die, but He took our sin upon Himself, and paid the penalty for us all (Rom. 5:8; Gal. 2:20; Isa. 53; 1 Pet. 3:18, 2:24). Jesus' blood destroyed the work of the devil, giving us overcoming power to resist sin and to live victoriously.

The following is a list of blood-bought benefits from Elizabeth Alves' book, *Becoming A Prayer Warrior*.[12] Jesus' blood:

1. Gives salvation. Births us into His kingdom, and keeps us from eternal damnation (Mark 16:16; John 3: 3,17).

2. Makes atonement for us, blotting out sins (Lev. 17:11; Rom. 5:11).

3. Redeems us. Our life is paid for in full, bought back from the power of sin and earth (Psalm 107:2; Eph. 1:7; Heb. 9:12; Rev. 5:9).

4. Justifies us. Acquits us of sin and guilt (Acts 13:38-39; Rom. 5:9).

5. Makes us righteous. Puts us back into right standing with God (Isa. 59:2; Rom 3:22; 23, 25; 1 John 1:9).

6. Gives sanctification. Sets us apart unto God at the time of salvation, as well as each day thereafter through Jesus' blood (1 Cor. 10:30; Heb. 10:10, 14).

7. Allows remission of sins. Sin was canceled (Rom. 3:24-25; Heb. 9:22).

8. Reconciles us. Accepting God's provision, we can now fellowship with Him in love (Rom. 5:10; Col. 1:20).

9. Gives overcoming power as we receive and use what has been delegated to us (Luke 10:19; Rev. 12:11).

10. Provides deliverance. Releases us from powers of darkness, and sets us free (2 Cor. 2:14; Col. 1:13).

11. Releases forgiveness. Pardons sins (Col. 1:14; 1 John 1:9).

12. Establishes a new covenant. Replaces old covenant of sacrifices with the perfect sacrifice, made through Jesus Christ (Heb. 7:22, 8:13, 9:15, 10:9, 12:24).

13. Cleanses us from all sin (1 John 1:7; Phil. 3:13-14).

When you pray, you can apply the blood. There's power in the blood of Jesus, and when properly understood and applied, you will understand that the devil cannot cross the bloodline of Jesus.

And they overcame him by the blood of the Lamb and by the word of their testimony, and they did not love their lives to the death (Rev. 12:11, 7:14).

NAME OF JESUS

The name of Jesus is our strong tower, which the devil cannot penetrate (Prov. 18:10). I have learned that one of the fastest ways to experience relief from a sudden spiritual attack is to call on the name of Jesus, which causes the enemy to flee.

You approach the throne of our heavenly Father by having a relationship with Jesus as your Lord and Savior. Jesus said in

John 14:6, "I am the way, and the truth, and the life. No one comes to the Father except through me." Jesus never sinned, making Him the Perfect Door to access the throne of a holy God. Acts 4:12 says:

> And there is salvation in no one else, for there is no other name under heaven given among men by which we must be saved.

He who knew no sin became sin for us, sacrificing His very life to pay the penalty to forgive our sins. As a result of humbling Himself to die on the cross to save us, Father God has highly exalted Jesus by giving Him the name that is above all names. Philippians 2:9-11 says:

> Therefore God also has highly exalted Him and given Him the name, which is above every name, that at the name of Jesus every knee should bow, of those in heaven, and of those on earth, and of those under the earth, and that every tongue should confess that Jesus Christ is Lord, to the glory of God the Father.

There is power in the name of Jesus. Everything must bow at Jesus' name. Demons flee when they hear the name of Jesus. Remember the 70 disciples came back rejoicing in Luke 10:17 saying that even the demons were subject to them *in Jesus' name.* When you pray in Jesus' name, His power is released to work on your behalf, causing the enemy to flee. You must have a genuine personal relationship with Jesus to operate your authority in His name. To develop this kind of relationship, you must intimately fellowship and commune with God. He is ever-present in your heart because of Jesus.

And whatever you ask in My name, that I will do, that the Father may be glorified in the Son. If you ask anything in My name, I will do it (John 14:13-14).

You did not choose Me, but I chose you and appointed you that you should go and bear fruit, and that your fruit should remain, that whatever you ask the Father in My name He may give you (John 15:16).

And in that day you will ask Me nothing. Most assuredly, I say to you, whatever you ask the Father in My name He will give you. Until now you have asked nothing in My name. Ask, and you will receive, that your joy may be full. In that day you will ask in My name, and I do not say to you that I shall pray the Father for you (John 16:23-24, 26).

In the verses above, Jesus told His disciples to pray to the Father, in His name. What is so important about Jesus' name?

1. His name encompasses all that He is, including His character, attributes, nature and authority.

2. God has placed Jesus' name above every name in heaven, on earth and beneath the earth. At the mention of Jesus' name, every knee must bow and every tongue must confess that Jesus is Lord. If you are in Christ Jesus, you can boldly approach God's throne of grace and mercy and obtain what you desire. God sees you in right standing—or as authorized by Jesus' name as a joint heir—because you are covered by the blood of Jesus. In spiritual warfare, you don't win in your name, but in the name of Jesus, the Son of God, God Incarnate.

For example, David fought Goliath "in the name of the Lord of hosts, the God of the armies of Israel" and prevailed because David called on the name of the Most High God, who released His supernatural power to help David rout the enemy (1 Sam. 17:45-52).

3. When you pray in Jesus' name, you represent Jesus before the Father. It's like Jesus has sent you to the Father's throne to pray His prayers because you're in union with Him. Jesus has given you "power of attorney" in His name. His blood is the seal of authority that gives you access to the Father's throne. You are not approaching Father's throne based upon your righteousness that is like filthy rags. You have access to the Father because you are now the righteousness of God in Christ Jesus (2 Cor. 5:21).

You are a child of God and a joint heir with Christ Jesus granted the full rights and privileges to approach your Father's throne to receive by faith. Abba Father loves you just as much as He loves His only Begotten Son Jesus. In truth, God's love sent Jesus to die on the cross for our sins. Never doubt the Father's love for you because God is love. He accepted and validated you as His own in Christ Jesus before the foundation of the world. When you pray in Jesus' name as He has commanded you, expect signs to follow you just like they followed Jesus when He lived on earth. In Mark 16:15-18, Jesus said to His disciples:

Go into all the world and preach the gospel to every creature. He who believes and is baptized will be saved; but he who does not believe will be condemned. And these signs will follow those who believe: In My name they will cast out demons; they will speak with new tongues; they will take up serpents; and if they drink anything deadly, it will by no means hurt them; they will lay hands on the sick, and they will recover.

When you pray in Jesus' name, you have your Father's undivided love and attention. He will respond by releasing His power to save, deliver and restore His people.

PRAISE

Praise is a formidable weapon to magnify the Lord, to obtain victory in spiritual warfare and to encourage yourself in the Lord. Why praise?

- It blesses and magnifies our God (Psalms 34:1-3, 103, 149, 150).

- It's the protocol for approaching the throne of God to make your request known (Psalm 100:4; 2 Chron. 31:2).

- It defeats the devil (Psalm 8:2; 2 Chron. 20:21-30; Psalm 149; Acts 16:25-26).

- It releases joy, which is your strength (Isa. 61:1-3; Neh. 8:10).

- It is the highest form of faith because you're thanking and praising God in advance, before you have received your answer in the natural realm. Don't wait until you feel like praising God. Do it by faith. Your emotions will follow and align with your spirit man (Psalm 42:5-11).

Use the weapon of praise to lay the foundation for your victory. You will naturally flow into worshiping God when you render unto Him all the praise due unto His name. When you praise God in the midst of pain, this is called a "yet praise". It is the type of praise that the Psalmist David gave unto God during one of his darkest moments. King David says in Psalm 42:5:

Why are you cast down, O my soul? And why are you disquieted within me? Hope in God; For I shall yet praise Him, the help of my countenance and my God.

Another striking demonstration of "yet praise" can be found in Acts 16:25. Paul and Silas had been unjustly accused, beaten and thrown into prison. But at midnight, in pain and chained, they began to pray and sing unto God. The result was a miraculous breakthrough.

But at midnight Paul and Silas were praying and singing hymns to God, and the prisoners were listening to them. Suddenly there was a great earthquake, so that the foundations of the prison were shaken; and immediately all the doors were opened and everyone's chains were loosed.

A key to note is that singing is a part of your prayer language. God likes you to sing to Him, so whether you think you can sing or not, make a joyful noise unto the Lord and watch Him show up and rout the enemy.

Another example of the power of praise is 2 Chronicles 20:20-26. In this passage, we find King Jehoshaphat of Israel in a lot of hot water. He had not one, but three enemies preparing to attack Israel. Even though King Jehoshaphat was initially afraid, he put his emotions in check and called a fast for the entire nation, including the animals.

God responded by downloading a war strategy to Prophet Jahaziel. God gave them an unusual battle plan. He told King Jehoshaphat to let the singers and those who praise (dancers) lead the army with music, singing and dancing. (The word "praise" in verse 21 is the root word "halal" which means, "to shine, rave, boast, make a fool of, to act like a madman, be worthy of praise.") Praise is animated, free, joyful and demonstrative—not stiff, formal, confined, contracted or restrictive. Let's look at the strategy God gave to King Jehoshaphat:

And when he (King Jehoshaphat) had consulted with the people, he appointed those who should sing to the Lord, and who should praise in the beauty of holiness, as they went out before the army and were saying:

"Praise the Lord, For His mercy endures forever."

Now when they began to sing and to praise, the Lord set ambushes against the people of Ammon, Moab, and Mount Seir, who had come against Judah; and they were defeated. For the people of Ammon and Moab stood up against the inhabitants of Mount Seir to utterly kill and destroy them. And when they had made an end of the inhabitants of Seir, they helped to destroy one another.

So when Judah came to a place overlooking the wilderness, they looked toward the multitude; and there were their dead bodies, fallen on the earth. No one had escaped.

When Jehoshaphat and his people came to take away their spoil, they found among them an abundance of valuables on the dead bodies, and precious jewelry, which they stripped off for themselves, more than they could carry away; and they were three days gathering the spoil because there was so much. And on the fourth day they assembled in the Valley of Berachah, for there they blessed the Lord; therefore the name of that place was called The Valley of Berachah until this day. Then they returned, every man of Judah and Jerusalem, with Jehoshaphat in front of them, to go back to Jerusalem with joy, for the Lord had made them rejoice over their enemies. So they came to Jerusalem, with stringed instruments and harps and trumpets, to the house of the Lord (2 Chronicles 20:20-26).

Like singing, dancing can be a part of your prayer and praise language. A good way to increase your faith in the power of praise is to read, meditate and study all the Scriptures about praise. The book of Psalms is a great place to start. Then minister praise unto God in your secret place and watch how your heavenly Father will inhabit your praises by releasing heaven on earth.

Scriptures for meditation: Psalm chapters 8, 9, 29, 33, 34, 47, 65, 66, 68, 89, 92, 95–100, 104–107, 111, 113, 117–118, 134–136, 138 and 145–150.

WAYS TO PRAISE

Singing:

Psalm 95:1—Oh come, let us sing to the Lord! Let us shout joyfully to the Rock of our salvation.

Psalm 96:1-2—Oh, sing to the Lord a new song! Sing to the Lord, all the earth. Sing to the Lord, bless His name; Proclaim the good news of His salvation from day to day.

Psalm 104:33—I will sing to the Lord as long as I live; I will sing praise to my God while I have my being.

Shouting:

Psalm 47:1—Oh, clap your hands, all you peoples! Shout to God with the voice of triumph!

Psalm 95:1-2—Oh come, let us sing to the Lord! Let us shout joyfully to the Rock of our salvation. Let us come before His presence with thanksgiving; Let us shout joyfully to Him with psalms.

Psalm 98:4—Shout joyfully to the Lord, all the earth; Break forth in song, rejoice, and sing praises.

Dancing:

Psalm 30:11—You have turned for me my mourning into dancing; You have put off my sackcloth and clothed me with gladness,

Psalm 149:3—Let them praise His name with the dance; Let them sing praises to Him with the timbrel and harp.

Psalm 150:4—Praise Him with the timbrel and dance; Praise Him with stringed instruments and flutes!

2 Samuel 6:14—Then David danced before the Lord with all his might; and David was wearing a linen ephod.

Lifting Hands:

Psalm 63:4—Thus I will bless You while I live; I will lift up my hands in Your name.

Psalm 134:2—Lift up your hands in the sanctuary, and bless the Lord.

Clapping Hands:

Psalm 47:1—Oh, clap your hands, all you peoples! Shout to God with the voice of triumph!

Isaiah 55:12—For you shall go out in joy and be led forth in peace; the mountains and the hills before you shall break forth into singing, and all the trees of the field shall clap their hands.

Standing:

2 Chronicles 29:26—The Levites stood with the instruments of David, and the priests with the trumpets.

Exodus 33:10—All the people saw the pillar of cloud standing at the tabernacle door, and all the people rose and worshiped, each man in his tent door.

Bowing, Kneeling:

Psalm 95:6—Oh come, let us worship and bow down; Let us kneel before the Lord our Maker.

2 Chronicles 7:3—When all the children of Israel saw how the fire came down, and the glory of the Lord on the temple, they bowed their faces to the ground on the pavement, and worshiped and praised the Lord, saying: "For He is good, For His mercy endures forever."

2 Chronicles 29:29—And when they had finished offering, the king and all who were present with him bowed and worshiped.

Prostration:

Revelation 4:10—The twenty-four elders fall down before Him who sits on the throne and worship Him who lives forever and ever, and cast their crowns before the throne... .

Revelation 19:4—And the twenty-four elders and the four living creatures fell down and worshiped God who sat on the throne, saying, "Amen! Alleluia!"

YOUR TESTIMONY

The most powerful voice in the world is your own, whether sharing your testimony with others or encouraging yourself in the Lord. Your testimony is a surefire way to increase the faith of others to confess Jesus as Lord and to increase your faith, bringing defeat to the kingdom of darkness (Rev. 12:11).

PERSONAL RELATIONSHIP WITH JESUS

You must have a genuine, personal relationship with Jesus Christ to defeat the enemy and his cohorts. You must have faith in Jesus for yourself. Without a personal, sincere spirit-to-spirit relationship with Jesus, you are no match for the demonic realm. This is because the believer must "be strong in the Lord and in the power of His might" (Eph. 6:10). Remember the Seven Sons of Sceva. They had good intentions to cast out demons from a man, but when the demons recognized that they had no spirit-to-spirit relationship with Jesus, they beat them severely.

Then some of the itinerant Jewish exorcists took it upon themselves to call the name of the Lord Jesus over those who had evil spirits, saying, "We exorcise you by the Jesus whom Paul preaches." Also there were seven sons of Sceva, a Jewish chief priest, who did so. And the evil spirit answered and said, "Jesus I know, and Paul I know; but who are you?" Then the man in whom the evil spirit was leaped on them, overpowered them, and prevailed against them, so that they fled out of that house naked and wounded (Acts. 19:13-16).

ARMOR OF GOD

The armor of God is Jesus Christ, our Lord and Savior. Apostle Paul exhorts us to put on the whole armor of God. This means to put on and keep on the mind of Christ. How do you do this? By practicing the disciplines of our faith until you are conformed into the image of Christ Jesus.

The disciplines include prayer and communion with God, fasting, thanksgiving, praise and worship, meditating, studying and reading your Bible, and sitting under sound doctrine. Our disciplines also include witnessing and testifying to others about God's goodness and fellowshipping with other believers. The disciplines of our faith must become a part of your lifestyle, if you are to be conformed into the image of Christ Jesus and keep the enemy beneath your feet.

Wearing the armor of God means that when you confessed Jesus as Lord, you put off the old man of the flesh or carnality, and you put on the new man, the spirit man, or the hidden man of the heart. The armor of God enables you to commune spirit-to-spirit with Almighty God, transferring the strength that you need into your heart (spirit man and mind).

Wearing your armor means you continually abide in Christ Jesus and He abides in you. In Ephesians 6:12-18, Apostle Paul makes it plain that in order to defeat the devil, you must "keep on the whole armor of God". This means you must continually operate in the integrity of God.

Let's look at each piece of the armor of God, keeping in mind that all the pieces synergistically work together like the parts of your body with each joint supplying. When you wear the whole armor of God, you wholly function—spirit, soul and body and the enemy has no place in you. Ephesians 6:12-18 says:

Finally, my brethren, be strong in the Lord and in the power of His might. Therefore take up the whole armor of God, that you may be able to withstand in the evil day, and having done all, to stand.

Stand therefore, having girded your waist with truth, having put on the breastplate of righteousness, and having shod your feet with the preparation of the gospel of peace; above all, taking the shield of faith with which you will be able to quench all the fiery darts of the wicked one. And take the helmet of salvation, and the sword of the Spirit, which is the word of God; praying always with all prayer and supplication in the Spirit, being watchful to this end with all perseverance and supplication for all the saints.

Eph. 6:14—Stand therefore, having girded your waist with truth

The truth is the infallible, inerrant, immutable, eternal Word of God. The believer must keep on the belt of the truth of God's Word because it's the "word of God's power" that holds the universe together. You gird your waist with truth by immersing yourself in the Bible, until it transforms your thinking into the Kingdom of God paradigm.

Initially, I increased my faith in God and improved my image by standing in front of a mirror and confessing the "I am Scriptures" from the Bible over my life and other faith-filled confessions. I then acted upon those words by doing what I feared. My faith and confidence in my identity in Christ Jesus appeared to have skyrocketed. What really happened is that my old thinking was renewed by the mind of Christ. I was thinking like a Son of faith and not a slave to fear.

You are the prophet of your life. Therefore you and only you are responsible for where you are in life. If you don't like what you see, change your way of thinking by eating and digesting the Scriptures in the area you desire growth, just like eating natural food to strengthen your body. Begin confessing the promises, dreams and visions that God has given you to steward in this earth realm. You must consistently do the work! And you're not alone. Ask Holy Spirit to give you His grace that is sufficient when you get weak. Every day look at yourself in the mirror and decree, declare or confess the truth of God's promises over your life and family. Prophesy over your life until you fulfill your prophetic destiny. You must war in the spirit—decreeing and declaring God's Word over your life for your destiny to manifest.

If you have not done so already, write and confess a faith-filled confession that covers your family, associates, partners and your life. When you decree it by faith and act upon it, it will come to pass.

Eph. 6:14—Having put on the breastplate of righteousness

Putting on the breastplate of righteousness means you know who you are in Christ Jesus. You understand that the Father has given you access to His throne, not based on your works, but based on faith by grace in Christ Jesus. You have been granted full rights and privileges to approach your Father's throne to receive, according to His will.

The revelation of being the righteousness of God, or being in right-standing with God in Christ Jesus, was a game-changer for me. Once I understood that Jesus exchanged His sinless robe of righteousness by faith for my filthy unrighteousness, I was free indeed.

No longer could the filthy rags of sin, guilt and legalism bind me. The gift of righteousness freed me from condemnation. I am able to guard my heart and resist the enemy's tormenting lies and ignore the haters he sends to distract me from my purpose. The breastplate of righteousness has enabled me to daily crucify the old man or old way of thinking and yield to Holy Spirit, who leads and guides me into all truth (John 8:32, 16:13-15).

Eph. 6:15—And having shod your feet with the preparation of the gospel of peace

Be prepared to share the good news of the gospel and your testimony whenever the opportunity arises. Bring peace wherever you go. Shalom, nothing missing and nothing broken. You must be a peacekeeper, not a peacemaker. A peacekeeper confronts evil or evildoers in love. Never condone sin or turn the other way like you don't see it. Pray for spiritual discernment, wisdom and courage to use the right approach when confronting wrongdoers, whether in the church or marketplace. You must allow the peace of God to garrison and guard your heart and mind in the midst of spiritual warfare. Stay in the eye of the storm, where the enemy cannot touch you. In this way, you will sidestep the enemy's hidden traps laid along the path of your divine assignment. The peace of God will help you finish strong so you can say like Apostle Paul, "I have fought the good fight, I have finished the race. I have kept the faith. Finally, there is laid up for me the crown of righteousness, which the Lord, the righteous Judge, will give to me on that Day, and not to me only but also to all who have loved His appearing" (2 Tim. 4:7-8).

Eph. 6:16—Above all, taking the shield of faith with which you will be able to quench all the fiery darts of the wicked one

Without faith, it's impossible to please God. Faith is having confidence that God will do what His Word says, and what He speaks to your heart (rhema) based upon His written Word. God rewards the believer that diligently seeks after His heart and ways. To seek God means you put Him and His Word first place. You measure everything by the plumb line of God's integrity, character and His Word.

In the midst of a test, you might feel fear or pain, but you deal with it by speaking or superimposing the promises of God over that challenging situation. You call things that be not as though they were (Rom. 4:17). Your faith in God is your confidence in His integrity to do what He has promised in His Word, and what He has personally spoken to you. You become a channel for God's laser-like power to invade the earth and strike the mark, advancing His kingdom. Are you fully persuaded that what God has promised, He can perform? Then continue to fight the good fight of faith in spite of what your five senses perceive. You walk by faith and not by sight, and you are more than a conqueror in Christ Jesus.

Eph. 6:17—And take the helmet of salvation

You possess the mind of Christ, who has translated you from the kingdom of darkness into the kingdom of His marvelous light. The helmet of salvation refers to your understanding your totality in God. The battle is in the mind. The enemy cannot attack God, therefore He attacks God's children in their minds and bodies to steal their godly inheritance or salvation package. To activate the mind of Christ in your thinking so you can possess your inheritance, you must renew your mind to cast down every thought contrary to your prophetic destiny. You renew your mind by the washing of the water of God's Word or meditation, which is the believer's Constitution. As you continue to meditate the Word of God in intimate prayer and communion in your secret place, you will enlarge your territory first internally and then externally.

The word "salvation" is derived from the Greek word "soteria". It not only encompasses Messianic salvation as in being born-again and inheriting eternal life, but it also means deliverance, preservation of physical life, safety and protection from the enemy. Salvation encompasses health, wealth, right relationships and everything that pertains to life and godliness. However, to take your mountain, you must continually meditate and confess the Scriptures and act upon them. Your trust and faith in God will cause the favor already upon your life to attract the answers and solutions you need.

Eph. 6:17—And the sword of the Spirit, which is the Word of God

Learn to wield the sword of the Spirit like Jesus did in the wilderness, defeating the enemy (Matt. 4:1-11; Luke 4:1-15). Wholly dependent upon Holy Spirit while in the wilderness, Jesus defeated the devil by decreeing the "It is written" Scriptures, even though He was exhausted from fasting for forty days and nights.

One word from God can change your life forever. This is because God's Word is spirit and life. The spirit realm supersedes, displaces, or replaces the natural realm. The spirit realm is the causal realm. Everything you see was created by faith-filled words. These words are like keys that open doors in the heavenly realm to transfer what you desire or need into the earth. To bring your needs or desires from the spiritual realm into the natural, mix your words with the God-kind of faith and take action (Mark 11:22-26).

The sword of the Spirit (rhema) or spoken Word of God is based upon the foundation of the written Word of God (logos). The "rhema" agrees with the "logos." Jesus meditated, studied and read the Scriptures (Torah) to activate God's mind and ways in His heart. This is one reason His prayers and actions produced amazing results (signs, wonders and miracles). As God's Sons in the earth, you and I must operate in the same way, if we desire to please our heavenly Father and glorify Jesus.

As you store God's Word in your heart through meditation and study, Holy Spirit will pull out of you a "rhema" for you to decree that will cause the enemy to flee for a season just like he fled from Jesus. No one can wield your sword of the Spirit to keep the enemy beneath your feet except you. God has given you His authority in Jesus' name. So act now!

Eph. 6:18—Praying always with all prayer and supplication in the Spirit, being watchful to this end with all perseverance and supplication for all the saints

Watching and praying is how you partner with God to establish His kingdom on earth. It is wise to watch and pray to guard your predestinated destiny, family, leaders, state, nation, businesses, work place, ministries and the body of Christ.

Apostle Paul exhorts us to always pray with supplications in the Spirit for the saints (Eph. 6:18). This means we must diligently and daily commune with God in order to pray His prayers back to Him and hit the bullseye. The Holy Spirit inspires supplications, which are earnest, sincere requests from the heart of God. Ask God to anoint you with the spirit of grace and supplication, so you can accurately and fervently pray until His will is done on earth as it is in heaven (Zech. 12:10).

Praying in the Spirit also means to pray in your heavenly prayer language or tongues. Again, this type of praying recharges and strengthens your spirit man, so you are set on ready at all times to minister to others from the overflow. It also enables you to pray the mysteries of God into the earth realm for your life and other situations.

Finally, quitting is never an option for the believer involved in spiritual warfare. You must put on and keep on the whole armor of God. You must not become entangled in the things or distractions of the world if you want to be an effective soldier in the army of the Lord. Every believer does not desire to go deeper in God. If you do desire to go deeper, you cannot be fearful, complacent, passive or apathetic. These qualities do not describe a godly king-priest that serves the Most High God.

What you tolerate will proliferate. If you don't like your life, create a new reality on the canvas of your mind by decreeing the promises of God with faith in your heart and taking action until your change comes to pass. You cannot qualify for what you do not pursue in prayer by faith and strategic action.

Continue to seek God's face and not His hand by communing with Him in prayer, so you know His ways. Continue to renew your mind with the Word of God, so you operate with the mind of Christ, compelling you to step out and take action. Continue to wait upon and minister to the Lord in Spirit and truth, so you discern the right spiritual weapon to wield at the right time, always winning the victory!

But thanks be to God, who gives us the victory through our Lord Jesus Christ (1 Cor. 15:57).

SECTION IV
PRAYERS & DECREES

CHAPTER 15

DECREE A THING

You shall decree a thing and it shall be established unto you and the light will shine on your ways. —Job 22:28

Believe in your heart when you say these prayers and make these decrees for your family, others and yourself. Then watch God answer your prayers. As you pray or decree, use your sanctified imagination to envision God's glory being released to bring change into the lives of your family, friends, leaders, churches, regions and nations, and in your own life.

God says in 2 Chronicles 7:14, *"If My people who are called by My name will humble themselves, and pray and seek my face, and turn from their wicked ways, then I will hear from heaven, and will forgive their sin and heal their land."* Will you be the one that God can depend on to pray now, so that He can heal the land?

❧ PRAYERS OF VICTORY ☙

THANKSGIVING & PRAISE

Father, in the name of Jesus and by the power of Holy Spirit, I thank you for this day that you have made and I rejoice and am glad in it. You are my loving, caring, sharing heavenly Father and I exalt your name forever.

I praise you Lord for what you have done, are doing and shall continue to do in and through our lives for your glory. I give you all the honor, glory and praise that is due your name. Thank you for blessing us to see a new day and a new beginning. Thank you for saving my family, the Body of Christ, and me—restoring us into the kingdom of God by faith in the precious blood of Jesus. You are our God and we are your people, the sheep of your pasture. You alone are worthy to be praised. You are the Most High God, Jehovah, the Great I Am that I Am, Creator of the universe, and I exalt your name forever. I give You all honor, glory, power and praise. In Jesus' name. Amen (Psalm 118:24; Rev.4: 11).

WORSHIP WITH THE NAMES OF GOD

I worship you Father for who You are—*Jehovah Elohim*, our Lord God. You are *Adonai*, my Lord and Master. You are *El Elyon*, the Most High God, and the Highest Sovereign in the universe. You are *El Olam*, our Everlasting Father, the *Alpha* and the *Omega*, the beginning and the end. *El Roi*, I worship You as the Strong One who sees and knows all things concerning our lives.

You are *Jehovah,* the Self-Existent One, the Great I Am that I Am, and You are everything we need. You are *El Shaddai*, the Almighty God, the All-Sufficient One, and the Many-Breasted One that nourishes and supplies all of our needs. You are *Jehovah Jireh,* our God who sees ahead and provides all that we need, far over and above all that we can ask, think, dream or imagine, according to your power working in us.

You are *Jehovah Nissi*, the Lord our banner, and your banner over us is your love that never fails. You are *Jehovah Raah*, the Lord my Shepherd. I shall not want for You make me and my family and those connected to us to lie down in green pastures, which is the abundance of your blessings overtaking us.

You *are Jehovah Shalom*, the Lord God our peace that surpasses all understanding; nothing missing, nothing broken. You guard our hearts and minds. You are *Jehovah Shammah*, the Lord who is ever present and who never leaves us nor forsakes us. You are *Jehovah Tsidkenu*, the Lord God our righteousness. You became sin for us that we might be made the righteousness of God in Christ Jesus. You are *Jehovah Rapha*, the Lord my Healer. You heal all of our diseases from the top of our heads to the soles of our feet. You make us whole. You are *Jehovah M'Kaddesh*, the Lord God our Sanctifier, who makes us holy. We cry out with the angels, "Holy, Holy, Holy, Lord God of Hosts, heaven and earth is filled with your glory."

I worship you *Jehovah Sabaoth*, the Lord of hosts, who dispatches angels to war, protect, guard and minister on our behalf. You are *Jehovah G'molah*, the Lord our Recompense, who avenges us and restores everything that has been stolen from us, going back to the Garden of Eden. You avenge us for You are a just God who abhors injustice and unbalanced scales. You are *Jehovah Gibbor*, the Mighty God, the Man of War, who shoots forth your arrows against our enemies, demolishing every demonic assignment! You are *Jehovah*, the Great I Am that I Am and You are everything I need. Be glorified, oh God! To You belong all glory, all honor and all praise forevermore. In Jesus' name. Amen (Gen. 1:1, 15:2, 14:17-20; Isa. 40:28-31, 16:13; Psalm 118:24, 145:1, 86:12; Rev. 4:11; Ex. 3:14-15; Gen. 14:22, 22:13-14; Ex. 17:15; Psalm 23:1; Judges 6:24; Ezek. 48:35; Jer. 23:6; Ex. 15:26, 31:13; Isa. 6:1-3; Jer. 51:6; Psalm 24:8).

FOR HUSBAND

Father, in the name of Jesus and by the power of Holy Spirit, I thank and praise you for this is the day that the Lord has made and I will rejoice and be glad in it. You are my loving, caring, sharing heavenly Father and I will exalt and praise your name forever.

I come boldly before your throne of grace to thank you for my husband, who is a man after your own heart. He is a man of valor, wisdom, wealth and health. He is head over heels in love, first with You, and then with me. His eyes are for me only. Another he will not follow.

Re-ignite his passion for your presence, so that our marriage is renewed. Help him to be patient and understanding with our family. Knit our hearts together as one in the Spirit of a covenant bond that is impenetrable. Increase his love and desire for your presence and your Word, oh God.

I say that my husband is blessed like faithful Abraham and He walks in divine health and unlimited wealth. He lives to be a good, old age—full of strength and stamina. Renew his youth like the eagle.

Father, as he seeks first your kingdom and righteousness, bless him with wisdom, knowledge, understanding, witty ideas, inventions, books, real estate, divine partnerships, education, successful business endeavors and promotion to advance your kingdom.

I thank you that because my husband is a cheerful tither and giver, You open up windows from heaven and pour out continual blessings into His life. He is blessed to be a blessing. My husband always has more than enough, for You are His shepherd and he lacks for no good thing. He has favor with You, therefore He has favor with man. He walks uprightly before you, and you give Him the desires of His heart.

My husband abounds in Your grace, receiving favor and earthly blessings, so that he always has all sufficiency in all things, never requiring aid or support. He is furnished in abundance for every good work. Wealth and riches are in my husband's storehouses. He lays up an inheritance for his children, grandchildren and future generations.

He's the head and not the tail, above only and never beneath and blessed to be a blessing. He's more than a conqueror in Christ Jesus. He leaps over walls and runs through troops. He pursues by the Spirit and recovers all that has been stolen from His bloodline, in Jesus' name.

I decree and declare that my husband finishes strong and in a spirit of excellence every God-given assignment on time, under budget and on target. I decree that my husband fulfills his divine purpose and destiny on earth, so that he will hear You say on that great day, "Well done good and faithful servant. You have been faithful with a few things, now I will put you in charge of many." In Jesus' name. Amen (Psalm 118:24, 145:1; Heb. 4:16; Acts. 13:22; Judges 6:12; Psalm 112; Matt. 22:37-40; 1 Pet. 4:8; Eph. 4:2-3; Ecc. 4:12; Mark 10:9; Deut. 18:18-20; Psalm 103:5; Gal. 3:13-14; Gen. 25:8; Matt. 6:33; Psalm 23:1; Mal. 3:10-11; Eph. 1:17-18, 3:20; 2 Cor. 9:6-8; Deut. 28:1-14; Gen. 12:1-3; 2 Cor. 12:9; 3 John 2; Psalm 5:12; Jer. 29:11; Matt. 25:23).

FOR WIFE

Father, in the name of Jesus and by the power of Holy Spirit, I thank and praise you for this is the day that you have made. I will rejoice and be glad in it. You are my loving, caring, sharing heavenly Father, and I will exalt and praise your name forever.

I come boldly before your throne of grace to thank you for my wife, who is a virtuous woman. She is more than enough for me and my family. Give her wisdom to build our home, to care for our family, and to pursue a career, if she decides, as I work along with her, so she has no fear of lack. We rise up and call my wife blessed because she fears You above all. Let the law of kindness come from her lips.

Strengthen her where she is weak. By your stripes, I call her healed: spirit, soul, body, mind, will and emotions. Father, I ask you to supply my wife's every need—spiritually, emotionally, mentally, physically and financially. Let her be ravished with love for me only.

My wife always abounds in God's grace, receiving favor and earthly blessings, so that she always has all sufficiency in all things, never requiring aid or support. She is furnished in abundance for every good work. Wealth and riches are in her storehouses. She lays up an inheritance for our children, grandchildren and future generations.

I thank you that my wife has favor with You, therefore she has favor with man. She walks through open doors of success always abounding, and every door of failure has been closed. She shall not know defeat. Your favor surrounds my wife like a shield, attracting everything she needs to fulfill her purpose and destiny.

I decree and declare that the purpose for which you have created my wife on the earth, she will fulfill and hear you say on that great day, "Well done good and faithful servant. You have been faithful with a few things, now I will put you in charge of many." In Jesus' name. Amen (Psalm 118:24, 145:1; Heb. 4:16; Prov. 31:14-30; 1 Pet. 2:24; 2 Cor. 9:6-8; Deut. 28:1-14; Gen. 12:1-3; 2 Cor. 12:9; 3 John 2; Psalm 5:12; Jer. 29:11; Matt. 25:23).

FOR CHILDREN

Father, in the name of Jesus and by the power of Holy Spirit, I thank you and praise you for this is the day that you have made. I will rejoice and be glad in it. You are my loving, caring, sharing heavenly Father and I will exalt and praise your name forever. You are worthy to be praised.

I come boldly before your throne of grace to pray for my child(ren)/grandchildren. I thank you that as I pray by faith and put you in remembrance of your Word concerning my children that you will watch over your Word to perform it. I cast the cares concerning my children upon you, for you care for them deeply and lovingly.

No weapon formed against them will prosper and every tongue that rises against my children in judgment, you will condemn and show to be in the wrong. I cancel every plot, plan and ploy of the enemy against my children, and I decree the enemy's tactics backfire on him and work out for their good.

Our children are a gift from You, Father. Great is their peace and undisturbed composure. Thank you, Father, for contending with those who contend with our children. Thank you that their angels behold your face daily for instructions concerning them. The angels are continually encamped around our children/grandchildren to protect them from all hurt, harm and danger, seen and unseen.

Give them grace to resist temptation and deliver them from the evil one. I say our children possess the gates of their soul. They walk by the Spirit and not by the flesh. I declare that our children are obedient and respectful to their parents and those in authority over them. They choose life and not death. They speak life and not death. They love you, Lord, with all their heart, mind,

266 | PRAY NOW

soul and strength, and they love their neighbors as they love themselves.

I apply the blood of Jesus to cover our children. I draw the bloodline of Jesus above their heads, beneath their feet and around them as a hedge of protection. I rebuke satan and demon power from every area of their lives, in Jesus' name. I say my children are loosed from the enemy's influence.

I decree and declare that favor continually surrounds our children like a shield, attracting to them everything that pertains to life and godliness. I call into their lives the right godly spouses, academic, athletic and arts scholarships, promotions, witty ideas, inventions, divine connections, books, real estate, financial and material wealth. They have favor with those in authority over them—who use their power, position, wealth and influence on their behalf.

I speak Shalom over our children—nothing missing, nothing broken. They walk in divine health. I rebuke every spirit of infirmity and sickness and disease from their bodies and souls. I rebuke premature death, accidents and destruction from my children and future seed. They are shown to be ten times smarter in their studies, especially in math and sciences. They will fulfill their purpose and destiny on earth, in Jesus' name.

I bind and rebuke every counterfeit spirit of the opposite sex from entering into their lives. I bind and rebuke the spirits of disobedience, rebellion, lust, sexual immorality, emotional instability, mental illness, OCD, poverty, low self-esteem, shame, fear, guilt, co-dependency, addictions, depression, sickness and disease, infirmities and every evil spirit.

I bind and rebuke from my children and future seed every hindering, seducing, familiar and lying spirit, and I command them, in Jesus' name, to get away from my children now. I bind and rebuke the spirits of python that would try to choke my children's destinies. I break every unhealthy soul tie from their lives. I serve the enemy notice that he's powerless, inoperative and ineffective to come against our children in any way, in Jesus' name.

I decree that our children are the righteousness of God in Christ Jesus. They prosper spirit, soul and body, mind, will, and emotions. They increase more and more, them and their children. They are the head, and not the tail, above only and never beneath, because they obey God. They are quick to repent when they sin because they love God. They are blessed to be a blessing. They glorify You, Father, with how they live. They are a righteous seed. In Jesus' name. Amen (Psalm 118:24, 145:1; Heb. 4:16; Jer. 1:12; 1 Pet. 5:7; Isa. 54:17; Psalm 127:3; Isa. 54:13; Gen. 22:17; Psalm 91:11-12; Matt. 6:13; Luke 21:19; Gen. 22:17; Eph. 6:1-3; Deut. 30:19; Prov. 18:21; Matt. 22:37-40; Ex. 12:7, 13; Rev. 12:11; Psalm 5:12; 2 Pet. 1:3; Rom. 4:17; 3 John 2; 2 Pet. 2:24; Dan. 1:17, 20; Eph. 1:11-13; Jer. 29:111; Cor. 5:21; 3 John 2; Psalm 115:14; Deut. 28:13-14; Gen. 12:2).

SAFETY & PROTECTION FOR FAMILY

Father God, I thank you for continually encamping angels of protection around my family and me, protecting us from all hurt, harm and danger. I decree that this is a day of victory, power, success, safety and strength for us. No weapon formed against us will prosper and every lie spoken against us You will expose. I decree that our children, grandchildren and future seed are righteous seed and that you contend with those that contend with our children.

Great is the peace and undisturbed composure of our children, grandchildren and future seed. I evict every counterfeit spirit and thought from their hearts and souls (mind, will and emotions). I rebuke in Jesus' name every familiar, seducing, lying and hindering spirit now and in the future from derailing our children and future seed from fulfilling their purpose and destiny. I decree that every trap set for our children backfires on the enemy and works for our children's good.

I command the fire of God to burn every iniquitous pattern of thinking and behavior from the souls of our family, so that we serve the Lord all the days of our lives. I decree that our children live to be a good old age full of strength, health and stamina, advancing the kingdom of God. Our entire household is saved now, in Jesus' name.

I serve the enemy notice that he's powerless and inoperative to come against my family or me this day or any day because we abide in the secret place of the Most High, and under His shadow we are protected. Lord, You are our refuge and our fortress and you deliver us from every trap of the enemy. Every germ that touches our bodies dies on contact because of the anointing upon our lives. Sickness, disease and infirmity are far from us.

A thousand may fall at our side and ten thousand at our right hand, but destruction will not touch my family or me. Only with our eyes will we behold and see the reward of the wicked because we obey our Father God. Thank you Father for your promise that you will be with us in trouble and deliver us, for you always cause us to triumph. In Jesus' name. Amen (Psalm 91:11; Isa. 54:17; Prov. 11:21; Isa. 49:25; Isa. 54:13; Job. 22:28; Rom. 8:26-28; 1 Kings 1:10; Gen. 25:8; Phil. 1:6; Acts. 16:31; James 1:5-6; Psalm 5:12; Deut. 28:13, 30:9; Luke 10:19; Psalm 91; Phil. 4:19; Psalm 91:7-8; 2 Cor. 2:14).

SALVATION

Father, I thank you and I praise you for this is the day that you have made and I will rejoice and be glad in it. You are my loving, caring, sharing heavenly Father and I exalt and praise your name forever.

I come boldly before your throne of grace to pray for salvation for (name). In Jesus' name and by the power of Holy Spirit, I bind every mind-blinding enemy from operating in the life of (name). I command satan to desist in his maneuvers against (name) now. I decree (name) is loosed from the deception, accusations and temptations of the enemy.

Remove the scales from the eyes of (name). Set righteous laborers upon (name)'s path that will share the good news of the gospel in such a way that (name) will believe and confess Jesus as Lord.

You said in your Word that you don't want any to perish. You also said you would save the lost by the cleanness of the hands of the intercessors. So Father, I'm asking you right now to save (name). I claim (name)'s soul for the kingdom of God. I thank you and praise you for saving them. In Jesus' name. Amen (Psalm 118:24, 145:1; Heb. 4:16; Matt. 18:18; Acts. 9:18; Matt. 9:38; Rom. 10:9-10; 2 Pet. 3:9; Job. 22:30).

BAPTISM OF THE HOLY SPIRIT

Father God, I thank you for saving my soul by faith in Christ Jesus. You said in your Word that if we, being natural know how to give good gifts to our children, how much more will You, our heavenly Father, give the gift of the baptism of the Holy Spirit with the evidence of speaking in tongues to them who ask you. Right now, I ask You to fill me with the Holy Spirit with the evidence of speaking in tongues. I believe I receive this gift now, in Jesus' name. Amen (Luke 10:13; Acts 2:4).

(Now open your mouth and begin to pray, allowing Holy Spirit to give you utterance. Pray daily using your heavenly prayer language (tongues) to commune with God, to be a witness of the gospel of Jesus Christ, to minister to others and to increase your faith and strengthen your spirit man.)

INNER HEALING

Father, I thank You for Who You are, the Creator of heaven and earth and everything therein. I magnify and give reverence to your holy name, for You are faithful, and You alone are worthy to be praised.

I invoke your name Jehovah Rapha. You are my Healer. Right now, in Jesus' name, I bind every spirit of rejection, shame, schizophrenia, OCD, mental illness, anxiety disorders, pain, trauma, abuse and bondage from operating in my life, my family members, or the lives of my sisters and brothers in Christ Jesus. I break every stronghold in their minds, emotions and wills and in my own.

I take authority in Jesus' name and cast out every evil spirit from my spirit, soul and body—subconscious mind, emotions and memories. I am loosed now from the effects and trauma of these evil spirits. By Jesus' stripes I am healed. I release the healing power of God to saturate me from the top of my head to the soles of my feet and from the inside out.

I release God's peace and love to cover me now. I speak God's peace over myself—Shalom, nothing missing, nothing broken. In Jesus' name. Amen (Psalm 145:3, 146:6; Ex. 15:22-26; Mark 16:15; 1 Pet. 2:24; Judges 6:24).

HEALTH & HEALING

Father, in the name of Jesus and by the power of Holy Spirit, I thank and praise you, for this is the day that you have made. I will rejoice and be glad in it. You are my loving, caring, sharing heavenly Father, and I will exalt and praise your name forever.

I come boldly before your throne of grace to obtain mercy for those who need healing or creative miracles. I invoke your name, *Jehovah Rapha.* You are our Healer. Thank you by faith in Jesus' name for redeeming us from the curse of the law, which includes sickness and disease.

I send your Word now to heal sick bodies, minds and emotions, according to Isaiah 53:5 and 1 Peter 2:24, which says by Jesus' stripes we are healed. I bind and rebuke the spirits of infirmity in the bodies, minds, emotions and memories of your people. I call your people loosed from the spirit of sickness and disease and from the effects of every infirmity, in Jesus' name.

I curse and command all bad cells in your body to die and to be discarded now. I command fresh, new white blood cells to multiply and devour all bad cells. I command your immune system to be strengthened, in Jesus' name.

I speak to the electrical, chemical, hormonal and magnetic frequencies in your body to operate in divine harmony. I curse and command all prions (bad proteins) to die and leave your body now.

I curse diabetes and related issues, heart disease, cancer, Alzheimer's, dementia, high blood pressure, respiratory diseases, acid reflux, glaucoma, macular degeneration, periodontal gum disease, arthritis, back pain and disc degeneration, migraine headaches, stress, osteoporosis, multiple sclerosis, autism, Tourette Syndrome, STDs, AIDS, nerve disorders, phobias, psoriasis, eczema, every hereditary disease and every unnamed disease, in Jesus' name.

I release the creative, miracle-working power of God to penetrate your body, mind and emotions, creating new body parts to replace broken ones.

I command new organs of every kind to be installed inside of your body now, in Jesus' name. I command new bladders, kidneys, livers, hearts, spleens, valves, arteries, prostates, female organs, retinas, corneas and veins to come forth now, in Jesus' name. I decree new bones, joints, ligaments, tendons, cartilage, tissues, glands, marrow, blood cells, enzymes, amino acids to be made whole now, in Jesus' name!

Every hereditary and unnamed disease and every virus and bacteria, I curse you at the root and command you to die. You will not come upon God's children or (name)'s body, mind or emotions, in Jesus' name.

Thank you, Father, for healing your people. I worship you for who You are, Jehovah Rapha— our God that Heals. Jehovah, the Great I Am that I Am. I give you all the reverence and all the glory, for your name is worthy to be praised. Your Word will not return to You void, but it will accomplish and perform your purposes. Father, go beyond this prayer to meet every unspoken need. In Jesus' name. Amen. Thank You for making us whole and giving us the gift of divine health by faith. In Jesus' name. Amen (Psalm 118:24, 145:1; Heb. 4:16; Ex. 15:25-26; Gal. 3:13-14; John 14:16; Isa. 53:5; 1 Pet 2:24; Matt. 18:18; Mark 11:23; Isa. 55:10-11; Psalm 91).

PROSPERITY & STEWARDSHIP

I thank you, Father, for your goodness. I bless your holy name. You alone are worthy to be praised. Thank you for your provision, Jehovah Jireh. Thank you for prospering us: spirit, soul (mind, will, emotions, imagination, intellect) and body as your covenant people.

I command every demonic spirit to depart from our souls, so that we believe, think and attract abundance as sons and daughters of God. Father, release your fire to burn to ashes every limiting belief system, and send a fresh wave of momentum that causes us to move forward into our destiny, to save nations and to create heavenly solutions that solve earthly problems.

Increase our hunger and thirst to meditate your word, so that our minds are renewed and we operate in our dominion authority as kings and priests to subdue and replenish the earth. I decree that we sow seeds of faith and harvest crops of victory in every test, trial and tribulation. Help us to see ourselves as giant-slayers and deliverers of the lost, hurting, naked, prisoners, poor, orphans and widows.

I decree we think big because we serve a BIG God who loves people. We prosper spiritually, emotionally, mentally, physically, financially, materially, relationally, socially, psychologically, and in every way because we are citizens of heaven where there is abundance. I decree we have the spirit of power, love and a sound mind. There is no fear here! Greater are You in us than he that is in the world.

I decree that our families and those connected to us are faith-filled believers anointed by God to release signs, wonders and miracles into the earth. We take the land wherever our feet tread. When we decree a thing, it comes to pass because we are kingdom shifters, anointed to change the world around us to reflect the glory of heaven.

You are Jehovah Chayil, the Lord of Wealth, who gives us wisdom, favor, power, revelation knowledge, influence, virtue and wealth to establish your covenant on earth. I rebuke the spirit of mammon and idolatry from our lives, so that Jesus alone is Lord of our wealth and riches. Help us to multiply the wealth you have entrusted to us, so that we are a blessing to our families and those in need.

Everything belongs to You, oh God, and we surrender our lives, gifts, talents, skills, abilities, and financial and material wealth to be used for your purposes like Father Abraham, Isaac and Jacob. Oh Father God, thank you for choosing to crown us with your glory and honor. Thank you for releasing heaven on earth through us, according to your purposes.

As a cheerful giver, I thank you for rebuking the enemy from my family, including our destinies, finances, relationships, businesses, careers, ministries and every endeavor. I decree that because we are cheerful, consistent givers, we have a covenant right with Almighty God to have sufficiency in all things, so that we require no aid or support and have provision for every good work. Wealth and riches remain in our storehouses.

I thank you, Lord, for teaching us the way we should go, so that we will profit and be a blessing to advance your kingdom. Give us an increasing appetite to share the gospel of salvation with the lost, to heal the sick, to reconcile the backslidden, to restore and cultivate right relationships, to set the captives free and to equip the body of Christ inside the four walls of the church and in the marketplace for the work of the ministry. Be magnified, oh Lord, who delights in prospering your people, for you are worthy to be praised.

I apply the blood of Jesus upon my family, and I draw the bloodline of Jesus above, beneath and around them and what you have entrusted to us. Lead us not into temptation, but deliver us from evil. I decree my family will fulfill the purpose for which each of us has been created, individually and collectively. I love you, Lord. I give you all the honor, glory and praise for who You are, my loving, caring, sharing heavenly Father. In Jesus' name. Amen (3 John 2; 2 Kings 1:10; Jer. 29:11; Josh. 1:8-10; Gen. 1:26-28; Matt. 25:14-30, 34-36; John 10:10; 2 Tim. 1:7; 1 John 4:4; Rom 5:17; Mark 16:17-20; 1 Chron. 10:10–13; James 1:27; Matt. 25:14-15; Psalm 8:4; 2 Cor. 9:6-10; Psalm 112:1-3; Isa. 48:17; Matt. 28:18-20; Psalm 35:27; Matt. 6:13; Job. 22:28; Rev. 7:12).

FINANCIAL PROSPERITY

Father, in the name of Jesus and by the power of Holy Spirit, I thank and praise you, for this is the day that you have made. I will rejoice and be glad in it. You are my loving, caring, sharing heavenly Father, and I will exalt your name forever.

You are Jehovah, the Great I Am. You are everything we need. You are Jehovah Chayil, the God of wealth and power who gives us the ability to produce wealth, confirming your covenant, which you swore to our forefathers, Abraham, Isaac and Jacob.

Let your Chayil grace and glory, consisting of worship, wisdom, power, honor, favor, wealth and influence manifest in our lives for your Kingdom's sake.

All riches and honor come from You, oh Lord. In your hand is the power and might to make great and to give strength to all. Everything comes from You. Therefore I cheerfully give my tithes, offerings, first fruits and alms, for You are my Source. No other help I know.

You are our Shepherd and we shall not lack for any good thing. You supply our needs, according to your riches in glory in Christ Jesus. Great is your faithfulness.

You said in your Word that when we seek first the kingdom of God and Your righteousness, everything we need would be added to us. You are so good to us, Father, better than we could ever be to ourselves.

Forgive us for poor financial stewardship over that which you have entrusted to us. Forgive us for covetousness, greed, laziness, stinginess, fear and withholding from helping others. Give us a generous heart to give to those less fortunate, as you lead us by your Spirit. You are our Source. Thank you for your forgiveness Father.

I decree and declare that wealth and riches remain in our storehouses as we cheerfully give our tithes, offerings, first fruits and alms to honor your name. I thank you that as we give, we receive good measure, pressed down, shaken together and running over as men give unto us.

You promised in your Word that when we give our tithes, you would pour a blessing from the windows of heaven into our lives and rebuke the devourer for our sake. You promised, Father, that when we give offerings, you would bless us 30, 60 and 100-fold. You promised, Lord, that when we give you our first fruits, our storehouses will stay full and our vats will overflow with new wine. You promised, Father, that when we give alms to help the poor, that you will repay us. I thank you, Father, for blessing us to the full until we overflow to be a blessing. You are El Shaddai, the many-breasted One. Great is thy faithfulness from the rising of the sun to its going down. I give you all glory, all the honor and all the praise. In Jesus' name. Amen (Psalm 118:24, 145:1; Ex. 3:14-15; 1 Chron. 29:12; 2 Cor. 9:6-8; Psalm 23:1; Phi. 4:19; Matt. 6:33; 1 Jn. 1:9; Psalm 112; Luke 6:38; Mal. 3:10-11; 2 Cor. 9:6-10; Prov. 3:9-10; Prov. 19:17; Gen. 17:1; Lam. 3:23; Rev. 4:11).

LEADERS

Father, in the name of Jesus and by the power of Holy Spirit, I thank and praise you, for this is the day that you have made. I will rejoice and be glad in it. You are Alpha and Omega, the beginning and the end. You are everything we need. You are my loving, caring, sharing heavenly Father. I will exalt and praise your name forever.

I come boldly before your throne to obtain mercy and grace on behalf of our leaders. You tell us in your word to pray for those in authority over us, so that we may lead peaceable lives.

Bless our leaders both behind the four walls of ministries and in the marketplace with wisdom, understanding, knowledge, revelation, grace, favor and courage to make decisions that glorify You.

Protect their families, leadership teams, congregations, partners and intercessors from all hurt, harm and danger. Thank you, Father, for encamping your angels continually around them and their families. Bless them with traveling mercies, wherever they go. I speak peace and increase over them and their families. No weapon formed against them will prosper.

Expose all ungodly rulers and replace them with God-fearing men and women that will advance the Kingdom of God. Send them leaders like "Aaron and Hur" to hold up their hands, and to fast and pray for and with them, to do your will and to glorify You with their decisions.

Remove the scales from the eyes of those who have not yet confessed Jesus as Lord. Soften their hearts and send laborers to share the good news of the gospel with them. I pray for those who once walked with you to repent and come back to You, their first love.

Strengthen our governmental leaders to defend the oppressed, and to pass laws and legislation that advance your righteous causes. In Jesus' name. Amen (Psalm 118:24; Rev. 1:8; Heb. 4:16; 1 Tim. 2:1-3; Eph. 1:17-18; Psalm 91; Isa. 54:17; Ex. 17:12; Prov. 29:2; Acts 9:18; Matt. 9:38).

PROTECTION

Father, in the name of Jesus and by the power of Holy Spirit, I thank and praise you for your lovingkindness and tender mercies that are new every day. You are my loving, caring, sharing heavenly Father. I will exalt and praise your name forever.

I come boldly before your throne of grace to obtain protection. You are *Jehovah Gibbor*, the Man of War. Thank you for warring on behalf of my family and me, turning back the enemy at the gate. Thank you for shooting forth your arrows to defeat the enemy. Let the enemy be blown in four different directions like chaff in the wind, never to come together again.

I rebuke and veto all demonic interference launched against my family and me. I cancel every curse, hex, spell, jinx and idle word spoken against us. I command these words to fall to the ground and die. I appoint every curse to the footstool of Jesus.

No weapon formed against my family or me will prosper. In Jesus' name. Father, thank You for providing a continual hedge of protection around us and those connected to us, for we abide in your secret place. In Jesus' name. Amen (Psalm 145:1; Heb. 4:16; Lam. 3:23; Matt. 6:9; Isa. 42:13; Psalm 18:14, 35:5; Gal. 3:13-14; Isa. 54:17; Job 1:10; Psalm 91).

ISRAEL

Father God, I thank you and praise you for this day that you have made. I will rejoice and be glad in it. I come boldly before your throne of grace to pray for peace in Jerusalem and Israel.

Father, remove the scales from the eyes of your chosen people that they may confess Jesus as their Messiah, so that the Gentile and Jew are baptized as one in the Spirit.

Let the enemy's plots, plans and ploys targeted at Jerusalem and Israel backfire and work for the good of Israel. Let all Israel's enemies be ashamed, and let confusion cloud their way. Let your glory and might rest upon Israel so her enemies will see and know that because your hand rests upon her, no weapon formed against Israel will ever prosper. I praise and thank you, Lord, for giving Israel the victory by releasing ambushes against her enemies.

Father, raise up intercessors as houses of prayer that will not cease praying night and day for the salvation and protection of Israel until Jesus returns for the "one new man". In Jesus' name. Amen (Psalm 118:24, 122:6; Heb. 4:16; Acts 13:22; Rom. 10:9-10; Psalm 18; 2 Chron. 20:22-24; Isa. 56:7; Jer. 62:6-7; Eph. 2:14-16).

THE NATIONS

Father, in the name of Jesus and by the power of Holy Spirit, I thank and praise you for your lovingkindness and tender mercies that are new every day. You are my loving, caring, sharing heavenly Father. I will exalt and praise your name forever.

I stand in the gap and pray for the nations, according to 1 Timothy 2:1-2 and Psalm 2:8. I give thanks for kings and all that are in authority and ask that you will give them wisdom to make godly decisions. Keep our nation and others on the path of righteousness, so that there will be peace to spread the gospel of Jesus Christ and the kingdom of God. The heart of the king is in your hand, so turn it, Lord, where you desire.

I decree the leaders of every nation operate in a spirit of divine unity that will glorify You. Bless them and their families. Protect them from all hurt, harm and danger. No weapon formed against them will prosper. Blow the wind of your spirit into the four corners of the world to release divine transformation, revival and change, causing your kingdom to come on earth as it is in heaven.

Expose and remove all ungodly leaders and judges who stubbornly oppose your will and replace them with godly leaders. I ask for the nations as my inheritance, for you don't want any to perish, but all to have eternal life in Christ Jesus.

Father, send laborers and intercessors in these last days, filled with the spirit of wisdom and understanding, to uphold the hands of leaders everywhere. Thank You, Father, for bringing these things to pass. In Jesus' name. Amen (Psalm 145:1; Lam. 3:23; 1 Tim. 2:1-3; Psalm 2:8; Prov. 21:1; Isa. 54:17; Matt. 6:10; Psalm 2:8; Matt. 9:38; Prov. 14:34).

INTERCESSORS

Father I thank and praise you for this new day that you have made. A day of victory, power, success, strength and protection. You are the air that I breathe, and I want to thank you for waking me up to see a new day of your power. If I had 10,000 tongues to say thank you, this still would not be enough. Oh Mighty God, my Strength and my Redeemer. You are my merciful, loving, caring, sharing Father, and I come boldly before your throne on behalf of your intercessors—the burning ones who are called after your name to pray for your people. I thank you for their great sacrifice of love as they continue Jesus' present day ministry of intercession to birth your kingdom on earth as it is in heaven.

In the name of Jesus and by the power of Holy Spirit, I decree that Your love, peace, righteousness and joy now rests, rules and abides upon your intercessors to continue standing in the gap to pray for the salvation of souls. Let your kingdom come as a wave of glory through the prayers of your intercessors, prayer warriors and watchmen, releasing love, power, glory, majesty, salvation, healing and deliverance, financial prosperity, justice, restitution, restoration, transformation and vindication— in the seven mountains of culture: arts and entertainment, business, education, family, government, media and religion.

Father, raise up a new breed of intercessors in this season so full of your love and compassion for the nations that they eagerly take their place upon the wall of intercession, fervently and violently praying your desires into the earth because they intimately know you. Give them an insatiable appetite to seek your face and to eat your Word until their faith increases. Give them a hunger to see souls saved, starting with their own families, until every soul has had an opportunity to confess Jesus as Lord. Most of all give them an increasing revelation of your love for them, so they know and understand how powerful they are in You and how much you trust them to finish strong. Help their unbelief, Father, as they press into your presence with fasting and prayer, praying in tongues often to build up their faith to believe and do the impossible.

I decree strength for those who are weary; wisdom, revelation knowledge and clarity of purpose for those seeking answers and direction; comfort for those who have lost loved ones; divine health and healing for those who are sick in spirit, soul or body; financial and material increase for those in need and that desire to give; endurance to pass every test; joy for those fighting depression/oppression; and angelic protection from all demonic attacks for them and their families. I speak your peace over them. Shalom—nothing missing, nothing broken—driving out all fear, confusion, agitation and pressure.

I command the enemy to release, give up and return everything that he's stolen from them, their forefathers, children/grandchildren. I draw your bloodline as a continual hedge of protection above their heads and their family members, around them and their family members and beneath all of their feet. No weapon formed against them will prosper. Expose every lie of the enemy, bringing it to nothing.

Let other intercessors pick them up in the spirit, so they receive fresh spiritual and physical strength to complete their prayer assignments, according to your will. Give them balance in all of their ways, so they are instant in season and out of season. Keep them hungry for your presence. Keep the fire of intercession lit upon the altar of their hearts. Bless them to know and understand how precious they are to you. Reward them, Father, with the desires of their heart, for they are wholly devoted unto you.

I bless your intercessors, Father. I call them healed from the top of their heads to the soles of their feet—them, their families and connections. Be glorified though their lives of sacrifice and prayer as they humbly depend upon You, Holy Spirit, to pray divine prayers that strike the mark, glorifying Jesus and our Father. I decree that what they do always prospers.

Speak to them, Father, in dreams and visions, revealing your secrets, so they can strategically pray—thwarting the enemy's plots, plans and ploys and advancing your kingdom in these end times. It's in You that they live, move and have their being. Give them grace to continually thank, praise, worship, intercede and serve You all the days of their lives. I decree a finishing anointing upon them to finish strong, just like our Lord and Savior Jesus Christ, King of kings and Lord of lords. In Jesus' name. Amen (Ps. 118:24, 19:14; Ezek. 22:30; Matt. 6:10; Ex. 12:13; Rev. 12:11; Eph. 3:14-21; Job. 22:28-30; Is. 54:17; Lev. 6:12-13; Is. 53:5; Acts 17:28; 2 Tim. 4:7-8).

❧ DECREES TO CONFESS ☙

To decree a thing is to speak into the atmosphere a promise from heaven in agreement with God's Word until it manifests into the natural realm. For example, you can decree "Wealth and riches are in my house" (Ps. 112:3) when you have lack. You can decree "I am healed by Jesus' stripes" when you are sick (Isa. 53:5). You can decree "I am strong" when you feel weak (Joel 3:10). A decree releases God's kingdom from inside of you, to outside of you into the natural realm, manifesting heaven on earth.

Elizabeth A. Nixon says, "When we decree, "I am blessed" (inspired by Psalm 112:1), we establish the blessing while separating ourselves from anything purposed against it and destroying the plans of the enemy."[13] For example, when you decree "The joy of the Lord is my strength", you destroy the spirit of oppression/depression.

To declare is to state what you *already possess,* based on your covenant with God. For example, you can declare, "I'm the righteousness of God in Christ Jesus. I am saved by faith in the blood of Jesus. God loves me the same way He loves Jesus. I am crowned by God with glory and honor. I always triumph in Christ Jesus! The favor of God surrounds me like a shield."

To confess something means to speak in agreement with God's Word, not your human desires. It means to say what God is personally speaking to you from the Bible, not what your circumstances are speaking. A general faith-filled confession must be built upon the universal promises that God has made to all believers, as opposed to a personal confession where God is speaking directly to you.

Always begin your decrees, declarations and confessions by entering into God's presence with thanksgiving and into His courts with praise. Then flow into worshiping the Lord in spirit and truth.

THANKSGIVING

Father God, I thank you and praise for you this day that you have made. I will rejoice and be glad in it, not sad in it. I come boldly before your throne of grace to obtain mercy and to find grace when I need it. Your Word will not return unto you void, but it will accomplish what pleases You and prosper in the thing where you have sent it. I thank you God that you look over your word to perform it. Thank you for your faithfulness. You alone are worthy to be praised forevermore. In Jesus' name. Amen (Psalm 118:24; Heb. 4:16; Isaiah 55:8-12; Jer. 1:12; Lam. 3:22-23; Rev. 4:11).

BLESSING & PROSPERITY

Bless the Lord, oh my soul, and all that is within me. Bless his holy name. Bless the LORD, oh my soul, and forget not all his benefits. Father, you make me to lie down in green pastures, which are the abundance of your blessings overtaking me in every area of my life: spiritually, mentally, emotionally, physically, financially and relationally.

I am a tither and the windows of heaven are continually open, pouring out a blessing I can't contain. I'm a cheerful giver, and as a result, I always have all sufficiency in all things, requiring no aid or support and I am furnished in abundance for every good work. I am blessed to be a blessing.

Wealth and riches are in my house. I am the head and not the tail, above only and never beneath, blessed coming in and going out, for I am the seed of prosperous Abraham by faith in Christ Jesus.

Forgive my family, forefathers and me for every sin, transgression and iniquity that we have committed against you, oh God. Thank you for forgiving us. I nullify every legal right of the enemy to steal my wealth or the wealth of my ancestors. I decree and declare that every generational curse of poverty and lack is cast out of my bloodline now, by faith in Jesus' name.

I command poverty and lack to depart from my mother's and dad's bloodlines going back to the Garden of Eden, and from my spouse's bloodlines, (or if not married), from the bloodlines of the other parent of my children. No weapon formed against us will prosper.

I decree and declare that my family and I follow the leading of Holy Spirit, who teaches us the way we should go, so that we profit. You supply all of our needs according to your riches in glory in Christ Jesus. What we set our hands to do for you, oh God always prospers.

I release the following anointings for prosperity over my family, career, ministries, businesses, associates, partners, students and my life:[14]

- Seven-fold Garden of Eden anointing (Gen.1: 28, 30, 2:15)
- Joshua's anointing (Josh. 1:8-10, 6:1-3)
- Abraham's anointing (Gen. 12:1-3)
- Melchizedek's anointing (Gen. 14:18; Heb. 5:6-10)
- Joseph's anointing (Gen. 14:18)
- Jacob's anointing (Gen. 28:1, 30:43)
- Isaac's anointing (Gen. 26:1-14)
- King Uzziah's anointing (2 Chron. 26:5-15)
- Jabez's anointing (1 Chron. 4:10)
- Daughters of Zelophehad's anointing (Num. 27: 1, 7)

- David's anointing (1 Chron. 29)
- Solomon's anointing (2 Chron. 9)
- Jesus' anointing (Luke 8:1-3)

Let the Lord be magnified, who takes delight in prospering his children. I seek God's kingdom first and His righteousness and all the things that pertain to life and godliness are added to my family and me. The favor of the Lord surrounds us like a shield, opening doors of increase, resources and opportunities for advancement. Rules, regulations, policies, laws, judgments and decisions are changed or made in our favor.

This is a prosperous day, week, month and year for us and we shall not know defeat. My God always causes us to triumph. In Jesus' name. Amen (Gen. 28:1-14; Isa. 54:17, 48:17; Phil. 4:19; Luke 4:18-19; Deut. 8:18-20; Gen. 12:1-3; Psalm 112; 2 Cor. 9:6-10, 2:14).

PROTECTION

I decree and declare that my family and I abide in the secret place of the Most High God. You are our refuge and fortress. In You we trust, oh God. We find protection under your wings, for you are our shield and buckler. One thousand may fall at our side, ten thousand at our right hand, but death and destruction will not come near us.

Only with our eyes will we behold and see the reward of the wicked. No evil, sickness or disease can come near us, for you have given your angels a charge to keep us in all of our ways. The angels continually war on our behalf, protecting us from all hurt, harm and danger. I decree that the enemy is beneath our feet, for we are hidden in Christ Jesus, who has defeated the devil.

I declare my love for You, Lord. Because I know your name, whenever I call, You will answer and show me great and mighty things that I know not of. I decree that I will live a long, satisfying life because I honor You. Father, thank you that You are with me in trouble to deliver my family and me, so that no weapon formed against us will prosper. In Jesus' name. Amen (Psalm 91; Isa. 54:17).

FAMILY

I decree and declare that as for me and my house, we will serve the Lord. My spouse (if married) and my children are healthy, successful and prosperous. Great is the peace and undisturbed composure of my children, grandchildren and future offspring..

We walk in unconditional, unfailing love of God towards one another. We are quick to hear, slow to speak and slow to get angry. We quickly forgive each other, giving the enemy no place.

The peace of God rests in our hearts and in our home. Our home is holy ground. We operate in a spirit of unity, giving the enemy no place. The commanded blessing rests upon our family because we walk in love and unity.

We speak Words of life, not death, attracting the abundant life in Christ Jesus. God blesses our family exceedingly and abundantly above all that we can ask, think, dream or imagine, according to the power of Holy Spirit working in us. We humble ourselves before God, we resist the devil and He flees from us. In Jesus' name. Amen (Joshua 24:15; Psalm 128:3; Isa. 54:17; 1 Cor. 13; James 1:19; Matt. 11:25; Eph. 4:27; Psalm 133; Prov. 18:21; John 10:10; Eph. 3:20; Eph. 4:27).

FOR HUSBAND

(Confessed by Wife)

I decree that my husband is a mighty man of valor. What he puts his hand to do prospers. He is a man after God's own heart.

He daily walks in the wisdom of God. He is bold as a lion. He leaps over walls and runs over a troop. When God gives the command, He pursues, overtakes and recovers all. He is a good provider and faithful steward of all that he possesses, providing an inheritance to his children's children.

He commands his family after him as He follows Christ Jesus. He allows nothing and no one to distract him from loving God, his family and his wife. He is known in the "city gates". He deals wisely and with discretion. Wealth and riches remain in His house. His righteousness endures forever. In Jesus' name. Amen (Judges 6:12; Deut. 8:18-20; Acts 13:22; Eph. 1:17-18; Prov. 29:1; Psalm 18:29; 1 Sam. 30:8; 1 Cor. 4:2; Prov. 13:22; Gen. 18:19; Heb. 12:2; Prov. 31:23; Psalm 112:3, 5).

FOR WIFE

(Confessed by Husband)

I decree and declare that my wife is a virtuous woman. Her price is far above rubies. Strength and honor are her clothes. Wealth and riches are in her hands.

She does me good and not evil all the days of my life. She is a woman of God—wise, beautiful and kind. She is a holy woman, who looks well to the ways of her household.

What she puts her hand to do always prospers. She is a wealthy woman that leaves an inheritance to her children, grandchildren and future seed. She gives to the widow and the orphan. Kindness comes out of her mouth. She speaks words of life, not death. She is an enterprising woman who grows people, businesses, ministries and organizations. The words of her mouth can't be resisted or refuted, for she is a woman of great influence.

She is always ravished with love for me. She respects and admires me. She allows nothing to come before You, Lord, or me or our family. She is a woman to be praised because she worships the Most High God all the days of her life. In Jesus' name. Amen (Prov. 31, 13:22; Eph. 5:22:33).

HEALTH & HEALING

I decree and declare that my family and I walk in divine health, and by Jesus' stripes we are healed. We prosper spirit, soul and body—mind will and emotions. We operate with the mind of Christ, casting down every lie of the enemy and decreeing the promises of God.

I bind and rebuke every spirit of infirmity, and I command it to be uprooted from our bodies and souls and to be cast in the sea. I break every curse and rebuke every spirit of infirmity from my bloodline and the bloodline of my spouse, (or if unmarried, the other parent of my children) going back to the Garden of Eden.

I decree we are loosed from the effects of these infirmities and sickness and disease by Jesus' stripes. I release the healing, delivering anointing of God to rest in and upon us now in Jesus' name.

Any germ or virus that touches our bodies dies on contact because of the anointing of the blood of Jesus that covers us. In Jesus' name. Amen (3 John 2; Matt. 16:19; Isa. 53:5).

BREAKING CURSES

I decree and declare that I am redeemed from the curse of the law by faith in Christ Jesus. I break all generational curses of pride, fear, rejection, shame, mental illness, addictions, lust, whoredom, confusion, poverty, sabotage, infirmity, bondage, seducing spirits, dumb and deaf spirits, anti-Christ spirit, error, divination, familiar spirits, jealousy, lying, perversion, death, unhealthy soul ties, and every evil spirit, in Jesus' name.

I command all generational curses that entered into my life when I was conceived, while I was in my mother's womb or that entered through the umbilical cord, to get out of me now in Jesus' name, to get out of my spouse (or if not married, out of the father or mother of my children), and to get out of my children.

I command all ancestral curses of idolatry, pride, witchcraft, freemasonry and paganism, and hereditary curses of fear, rejection, shame, homosexuality, lesbianism, failure, anger, abortion, lust, infirmity, sickness and disease, covetousness, greed, poverty, violence, murder, meanness, perversion and codependency to get out of me, to get out of my spouse and to get out of my children now, in Jesus' name. I bind and rebuke every evil spirit and call my family loosed from the enemy's grip. I release the peace and love of Holy Spirit to fill up every vacated place in our hearts with a fresh anointing, in Jesus' name.

I break the power of all negative words, witchcraft prayers, hexes, spells, jinxes and every idle word that I have spoken, or that others have spoken against my family or me.

I break the legal rights of all generational spirits operating behind a curse in the name of Jesus.[15] You no longer have a right to operate in my life or my family, in Jesus' name.

I cancel all time-released curses and familiar spirits waiting up the road and around the corner in my future to derail me, or to derail my spouse or my children/grandchildren. I evict every evil spirit now, in Jesus' name.

I command the enemy to loose, spit out and release everything he has stolen from my family, ancestors and me in both of my parent's bloodlines, in Jesus' name. By the precious blood of Jesus, every curse is broken and I release the blessing.

I decree that my family and I walk in the blessing of Abraham by faith in Jesus, which includes financial and material provision to be a blessing. I increase more and more, me and my family.

I speak Shalom over my family relationships, finances, businesses, career, educational pursuits, ministries and partners—nothing missing, nothing broken. We are blessed to be a blessing, fulfilling our purpose and destiny to establish the kingdom of God. In Jesus' name. Amen (Gal. 3:13-14; Gen. 12:1-3; Jer. 29:11; Deut. 8:18-20).

I AM CONFESSION

I am who God says I am. The Greater One lives in me. I am the head and not the tail, above only and never beneath; blessed coming in and going out because I obey God. I am accepted in the Beloved. Great is His love for me, and my love for Him. I am more than a conqueror in Christ Jesus. I am the righteous (name), bold as a lion. Fear, failure, poverty, death and destruction are beneath my feet. I can do all things in Christ Jesus that God has commanded me to do. I walk in the Spirit of the Lord, in His dominion and authority, wisdom and understanding, counsel and might, knowledge and the fear of the Lord.

I walk by faith and not by sight. My family and I are hidden in Christ Jesus, so no weapon formed against us can prosper. Every tongue that has risen up against us in judgment, we shall condemn and show to be in the wrong, for this is our heritage as servants of the Most High God. We walk by the Spirit, so we do not fulfill the lust of the flesh.

God's grace is sufficient, therefore my strength never fails. I obey my heavenly Father, who delights in me, causing doors of success to open that no man can shut, and doors of failure to close that no man can open. I take new territory and enlarge the borders of my tent, advancing God's kingdom in my spheres of influence, beginning with my family.

I am an ambassador of Christ Jesus with a hunger to see souls saved, healed and set free. I am an advancer of the kingdom of God, spreading the good news of the gospel wherever I go and with my giving. I pray without ceasing, and what I pray for, led by Holy Spirit, comes to pass in due season.

I am a wise steward over the blessings God has entrusted to me. I reign in life as a king, ruling over my emotions and thought life. I am as Jesus is in the world, glorifying my heavenly Father because I do His will, not my own. It's not by might, nor by power, but by the Spirit of the Lord resting upon me, my family, associates, ministry partners, customers and students and associates, causing us to impact generations and nations for the kingdom.

I maximize my potential by obeying God, who always causes me to triumph in Christ Jesus. In everything, I give thanks to God for He is my Source. I lack no good thing, for wealth and riches are in my house to be a blessing. I obey God all the days of my life, fulfilling my godly purpose and destiny. In Jesus' name. Amen. (Based on the "I am Scriptures" found in the Bible.)

&

ENDNOTES

[1] Mattoon, Ron. *Treasure from Proverbs, Volume One*

[2] http://www.cwgministries.org/Four-Keys-to-Hearing-Gods-Voice

[3] http://www.relevantmagazine.com/god/practical-faith/when-god-doesn%E2%80%99t-answer-prayer

[4] Hagin, Kenneth, E. *The Art of Prayer*. Tulsa, Oklahoma: Faith Life Publications, 2000, pp. 9-15

[5] http://www.tbn.org/watch-us/our-programs/manna-fest-hosted-by-perry-stone

[6] Smith, Alice. *Beyond the Veil*. Ventura, Calif: Regal Books, 1997, p. 62

[7] http://www.prmi.org/blog/wp-content/uploads/2010/04/Nature-of-Demonic-Strongholds-From-Dunamis-Project-Man-Unit-6-L-8.pdf, Wagner, C. Peter, *Confronting the Powers*

[8] Spurgeon, C. H. *Spiritual Warfare in the Believer's Life*. Emerald Books, 1993, pp. 77-78

[9] Piper, John. *Desiring God*, 1996, p. 129, www.desiringGod.org

[10] Smith, Eddie. *Making Sense of Spiritual Warfare*. Bloomington, Minn., Bethany House Publishers, 2008, p. 139

[11] Trimm, Cindy. *The Rules of Engagement*. Lake Mary, Florida, Charisma House, 2008, p. 150

[12] Alves, Elizabeth. *Becoming a Prayer Warrior*. Ventura, Calif: Regal Books, 1998, p. 136

[13] Nixon, Elizabeth, A. *Psalms: Decrees That Renew Your Heart and Mind*. Lake Mary, Florida, Charisma House, 2014, p. 7

[14] Trimm, Cindy. *The Rules of Engagement*. Lake Mary, Florida, Charisma House, 2008, p. 36

[15] Eckhardt, John. C. *Prayers that Rout Demons*. Lake Mary, Florida, Charisma House, 2008, p. 23

NAMES OF GOD

The Names of God in the Bible reveal His character and nature. When we say or pray God's name(s), we invoke His presence, encounter His glory and we are strengthened.

"ELOHIM" (or Elohay)

The first name for God used in the Old Testament appears over 2,300 times. It is derived from the Hebrew root meaning "strength" or "power", and is plural in form to describe the One True God (Genesis 1:1) .

Elohay Kedem	God of the Beginning	Deuteronomy 33:27
Elohay Mishpat	God of Justice	Isaiah 30:18
Elohay Slichot	God of Forgiveness	Nehemiah 9:17
Elohay Marom	God of Heights	Micah 6:6
Elohay Mikarov	God Who Is Near	Jeremiah 23:23
Elohay Mauzi	God of My Strength	Psalm 43:2
Elohay Tehilati	God of My Praise	Psalm 109:1
Elohay Yishi	God of My Salvation	Psalm 18:46
Elohim Kedoshim	Holy God	Leviticus 19:2; Joshua 24:19
Elohim Chaiyim	Living God	Jeremiah 10:10
Elohay Elohim	God of Gods	Deuteronomy 10:17

"EL"

Another name used for God shows up about 200 times in the Old Testament. *El* is derived from *Elohim*, and is often combined with other words for descriptive emphasis.

El HaNe'eman	The Faithful God	Deuteronomy 7:9
El HaGadol	The Great God	Deuteronomy 10:17
El HaKadosh	The Holy God	Isaiah 5:16
El Yisrael	The God of Israel	Psalm 68:35
El HaShamayim	The God of The Heavens	Psalm 136:26
El De'ot	The God of Knowledge	1 Samuel 2:3
El Emet	The God of Truth	Psalm 31:6
El Yeshuati	The God of My Salvation	Isaiah 12:2
El Elyon	The Most High God	Genesis 14:18
Immanu El	God Is With Us	Isaiah 7:14
El Olam	The God of Eternity	Genesis 21:33
El Echad	The One God	Malachi 2:10

"ELAH"

A name for God that shows up 70 times in the Old Testament.

Elah Yerush'lem	God of Jerusalem	Ezra 7:19
Elah Yisrael	God of Israel	Ezra 5:1
Elah Sh'maya	God of Heaven	Ezra 7:23
Elah Sh'maya V'Arah	God of Heaven and Earth	Ezra 5:11

"YHVH" (also pronounced Jehovah or Yahweh)

Even though scholars aren't sure how to pronounce it, it is a Hebrew word that translates as "LORD"; it shows up approximately 7,000 times in the Old Testament. This name of God is also referred to as the "Tetragrammaton," meaning the "The Four Letters". YHVH is derived from the Hebrew verb "to be". It's the name God revealed to Moses at the burning bush—I AM WHO I AM (Exodus 3:14-15). Therefore, YHVH means "God's absolute being—the source of everything, without beginning and without end".

Jehovah Ahavah	The LORD is Love	1 John 4:8, 16
Jehovah Chesed	The LORD Who is Merciful	Exodus 34:6
Jehovah Elohim	LORD God	Genesis 2:4
Jehovah El'elyon	The LORD, the Supreme God	Genesis 14:18-19
Jehovah Hayah	The LORD, I Am that I Am	Exodus 3:14-15
Jehovah Kabod	The LORD, the King of Glory	Psalm 24:8-10
Jehovah Kadosh	The LORD, the Holy One	Exodus 3:14-15
Jehovah Quanna	The LORD, a Jealous God	Exodus 20:5
Jehovah M'Kaddesh	The LORD Who Sanctifies You	Exodus 31:13
Jehovah M'kadesh	The LORD Who Makes Holy	Ezekiel 37:28
Jehovah Magen	*The LORD Our Shield*	Genesis 15:1
Jehovah Or	*The LORD is My Light*	Psalm 27:1

Jehovah Yireh	The LORD Who Sees/Provides	Genesis 22:14
Jehovah Nissi	The LORD My Banner	Exodus 17:15
Jehovah Raah	The LORD My Shepherd	Psalm 23:1
Jehovah Rapha	The LORD Our Healer	Exodus 15:26
Jehovah Shaddai	The LORD is Mighty	Genesis 17:1
Jehovah Shalom	The LORD of Peace	Judges 6:24
Jehovah Shammah	The LORD is There	Ezekiel 48:35
Jehovah Tsedek	The LORD, a God of Justice	Isaiah 30:18
Jehovah Tzidkaynu	The LORD Our Righteousness	Jeremiah 33:16
Jehovah O'saynu	The LORD our Maker	Psalm 95:6
El Gibbor	The Mighty God	Isaiah 9:6
El Chaiyai	The God of my Life	Psalm 42:8
El Hakkavod	The God of Glory	Psalm 29:3
El Sali	God of my Strength	Psalm 42:9
El Emet	The God of Truth	Psalm 31:5
El Hakkadosh	The Holy God who sent the Holy Spirit	Isaiah 5:16

Sources: http://www.allaboutgod.com; http://www.streamsministries.com

APPENDIX B

PRAYER WATCHES

There are eight watches described in the Bible.

–1– **6AM-9AM**	This time is for declarations and utterances; equipment of service; transforming of minds; the time that God strengthens Christians.
–2– **9AM-NOON**	Time for forgiveness; healing of relationships; harvest; scientific and technological advances; exits and entry watch.
–3– **NOON-3PM**	Time that the promises of God are released; shaking of foundations; dwelling in the secret place of the most high; time to exercise God-given dominion.
–4– **3PM-6PM**	Time to transform history; time to remove veils, coverings of darkness; prayer hour of covenants; the hour of triumphant glory; the time for establishing kingdom.
–5– **6PM-9PM**	Time of meditation; time for divine judgments; time for deliverance; time for resurrection; time to pray for the economy; drown the walls of darkness; shake out all the wicked structures from our economic systems, educational systems, religious systems, political systems and all other systems.
–6– **9PM-MIDNIGHT**	Time for thanksgiving; time for visitation; the time when the Lord prepares you to receive many acts of change in the earth. Midnight is symbolic of intense darkness but God is the light in the darkness and releases strategy during this time.
–7– **MIDNIGHT-3AM**	Time for prayers of protection and strength to overcome; time for outpouring of the spirit of grace; to overcome every limitation of gifts and anointing; special time for divine governments; overruling human decrees to give an angelic release.
–8– **3AM-6AM**	Time to pray for freedom of the Bride. Angelic activity or intervention; the time when God releases the dew of heaven; time for blessings from heaven above; blessings of the deep that lie beneath; blessings of the womb; blessings of our fathers and ancestors. God has to bless His people.

Source: www.ezekielregiment.wordpress.com

APPENDIX C

APOSTOLIC PRAYERS

Ephesians 1:17-19— ...that the God of our Lord Jesus Christ, the Father of glory, may give to you the spirit of wisdom and revelation in the knowledge of Him, [18] the eyes of your understanding being enlightened; that you may know what is the hope of His calling, what are the riches of the glory of His inheritance in the saints, [19] and what is the exceeding greatness of His power toward us who believe, according to the working of His mighty power.

Ephesians 3:16-19— ...that He would grant you, according to the riches of His glory, to be strengthened with might through His Spirit in the inner man, [17] that Christ may dwell in your hearts through faith; that you, being rooted and grounded in love, [18] may be able to comprehend with all the saints what is the width and length and depth and height— [19] to know the love of Christ which passes knowledge; that you may be filled with all the fullness of God.

Philippians 1:9-11— ...And this I pray, that your love may abound still more and more in knowledge and all discernment, [10] that you may approve the things that are excellent, that you may be sincere and without offense till the day of Christ, [11] being filled with the fruits of righteousness which are by Jesus Christ, to the glory and praise of God.

Colossians 1:9-12—For this reason we also, since the day we heard it, do not cease to pray for you, and to ask that you may be filled with the knowledge of His will in all wisdom and spiritual understanding; [10] that you may walk worthy of the Lord, fully pleasing Him, being fruitful in every good work and increasing in the knowledge of God; [11] strengthened with all might, according to His glorious power, for all patience and longsuffering with joy; [12] giving thanks to the Father who has qualified us to be partakers of the inheritance of the saints in the light.

Romans 15:5-6, 13—Now may the God of patience and comfort grant you to be like-minded toward one another, according to Christ Jesus, 6 that you may with one mind and one mouth glorify the God and Father of our Lord Jesus Christ. 13 Now may the God of hope fill you with all joy and peace in believing, that you may abound in hope by the power of the Holy Spirit.

1 Corinthians 1:5-8— ...that you were enriched in everything by Him in all utterance and all knowledge, 6 even as the testimony of Christ was confirmed in you, 7 so that you come short in no gift, eagerly waiting for the revelation of our Lord Jesus Christ, 8 who will also confirm you to the end, that you may be blameless in the day of our Lord Jesus Christ.

1 Thessalonians 3:10— ...night and day praying exceedingly that we may see your face and perfect what is lacking in your faith? 11 Now may our God and Father Himself, and our Lord Jesus Christ, direct our way to you. 12 And may the Lord make you increase and abound in love to one another and to all, just as we do to you, 13 so that He may establish your hearts blameless in holiness before our God and Father at the coming of our Lord Jesus Christ with all His saints.

2 Thessalonians 1:11-12—Therefore we also pray always for you that our God would count you worthy of this calling, and fulfill all the good pleasure of His goodness and the work of faith with power, 12 that the name of our Lord Jesus Christ may be glorified in you, and you in Him, according to the grace of our God and the Lord Jesus Christ.

2 Thessalonians 3:1-5—Finally, brethren, pray for us, that the word of the Lord may run swiftly and be glorified, just as it is with you, 2 and that we may be delivered from unreasonable and wicked men; for not all have faith. 3 But the Lord is faithful, who will establish you and guard you from the evil one. 4 And we have confidence in the Lord concerning you, both that you do and will do the things we command you. 5 Now may the Lord direct your hearts into the love of God and into the patience of Christ.

Acts 4:29-31—Now, Lord, look on their threats, and grant to Your servants that with all boldness they may speak Your word, 30 by stretching out Your hand to heal, and that signs and wonders may be done through the name of Your holy Servant Jesus." 31 And when they had prayed, the place where they were assembled together was shaken; and they were all filled with the Holy Spirit, and they spoke the word of God with boldness.

Acts 1:8—But you shall receive power when the Holy Spirit has come upon you; and you shall be witnesses to Me in Jerusalem, and in all Judea and Samaria, and to the end of the earth.

Acts 2:17-21—And it shall come to pass in the last days, says God, That I will pour out of My Spirit on all flesh; Your sons and your daughters shall prophesy, your young men shall see visions, Your old men shall dream dreams. 18 And on My menservants and on My maidservants I will pour out My Spirit in those days; And they shall prophesy. 19 I will show wonders in heaven above And signs in the earth beneath: Blood and fire and vapor of smoke. 20 The sun shall be turned into darkness, And the moon into blood, Before the coming of the great and awesome day of the Lord. 21 And it shall come to pass that whoever calls on the name of the Lord shall be saved.'

PRAYERS FOR ISRAEL

Brethren, my heart's desire and prayer to God for Israel is that they may be saved (Rom. 10:1).

And so all Israel will be saved, as it is written: "The Deliverer will come out of Zion, And He will turn away ungodliness from Jacob; For this is My covenant with them, When I take away their sins" (Rom. 11:26-27).

For Zion's sake I will not hold My peace, And for Jerusalem's sake I will not rest, Until her righteousness goes forth as brightness, And her salvation as a lamp that burns (Isa. 62:1).

Old Testament Prayers for Israel: Isa 63:15-64:12; Dan. 9:4-19; Mic. 7:7-20; Hab. 3:2-19; Ezra 9:5-15; Neh. 1:4-11; 9:5-38; Psalm 44, 45:3-5, 65, 67, 79-80, 83, 86, 90:13-17, 102:12:22, 110:1-5, 122:6-7, 132:11.

Pray these prophetic promises over Israel and the Church: Deut. 4:27-31, 30:1-10, 31:29; Isa. 11:10-16, 29:14, 17-24, 30:18-33, 32:15-19, 33:2-6, 17, 35:1-10, 42:10-17, 43:1-7, 44:1-5, 45:17, 22-25, 51:3-11, 54:1-17, 56:6-8, 59:19-21, 60:1-6, 12, 66:7-14; Jer.3:14-20, 16:14-21, 31:1-14, 32:16-23, 32:37-42, 33:6-26, 50:4-5, 50:19-20, 34; Ezek. 11:17-20, 16:60-63, 20:33-44, 34:11-31, 37:1-28; Hos. 2:14-23, 3:5, 5:15-6:3, 11, 14:1-8; Joel 2:28-32, 3:17-20; Zeph. 3:8-20; Hag. 2:6-9, 21-22; Zech. 8:2-8, 12:10-13:6; Mal. 4:1-6.

Source: www.ihopkc.org

PRAYER, INTERCESSION & SPIRITUAL WARFARE

Elizabeth Alves	*Becoming A Prayer Warrior*
Abu Bako	*Praying through the Gates of Time*
Mike Bickle	*Passion for Jesus*
E.M. Bounds	*The Best of E.M. Bounds on Prayer*
Billye Brim	*The Blood and the Glory*
Suzette T. Caldwell	*Praying to Change Your Life*
Charles Capps	*Jesus Our Intercessor*
	The Tongue—A Creative Force
Mahesh and Bonnie Chavda	*Watch of the Lord*
Mahesh Chavda	*The Hidden Power of Praying & Fasting*
Paul Yongi Cho	*Prayer: Key to Revival*
Kenneth Copeland	*Prayer—Your Foundation for Success*
Kimberley Daniels	*Clean House, Strong House*
	Prayers That Bring Change
John Dawson	*Taking Our Cities for God*
Wesley L. Duewel	*Mighty Prevailing Prayer*
Dick Eastman	*The Hour That Changes the World*
John C. Eckhardt	*Prayers that Rout Demons*
John Eckhardt	*Prayers that Break Curses*
John Eckhardt	*Prayers that Bring Healing*
Charles Finney	*The Secret of Faith*
Francis Frangipane	*The Three Battlegrounds*
Jim Goll	*The Lost Art of Intercession*
Norman Grubb	*Rees Howells, Intercessor*
Jeanne Guyon	*Experiencing the Depths of Jesus Christ*
Kenneth E. Hagin	*Exceedingly Growing Faith*
	Bible Prayer Study Course
	Praying to Get Results
	The Art of Intercession
	The Believer's Authority
Lynne Hammond and Patsy Camaneti	*Secrets to Powerful Prayer*
Bill Hamon	*Prophets and Personal Prophecy*
	Prophets, Pitfalls and Principles
Harrison House	*Prayers That Avail Much for Mothers*

Suzette Hattingh and Gayle Claxton	*Prayer School Workbook*
Marilyn Hickey	*The Power of Prayer and Fasting*
Benny Hinn	*Good Morning Holy Spirit*
	The Anointing
Richard Ing	*Spiritual Warfare*
Mary Alice Isleib	*Effective Fervent Prayer*
Cindy Jacobs	*Possessing the Gates of the Enemy*
Joyce Meyer	*Battlefield of the Mind*
Andrew Murray	*Ministry of Intercession*
Stormie O'Martian	*The Power of a Praying Wife*
George Otis Jr.	*Spiritual Mapping*
Chuck D. Pierce & John Dickson	*The Worship Warrior: Ascending in Worship, Descending in War*
Chuck D. Pierce and Rebecca Wagner Sytsema	*Prayers That Outwit the Enemy*
	The Future War of the Church
	When God Speaks
Chuck D. Pierce	*Redeeming the Time*
	Reordering the Day
Frederick K.C. Price	*Faith's Greatest Enemies*
Jerry Savelle	*Prayer of Petition*
Dutch Sheets	*Authority in Prayer: Praying Power and Purpose*
	Intercessory Prayer
	Watchman Prayer
Ed Silvoso	*That None Should Perish*
Alice Smith	*Beyond the Veil*
Eddie Smith	*Making Sense of Spiritual Warfare*
R.A. Torrey	*How To Pray*
Elmer L Towns	*Fasting for Spiritual Breakthrough*
Cindy N. Trimm	*Commanding Your Day*
	Rules of Engagement
Peter C. Wagner	*Prayer Shield*
Barbara Wentroble	*Praying with Authority*
	Prophetic Intercession
Smith Wigglesworth	*Ever Increasing Faith*
	Wigglesworth on the Anointing

DELIVERANCE, INNER & PHYSICAL HEALING

Neil T. Anderson	*Victory Over the Darkness*
Pablo Bottari	*Free in Christ*
Rebecca Brown M.D.	*He Came to Set the Captives Free*
Drs. Henry Cloud and John Townsend	*Boundaries*
Gloria Copeland	*And Jesus Healed Them All*
Kimberley Daniels	*Clean House Strong House*
John Eckhardt	*Identifying and Breaking Curses*
Dr. Ana Ferrell Mendez	*Iniquity*
	Regions of Captivity
	Shaking the Heavenlies
Kenneth E. Hagin	*Bible Healing Study Course*
Frank and Ida Mae Hammond	*Pigs in the Parlor*
Robert D. Heidler, Th.M.	*Set Yourself Free*
Brian A. Holmes	*The Ties That Bind*
Larry Huch	*Free at Last*
Charles and Frances Hunter	*How to Heal the Sick*
Joan Hunter and Michael Hinson	*Healing the Whole Man Handbook*
Joan Hunter	*Healing the Heart*
John Paul Jackson	*Unmasking the Jezebel Spirit*
Chester and Betty Kylstra	*Restoring the Foundations*
Roberts Liardon	*God's Generals*
Neal Lozano	*Unbound*
Watchman Nee	*Spiritual Authority*
T.L. Osborn	*Healing the Sick*
Derek Prince	*Blessing or Curse*
	They Shall Expel Demons
Vito Rallo	*Breaking Generational Curses & Pulling Down Strongholds*
Oral Roberts	*If You Need Healing Do These Things*
Drs. Jerry and Carol Robeson	*Strongman's His Name...What's His Game?*
Liberty Savard	*Breaking the Power*
Randy Shankle	*The Merismos*

Alice Smith	*Delivering the Captives*
	Spiritual Intimacy with God
Eddie and Alice Smith	*Spiritual House Cleaning*
Eddie Smith and	*Strategic Prayer*
Michael L.Hennen	
Lester Sumrall	*Demons—The Answer Book*
Doris M. Wagner	*How to Cast Out Demons*
Henry W. Wright	*A More Excellent Way*
Lilian B. Yeomans M.D.	*Healing Treasury*

MINISTRY CONTACT INFORMATION

Karen L. Gardner, in association with Pure Freedom Ministries International and Pure Freedom Ministries Alaska, teaches and trains covering various topics, including prayer and intercession, liturgical dance, spiritual and motivational gifts, leadership, personal development and sales. To schedule conferences, seminars, speaking engagements or consulting, please contact us using the information below.

Contact Information:

Karen L. Gardner
Pure Freedom Ministries Alaska
P. O. Box 230571
Anchorage, AK 99523-0571

Phone: 907.317.2811

Email: purefreedom@gci.net

Websites: www.purefreedomministries.com

                www.purefreedomalaska.com

                www.praynowtraining.com

                www.eaglesprayer.com

Free Offer

Visit www.purefreedomministries.com to sign up for our newsletter and other free offers.